Our Man
in the Kitchen

OUR MAN
IN THE
KITCHEN

A SUPERB NEW COOK BOOK

written by

Hyman Goldberg

(formerly Prudence Penny)

and illustrated by

WILLIAM HOGARTH

The Odyssey Press

NEW YORK

641.5

G

The recipe on page 67 is from
The Art of India's Cookery
by Lakshamanan and Kaufman,
copyright © 1964 by William L. Kaufman
and Saraswathi Lakshamanan, and is reprinted
by permission of Doubleday & Company, Inc.

iv

Acknowledgments

I am grateful to many people for their help, but my most heartfelt thanks go to Mrs. Agnes Murphy, Food Editor of the New York Post, *for her advice and guidance; to Jennie and Paul Grossinger and the Chief Steward-Chef of their hotel, Henry Speckhardt; to Danny (Hideaway) Stradella and his Chef, Al Priest; to Harry Lee of the Peking Restaurant; to my wife, Naomi, for her painstaking editing of my recipes and her unfailing good judgment; to my son, Gabriel, for his courage in test-eating his way through this manuscript; and to Glenn Neville, who did not laugh too long when I told him I wanted to be* PRUDENCE PENNY; *but above all, to Vaudine Newell, wherever she is.*

H. G.

Introduction

$\mathcal{F}$or six months of my life, I was obliged to
laugh with seeming glee whenever some waggish
friend hailed me with cries of, "Hello there, Pru,
what's cooking?" It began when I became the cooking editor of the late, lamentable *New York Mirror,*
and continued through the period when I was the
cooking columnist of the *New York Journal-Amer-
ican.* On both of these newspapers, I hid behind the
name of a woman who never lived, although millions
of people all over the country really believed that
there was a lady, presumably a dear old lady, whose
name actually was Prudence Penny.

That by-line was invented early in the century by
the elder William Randolph Hearst, who believed,
no doubt, that the implication of parsimoniousness
in that pretty, alliterative combination would have
great appeal to the wily, parsimonious housewives
among his readers, and it probably did. My friends
and acquaintances thought it was extremely comical
that I should receive letters addressed to "Miss
Prudence Penny," which began either, "Dear Miss
Penny," or merely, "Madame," for some of them had
known me for most of the thirty-nine years during
which I had been a reporter and feature writer for
newspapers and national magazines.

I became Prudence Penny by asking for the job
on the sudden demise of the lady who had been
using that by-line on the *Mirror* for about twenty-

five years. The editors laughed when I sat down with them to ask for the job. "What the hell," one of them asked in his customary gentle manner, "do *you* know about cooking?" He had known me for many years, as a police and court reporter, covering fires, murders, and murder trials, and then as a feature writer, interviewing stars, and would-be stars, of TV, the movies, and the Broadway theater. So I told them about my secret life as a semi-professional and amateur cook.

I was brought up in restaurants and hotels which my father operated while I was growing up, in New York City and in the countryside of upper New York State, and since my father—a former blacksmith, with a temper as powerful as his muscular ability—was always beating up cooks, waiters, and dishwashers, and throwing them off the premises, my two brothers, two sisters, and I, youngest in the family, were continually dragooned into helping out in the kitchen. So I began cooking, in a sort of professional way, at an extremely early age. By the time I was six, I was an expert salad man and chicken-liver-chopper. I have always regarded cooking as a creative art and a great joy.

From the time I became a police reporter at the age of sixteen — that is too many years ago — I became exposed to cooking in many languages. Some of the recipes in this book are for dishes I learned to cook in my father's restaurants and hotels; most of them, however, I have picked up traveling in many places of the world, from friends and wives of friends, and from chefs in restaurants and hotels all over the world. Some of the recipes I have invented (though I have been disillusioned occasionally by discovering that some dish which I had thought original to me had already been done by some other cook, like somebody with the improbable name of Escoffier). All my life I have collected recipes from newspapers and magazines. And I have almost a thousand cookbooks, some of them very good ones.

All the time I was writing under the pseudonym of Prudence Penny I was galled not only by the fact that my friends thought it was excruciatingly funny to call me "Prudence," or even "Miss Prudence," especially in public places where people who didn't know me would look at me with eyebrows raised, but also because whenever it became necessary to introduce myself for professional purposes it took too long to explain the reason why a middle-aged, white-haired, somewhat portly man who was a long-time husband and father should masquerade under a woman's name.

In a restaurant where I had taken my wife to dinner one night, I ate a dish that was new to me. The menu called it "Breast of Capon, Mai Rose." I knew it had in it May wine, cream, the yolk of an egg, and various herbs and spices as part of the ingredients for the sauce. But I wanted the precise measurements, so after I paid the check I asked to see the *maître d'hôtel*. The name of the restaurant is not essential, but it is one of the better—and more expensive—ones in Manhattan.

"I am Prudence Penny," I announced when he arrived, smiling at me with that peculiar mixture of unctuousness and frosty superiority affected by such persons in such snob establishments. Immediately his expression changed. His face mirrored disbelief and, perhaps, dislike. My wife giggled wildly as I explained the situation to the man. I finally did convince him that I was not a confidence man of some sort, but it was a long and slightly embarrassing experience.

So, when the opportunity arose, I switched to another newspaper, the *New York Post,* and the *Des Moines Register and Tribune Syndicate,* which distributes my column, "Our Man in the Kitchen," to many other newspapers. Now when I am asked why I am no longer Prudence Penny, I say that I changed my name for business reasons.

In the many years that I have been reading and collecting recipes it has annoyed me mightily to see in newspapers, magazines, and books admonishments like:"...wash 6 tomatoes and slice them in quarters;" or: "...put a layer of sliced potatoes on the bottom of the pot;" or: "...fry the onions until they are transparent;" or: "...take the seeds out of a green pepper;" or: "...peel a medium-sized onion." And more than once, to my absolute dismay, I read in a recipe: "...break the egg."

It seems to me that this sort of writing in recipes is extremely offensive because it implies that people who cook are so cretinous that they have to be told to wash a tomato (why not, then, say, "First, wash your hands," or even, "First take a bath"). You will not be told, in the following pages, to do any such things, and I will take it for granted that when it comes to putting something into a pot or any other vessel you will put it on the bottom instead of trying to suspend the stuff in the middle by levitation. And as for frying onions "until they are transparent," well, did you ever try to read a book or a newspaper through a fried onion? Can't be done. And surely no one has to be told to "peel an onion"? Or, for goodness' sake, to "break an egg"? Certainly not you.

Another thing you won't find in this cookbook is trade names of the many, many food products on the market. Reputable newspapers and magazines—the ones I write for, among them—have strict rules about such practices, for very good reasons. But since there is fierce competition in the food field, the efforts by advertising and publicity people to get their brand names into recipes in newspapers, magazines, and cookbooks are just as fierce. And the temptations held out to writers of recipes are powerful ones. I know, because I have had to fight some pretty fierce temptations myself. My experience has been that most well-known brand-name products are good and there is very little variation—except, occasionally, in price—among the same products under the various brand names. It is another matter entirely with luxury, gourmet-packaged, canned, and frozen foods; there are variations in quality and excellence as great as the variations in price.

By all this I do not mean to impugn either the honesty or the ethics of food writers, most of whom —though too often, sadly, they are militant bores— are honest and sincere; where newspapers and magazines continually use trade names, it is due, usually, to pressure brought by the publication's advertising department, which has been pressured by the advertising or publicity people in the hire of the manufacturer, processor, or importer. I know, because one of the newspapers for which I formerly worked had an egregious advertising director who continually tried to exert pressure for the use of certain brand names. Though I look with suspicion, always, on recipe writers who habitually use brand names, I exempt, of course, those books which are published with the imprimatur of some food manufacturer, packer, or importer. Frank and open product-pushing of this sort is acceptable because it *is* frank and open; with the hidden pushers, it is not.

On this score, It would be well to pay closest attention to the people who write about wines and liquors. There is more phoniness in this field and more nonsense written in it than in any other branch of the food-and-drink racket. It is bad enough to be told that only a barbarian would drink red wine with fish and fowl, but some of these people tell us *which* vintner's wine should be drunk with which particular dish! Well, I like red wine better than I like white, and I will damn well drink red wine with anything I like. I mentioned this to the head of a great French vineyard one day, and he whispered to me, after looking around carefully, "And so do I." And he said it didn't make one particle of difference to a Frenchman from what kind of glass he drank what kind of wine, another matter these wine writers speak about with much lady-like fervor.

These writers on wine (writers?) have made wine-drinking seem like such an arcane, mystic subject, surrounded by so many taboos and fetishes, that millions of people are afraid to drink or to serve wine for fear of making a gaffe that would label them as unknowledgeable — than which there is no greater failing. Some day, perhaps, the American winemakers, and the foreign ones, too, will realize that these writers, whom they have cossetted for so long, are doing them a great disservice by making wine-drinking seem to most Americans a subject that is too time-consuming and difficult to master. Drink what you like, I say, with whatever food you like!

Table of Contents

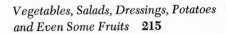

Appetizers

The well-paid advertising executive was overjoyed to run into an old college chum whom he hadn't seen since they had been to school together, and then the joy turned to embarrassment because the fellow told him a terrible tale of woe. He'd been unable to find work for months, his mortgage was going to be foreclosed, his wife had left him, and,oh, things were terrible. As a matter of fact, the fellow confided, he hadn't eaten for two days and he was terribly hungry. The advertising man gave the fellow his card, told him to call him up in the next week or so, and he would see what he could do about finding a job for him, and, meanwhile, just to tide him over, he gave the fellow $20. An hour later, he walked into his favorite restaurant and to his astonishment saw his impoverished college chum sitting at a table by himself, eating caviar and drinking champagne.

"This is terrible!" he shouted. "Do you think I gave you $20 to buy caviar and champagne?" The college chum sneered at his benefactor. "Listen," he said, "before I ran into you, I couldn't afford caviar and champagne. So then my luck changes, I run into you, and you give me $20, and now you're mad at me for having caviar and champagne. When the hell do you expect me to have caviar and champagne, anyway?"

There's nothing, to our mind, that comes near caviar for creating an appetite. For more caviar, is what we mean. Well, since we know very few people who can afford it—if they are not expense-account aristocrats—let us talk about the countless appetizers that almost everyone can afford, some made of herring, smoked salmon, and other fish; and some made of the eggs of fish which are less expensive than the true caviar, which comes, of course, from sturgeon from Russia and Iran. Every nation in the world, and every people, has wonderful appetizers, but it is the Scandinavians who have raised the appetizer—smorgasbord—to a fine art.

A man walking past a bakery saw a strange creature standing on the sidewalk looking into the window. He stopped and stared at the creature. "Excuse me," he said to the creature, "would you mind telling me what kind of a creature you are?" The creature smiled sweetly. "Not at all," it said. "I'm a Martian." The man goggled. "A Martian!" he exclaimed. "You mean from Mars?" The Martian sneered. "Of course," he said, "where else would Martians come from?"

They stared at each other, and then the Martian pointed at something in the bakery window. "I answered your question," he said. "Now answer one for me. What's that thing in there?" The man looked and saw the Martian was pointing at a bagel. "That's a bagel," he said. "We Earth people eat that." The Martian was astounded, so the man invited him into the bakery to try one.

He took a bite, chewed, and swallowed. "So what do you think of it?" the Earthman asked. The Martian looked thoughtful. "Well," he said finally,

"I'll tell you. With a little cream cheese and a piece lox it wouldn't be so bad."

They don't have bagels in Sweden, but they do have lox and cream cheese and they mix them together and call it:

RÖKTLAX

[SERVES THREE TO SIX]

½ pound lox, lax, or smoked salmon
1 3-ounce package cream cheese
1 or 2 tablespoons sour cream

dash of pepper
dash of Worcestershire sauce
1 tablespoon dill, chopped
pumpernickel or rye bread

Chop the lox into tiny bits and mix it up with the cream cheese and everything else except the chopped dill. Form it into a ball, and refrigerate it for hours and hours. Cut pumpernickel or rye bread in 1-inch rounds and spread with the mixture and sprinkle a little chopped dill on each one. Say, you know? Why not spread this lox and cream cheese on a bagel? It's great that way! Another thing you can do with lox, if you've got some handy, is serve a hot party appetizer of:

LOX AND POTATOES

[SERVES FOUR TO EIGHT]

5 potatoes
4 tablespoons butter
½ pound lox, sliced (of course)

1 onion, sliced thin
pepper

Peel the potatoes and cut them into thin strips. Get hold of a shallow baking dish, butter it up, and put half the lox slices into the dish, then all the onion slices, and put half the potato strips over them. Sprinkle a little pepper on the potato strips, then repeat the process with the rest of the lox, then the rest of the potatoes. Dot the top of the potatoes with the butter, sprinkle a little pepper over all. Preheat your oven to 375 degrees and bake the dish for about 40 minutes, when the top of the potatoes should be browned. Have plenty of potables on hand; everyone is going to have a grand thirst!

℞ 〈≡≡≡≡≈

The doctor looked at his patient's ankle and he was horrified. "My goodness," he exclaimed, "how long have you been walking around with this ankle? It's broken!" The man nodded. "Yes," he said, "I figure I broke it two weeks ago, when I tripped and fell downstairs."

"Two weeks ago?" the doctor cried out. "Why didn't you come to see me sooner?" The man shrugged his shoulders. "Well, you see, Doc," he said, "every time I tell my wife I don't feel well, she tells me to stop smoking." Here is a different way to make:

SMOKED SALMON WITH EGGS

[SERVES SIX TO EIGHT]

4 tablespoons butter
¼ pound smoked salmon (lox), chopped
1 medium onion, chopped
parsley
⅛ teaspoon pepper
6 eggs, beaten

Melt half of the butter in frying pan, fry the lox quickly, just long enough so it gets pale. Remove it from pan, and now wilt the chopped onion in the hot butter. Remove that, too. Add the rest of the butter to the pan, mix the parsley and pepper in with the eggs, and drop 2 tablespoons of the eggs into the pan. Put 1 teaspoon of chopped lox on the top of the egg, sprinkle with some chopped fried onion, and with a spatula, fold the egg over so the lox and onion are covered. Press the egg down lightly with spatula, then remove pancakes from pan. Keep doing this until you have used up the eggs, salmon, onions. Put a plate over a small pot of boiling water and put the pancakes on the plate, as you finish each one, so they'll stay hot.

They are wonderful as appetizers, cocktail party thirst-creators, late Sunday breakfast treats—any time at all. And they are good for Lenten fasters, too.

The small boy kept asking his father questions like "Why is that dog walking down the street?"—which the father could answer only by saying that he supposed the dog was visiting friends.

When the little boy asked why the sky was blue, his father sent him up to his room. The questions became more and more difficult for the father to answer and he was becoming quite desperate, for no father, of course, likes to look like an ignoramus to his son. But he was vindicated one day when his son asked him, "Daddy, why is the ocean so salty?" The father smiled patronizingly, and replied, to the boy's immense satisfaction, "Because, son, there live in the ocean millions and millions of herring."

This is the way the Swedish people in our neighborhood make:

BAKED HERRING

[SERVES TEN TO FIFTEEN]

4 fillets salt herring
6 potatoes
3 onions

½ teaspoon pepper
3 tablespoons butter
bread crumbs

Make sure there are no bones in the fillets and let them soak overnight in cold water. Next morning, drain them, cover with cold water again for several hours. Cut the herring into bite-size pieces. Peel the potatoes and slice them quite thin. Same with the onions. Now get hold of a baking dish, grease it and put in a layer of potatoes, dust it lightly with pepper, cover it with a layer of herring, and over that put a layer of onions. Keep repeating this process until you have used up these ingredients. NOTE: the top layer should be potatoes. Over that layer sprinkle your bread crumbs, dot with butter, and in a 375 degree oven, bake it for 45 minutes. If you like herring real salty, cut down on the soaking time. Best thing we know to go with this dish is a nice cold glass of beer. Or two. Except for the kiddies, of course.

With usual thoughtfulness, extreme care had been taken not to fill the drinking-water container on the Long Island Railroad train. Our friend was quickly annoyed and continued to be so when the elderly man next to her kept saying, after a fruitless trip to the water cooler (fruitless?), "Oh, my, my, my, I have such a terrible thirst!"

Finally, the train pulled into a station and our friend jumped off, got a cold bottle of soda pop and brought it to the elderly man, who gulped it down thirstily. Our friend sat back happily, certain that now the trip would be less annoying, when the man said, and kept saying, "Oh, my, my, my, was I thirsty!" You know what had made him so thirsty? A big plate of:

HERRING SALAD (that's what)

[SERVES SEVENTEEN TO TWENTY]

6 fillets salt herring
6 scallions, cut up
6 radishes, cut up
2 tomatoes, quartered
2 green peppers, chopped
1 cup lettuce, shredded
3 cold boiled potatoes, cubed

¼ cup cider vinegar
4 tablespoons salad or olive oil
¼ teaspoon ground black pepper

If you don't care too much for the taste of herring, soak it overnight in milk. If you do like herring, just wash it and cut it up into ½-inch pieces. Now cut up the scallions and radishes, quarter the tomatoes, and chop the peppers. Mix everything up with the lettuce, cubed potatoes, vinegar, and oil. Sprinkle with the freshly ground black pepper and refrigerate.

Sven Jensen had been courting Jennie Olsen for quite awhile, and though he was obviously deeply smitten with the pretty girl, and though she returned those feelings, neither of them was very articulate. One beautiful moonlit evening the couple sat on Jennie's porch and spent the time looking at the full moon, at each other, sighing, but saying nothing at all. Finally, Sven blurted out, to Jennie's great surprise, and to his own astonishment, "Jennie, will you marry me?" When Jennie recovered from her shock, she whispered, "Yes, Sven."

And then there was another long silence, which finally was broken by Jennie. "Sven," she said shyly, "don't you think you should say something else?" Sven looked at his beloved. "Aye think," he said bewilderedly, "aye say too much already." Maybe the Scandinavians don't talk very much, but they certainly know their appetizers, like:

ANCHOVIES AND EGGS

[SERVES EIGHT TO TEN]

1 small onion, sliced
2 tablespoons butter
1 can anchovy fillets
4 eggs
2 cups milk

1 tablespoon parsley,
  chopped
black pepper, freshly
  ground

Fry the sliced onion in butter until it is soft. Grease a baking dish—you can use the butter in which you fried the onion—and put into it the anchovy fillets, and on top of them the onion. Beat the eggs into the milk, add the parsley, and pour the mixture into the baking dish. Sprinkle with black pepper. In an oven preheated to 375 degrees bake the dish until the eggs are set, which will take about 30 minutes. This is a lovely cocktail appetizer, for it is a great thirst provoker.

We've given dinner parties in which each course was cooked with a different kind of booze, and it's great fun when your guests try to figure out just what booze was used in which dish, beginning with this cocktail accompaniment as an appetizer:

RUMMY ANCHOVY-EGGS

[SERVES SIX]

3 tablespoons butter
6 small mushrooms, chopped
2 small onions, chopped
1 teaspoon parsley, chopped
6 eggs, hard-boiled

pepper to taste
3 tablespoons Puerto Rican rum
6 anchovy fillets, chopped
6 toast rounds
bread crumbs

Melt half the butter in pan. Mix together the mushrooms, onions, parsley, and the yolks of the hard-boiled eggs, and sprinkle with a little pepper. Put the mixture into the pan, and cook it until the onions and mushrooms are soft. Halfway through the cooking, add the rum. Take it out of pan, mix in the chopped anchovies, and stuff the egg whites with the mixture. Now put the stuffed eggs on the rounds of toast, sprinkle them with bread crumbs, dot them with the remaining butter and put them in broiler, 3 inches from source of heat, until the tops are browned.

We heard about a woman who kept having trouble with her husband because he always expected her to have dinner right there on the table the minute he came home from work. The difficulty was that he always came home at different times. One night, though, she cured him of his complaining. He came home as usual, grumbling because he had to wait for his dinner, and then he shouted, "Never mind, never mind, I'm going out to have dinner in a restaurant."

His wife came to the door and stopped him. "Wait," she said, "for just five minutes." He looked at her with suspicion. "Five minutes?" he asked. "What's going to happen in five minutes?" His wife smiled. "Just give me enough time to go to the kitchen and throw out everything I've prepared," she said, "and I'll go to the restaurant with you." He never complained about waiting for dinner again, because it cost him $18 in the restaurant, for his wife had a triple portion of:

CAVIAR BLINIS

[SERVES FIVE TO TEN]

1 cake yeast
1 cup lukewarm water
¾ cup flour
1 cup buckwheat flour
1 cup milk, hot
3 eggs, separated
⅛ teaspoon salt
1 teaspoon sugar

3 tablespoons melted
    butter
¼ cup sour cream
lots more sour cream
lots more melted butter
caviar (as much as you can
    afford)

In a bowl, dissolve the yeast in the cup of luke-warm water. Stir in ½ cup of the flour and ¼ cup of the buckwheat flour, combining everything thoroughly. Cover the bowl with a towel, set in a warm, draft-free place, and let it stand for about 3 hours. Now add both remaining flours, mix everything together, cover it again with the towel and let it stand for 1½ hours. Add the cup of hot milk to the raised batter, and combine it well. Now beat the egg yolks, the salt and sugar, and add the melted butter. Beat the egg whites unmercifully until they are stiff. Fold the stiffened egg whites into the sour cream and combine both mixtures with the batter. You know what to do now? You cover it with a towel again and let it stand for one more hour, for goodness' sake! (You know, *you* don't have to stand around watching this stand around; go read a book, go for a walk, do something constructive, like taking a nap, maybe.)

When you get back to the batter, get a pan good and hot, grease it lightly with very little butter and drop a spoonful of the batter on it for each blini. The batter should be quite loose. Brown the blinis on both sides and as you finish a batch, put them on a large plate which rests on a pot of hot water, so they'll stay warm.

When they're all done, bring them to the table, where there should be a pitcher of hot, melted butter, lots of sour cream, and caviar. Whole, black caviar is fantastically expensive, because it comes from Russia or Iran; pressed caviar, which is made of crushed black caviar, is not *quite* as expensive; red caviar (which is salmon, not sturgeon, roe) is pretty reasonable. Douse the blinis with butter, slop on sour cream, and top with the caviar.

"Why are you so late this morning?" Suzanne LeRoy, the Sunday school teacher, asked the small boy.

"Because," said the boy, "I asked my father if I could go fishing, and he said I couldn't, that I had to come here instead."

Miss LeRoy beamed approvingly. "Your father was absolutely right," she said. "And did he explain the reason why it would be wrong to go fishing on Sunday?"

"Yes," said the small boy, "he said I had to go to Sunday school because there wasn't enough bait for the both of us."

If you ever catch flounder, or buy it, here's how to make:

COLD BAKED MARINATED FISH

[SERVES THREE AS MAIN COURSE, TWELVE AS APPETIZER]

3 flounder fillets	1 egg, beaten
1 teaspoon salt	1 cup cracker meal

SAUCE

1 large onion, sliced	¼ cup vinegar
2 cloves garlic, chopped	1 teaspoon salt
1 tablespoon butter	2 tablespoons sugar
1½ cups water	2 tablespoons mixed
1 can condensed tomato	pickling spices, in
soup	cheesecloth bag

Wash, dry, and salt the fillets. Cut each slice into 4 pieces. Now grease a large aluminum pan, lightly. Dip each piece of fish into beaten egg, roll it in cracker meal, getting it coated on each side. Put the pieces of fish in the pan, side by side, and bake for 40 minutes in oven preheated to 350 degrees, turning the fish pieces once. While the fish is baking, make the sauce. Slice and brown the onion and garlic in the butter, pour the 1½ cups of water into the pan and bring it to a boil. Now add the tomato soup, vinegar, salt, sugar, and pickling spices, which should be crushed and tied up in a little cheesecloth bag. Bring it all to a boil, and keep stirring it for about 5 minutes. When the fish is baked, put it into a crock, or other container that will withstand heat, pour the sauce over the fish, and let it cool. Refrigerate it for at least a day. This could be a main course, but it is great for creating an appetite for food or drink.

The young married couple was getting nowhere at all figuring out a budget, so they agreed
that each of them would keep a strict accounting of
money received and money spent. When the young
husband cashed his next paycheck he gave his wife
$50 and told her to write down what happened to
the money. He would do the same thing, and in
that way they could work out some sensible system
of budgeting their money. The following week he
asked his wife to show him her records. She proudly
brought forth a little notebook where the man read:
"Received $50. Spent every cent." Some of it she
spent on:

LOBSTER FRITTERS

[MAKES FIFTEEN OR SO]

1 cup flour	2 eggs, beaten
1 teaspoon baking powder	2 tablespoons butter,
¼ teaspoon salt	melted
⅛ teaspoon pepper	1 cup lobster meat
⅛ teaspoon paprika	1½ cups oil
½ cup milk	

Combine the flour, baking powder, salt, pepper,
and paprika by sifting. Add the milk slowly, stirring
all the time, then the eggs, and then the melted butter and lobster meat. (You can use meat from lobster
tails, and chopped shrimp are great this way, too.)
Now heat the oil and drop the mixture into the oil
by the spoonful. Brown the fritters on both sides
and drain them. Serve this with lemon wedges and:

TARTAR SAUCE

4 tablespoons mayonnaise	1 tablespoon onion juice
1 clove garlic, pressed or	1 teaspoon capers, minced
mashed	1 teaspoon parsley,
1 small sweet pickle,	chopped
minced fine	

Mix everything together violently and refrigerate for a couple of hours, at least. Or, better yet, put everything into a blender and agitate it severely. Or, for variety in your sauces, try:

SAUCE BÉARNAISE

¼ cup butter
1 egg yolk
1½ teaspoons lemon juice
salt to taste

½ teaspoon onion, chopped
1 teaspoon parsley, chopped
1 teaspoon thyme

In a double boiler, put one-third of the butter with the egg yolk and lemon juice. Stir it like mad, and don't let the water come anywhere near a boil! Add the salt, onion, parsley, and thyme, and then, slowly, the rest of the butter, stirring steadily. If it separates (heavens forfend!), add a little hot water and stir, stir, stir.

The Mexican gardener employed by Mitzi Gaynor to take care of her lovely lawns and gardens in Beverly Hills announced proudly one morning that he and his wife had adopted a baby. "That's nice," said Mitzi. "What kind is it?" She meant, of course, was it a boy or a girl. When the man replied, "A Jewish boy," Mitzi was not surprised, because she knew her gardener wanted to lower himself by becoming a gag writer for TV comedians.

"Why not a Mexican boy?" she asked, nevertheless bracing herself. "Because," said the Mexican gardener, "Jewish boys take care of their old parents." If you want your guests to think you take good care of them, give them this hot appetizer:

GUACAMOLE

[A SPREAD FOR TEN TO FIFTEEN]

2 avocados
1 tomato
1 small onion
2 cloves garlic
2 teaspoons chili powder, or 1 chili pepper

2 tablespoons olive oil
3 tablespoons lemon or lime juice
salt and pepper
chopped red pepper flakes (optional)

Peel, seed, and slice the avocados. Peel the tomato and chop it and the onion very fine. Now mash the avocados and mix together with the onion and tomato. Press the garlic cloves, stir into the mixture. Add the olive oil, lemon or lime juice, chili and salt and pepper. Crumble the chopped red pepper flakes—be careful, they're real hot, so watch out how much of this you use—and add this to the mixture. The spread should be as smooth as you can get it. Of course, if you have an electric blender, it's a cinch. Just toss everything into the blender and let it run on high. Then stop the blender, scrape the stuff down to the blades, and let it run slowly until it is all smooth. Refrigerate. Serve this with unsalted crackers, as a dip. Mexicans eat it with tortillas.

The boy called his father, at home in the Bronx, from Los Angeles, where he was attending the University of California. "Pop," the boy said, "I'm in a jam, and I need $150 right away." His father shouted back, "There's something wrong with this connection, I can't hear a word you're saying!" So the boy spoke louder. "I need $150 right away," he shouted. "This is terrible," said the father, "we have a very bad connection."

At this point, the operator broke in. "I can hear him all right," she said. "You can hear him, hey?" said the father. "So okay, lady, you send him the $150." If your son is in college, far from home, he will keep calling long distance and telegraphing for you to send him some homemade:

KNISHES

[MAKES FIFTEEN TO TWENTY]

6 tablespoons chicken fat or butter
1 small onion, minced
4 cups potatoes, mashed
3 eggs

½ cup flour (potato flour is best)
1 teaspoon salt
¼ teaspoon pepper

We know a fellow named John Muth who says he can't ever eat anything that he never ate before he was 12 years old, isn't that silly? But one time we induced him to eat a knish, and he said, "Knishes are delicious," but the trouble was he didn't pronounce it right—he left off the "k," which is a terrible thing to do. About this fellow, Muth, you know, he was born in New York, and has lived there all his life, more than 40 years, and he has never eaten pastrami! That's like being a Roman and never eating spaghetti, for goodness' sake! Oh, well, let's get back to the knishes.

What you do first is hot up half the butter or chicken fat and sauté the minced onion until it is soft, then remove it from the pan and let it cool. Now you mix together the mashed potatoes, the eggs, flour, salt and pepper, and then the onion. Knead it until it is all nice and smooth.

You know what the beauty part about knishes is? The beauty part about knishes is that you can put into them almost any kind of stuffing you like. As a matter of fact, what you should do is have several different kinds of stuffing when you make a batch of these potato knishes to serve with drinks at a party. What you do is break off little hunks and roll them into balls a little smaller than ping pong balls. Make a dent with your thumb—or your pinky —fill the dent with your stuffing, close the dent up.

Now you grease a pan or a baking sheet, and bake the knishes in an oven preheated to 375 degrees until they're browned.

For stuffings, you can use chopped liver mixed with fried onions; rolled anchovy fillets; chopped nuts, shrimp, or lobster; a clam or an oyster; chopped hard-boiled eggs; chopped chicken, any kind of chopped meat, cheese—oh, just about anything at all! That's the beauty part of knishes! You can have them all made up before your guests arrive, pop them into the oven when they show up, and by the time your company is ready for their second booze, the knishes will be ready, too!

A friend of ours named Joe McCarthy—he's a writer and never was a U. S. Senator—who is a prominent father, tells us about another fellow out on Long Island where he lives—it is a particularly fecund area—who has a new set of twins.

This man does, of course, love his children, but the duplicates his wife just presented him with are a source of much annoyance to him—because whenever he wheels them around town in their baby carriage someone is bound to simper up to him in order to "ooh" and "aah." And invariably they ask, brightly, "Are they twins?" This gambit has bored his friend so much that now the man snarls, "No, they aren't twins: I have a wife and a mistress." At least once a good wife should try:

PIROSHKI

[MAKES FIFTEEN TO TWENTY]

2 cups flour
½ teaspoon baking powder
½ teaspoon salt
¼ cup shortening
1 egg
4 tablespoons ice water

Sift the flour, baking powder, and salt and work in the shortening with your hands, the way your mother used to do, and the way we do, or use a pastry blender if you want to. Beat up the egg with the ice water and then add it to the flour mixture and knead it. Roll dough out about ⅛ inch thick and cut out 3-inch circles. The wonder of *piroshki* is that the varieties are limited only by your imagination, for they can be filled with virtually anything you like—meat, fish, potatoes, fruits, nuts, anything, maybe, except gin, and we're not too sure you can't have a ginny *piroshki*. After you put whatever filling you choose, by the tablespoon, in the center of each circle of dough, moisten your fingers, fold the dough, and press the edges together. Put the *piroshki* on a greased baking sheet and bake them for 15 minutes, or until they're browned, in an oven preheated to 400 degrees. The filling we like best is:

CHICKEN LIVER-MUSHROOM FILLING

½ pound chicken livers
¼ pound mushrooms
1 large onion, chopped
4 tablespoons chicken fat
1½ teaspoons salt
¼ teaspoon coarse black pepper

Wash the livers in cold water, remove membranes. Chop up the mushrooms. Fry onions and mushrooms in fat until they are brown, then sauté the chicken livers gently—they are delicate little things and should not be overcooked—and then chop everything up together, adding seasoning. Some like their *piroshki* filling to be quite smooth, others like it somewhat coarse. Do it the way you like.

The boy was home from college with a degree in business administration and he looked over his father's establishment. At the end of the first day, he went to his father. "Listen, old Daddy," he said in his obnoxious way, "the way you run your business is a scandal. I'm going to take over the office and straighten things out." A week later, the man's wife woke in the middle of the night to see her husband pacing the floor, muttering to himself. "What's the matter?" she asked. "Oh," he said, "it's terrible. Our son tells me, after a week of studying the books in my office, that I'm on the brink of bankruptcy." His wife sneered. "Listen, the business is just the way it always was," she said. "We live well, we pay our rent, we put our son through college. The only difference is our son and his fancy education. Give him some money and send him away and everything will be all all right, like it was before." If you have leftovers, and everybody always has from big meals, everything will be all right if you make:

MEAT BLINTZES

[MAKES ABOUT TEN]

4 eggs	water
salt and pepper	fat
1 cup cake flour (matzo flour is best)	

Beat the eggs with salt and pepper—maybe 1 teaspoon salt and a ¼ teaspoon pepper. Add the flour slowly to the eggs, beating, and add enough water to make a thin batter. It *must* be a thin batter, see? Now get hold of a small frying pan, grease it very lightly, get it good and hot, but not smoking. Drop in 2 tablespoons of the batter and QUICKLY turn the pan so the bottom is entirely covered by a thin layer of the batter. Fry it until the edges turn away from the sides and bottom of the pan and turn it out when the bottom is golden brown. Keep repeating this process until all the batter is used up. The secret in making these *bletlach,* or leaves, is to have the pan just hot enough, and very lightly greased. It is best to grease the pan by dipping a paper napkin in melted fat and rubbing the pan lightly with the fat-soaked napkin. When you've got the leaves all done, make the:

BLINTZ FILLING

2 cups cooked chicken, meat or liver, chopped	2 eggs salt and pepper
4 tablespoons onion, chopped	

Mix all the ingredients, and put a heaping tablespoon in the center of each leaf *(bletel),* on the browned side up. Roll them all up and tuck in the ends securely. Fry the blintzes in hot fat until they are well and truly browned and crisp, and you've got a *meichel fah der beichel,* which translates fairly roughly into "a yummy for the tummy."

*A*fter having painted all the horrors and evils of addiction to strong waters, the temperance lecturer decided to point up his lesson by citing the superior wisdom over man of the beasts of the field.

"I had an old jackass which I used on my farm for plowing the fields," he told his audience, "and one day after the jackass had worked from sunup to sundown, I put before him two pails. One contained rum, and the other water. Which do you think that jackass drank from?"

"The pail of water," shouted a man in the rear of the auditorium. "Correct," said the lecturer, "and do you know why?"

The man who had answered him stood up unsteadily and shouted back, "Yes," he said as he walked out of the hall, "because he was a jackass!"

You'll never be called that if you serve this hors d'oeuvre which we first tasted at a Caribbean party:

CHICKEN SAUSAGE

[WILL SERVE FIFTEEN TO TWENTY]

1½ pounds chicken breasts
½ pound boiled ham
¼ pound chicken livers
¼ cup water

6 eggs, beaten
¼ teaspoon nutmeg
¼ teaspoon pepper
½ teaspoon salt
¾ cup cracker crumbs

Cut meat from chicken breasts, reserving bones; grind chicken and boiled ham together through finest blade of meat grinder. Boil chicken livers in water with ¼ teaspoon salt for 5 minutes, then drain and chop fine. Mix 3 eggs with nutmeg, pepper, and salt, add chopped liver, and combine all this with the ground chicken and ham, including 3 tablespoons of the cracker crumbs. Put mixture on sheet of waxed paper, and shape it into a roll about 12 inches long and 2½ inches thick. Now sprinkle it all over with the remaining crumbs, dip it in the remaining eggs, and cover it with more crumbs.

Put the roll on a cloth long enough to cover it, sprinkle on any remaining crumbs, then roll it up in the cloth and tie the ends.

Make stock by boiling chicken bones with 5 tablespoons salt in 4 quarts of water in a rectangular pan large enough to hold roll of chicken meat. After you have made the stock, cook the roll of meat —in cloth—for one hour, turning it once. Now take it out of stock, let it cool, then remove the cloth. Refrigerate it until the next day, slice it thin, and serve it cold on toast.

In the spring of each year, the Japanese in the old days used to have a pretty little festival to honor their poets, all of whom were held in great esteem, and to pick the Poet of the Year. Competing poets chose a spot along one of the winding brooks in the Imperial Palace grounds, and when they were all lined up, a large goblet of *sake*, which is a sort of wine made from rice, was floated down the stream. As it came to the first one in line, he grabbed it out of the water, gulped a slug of *sake*, and recited an impromptu poem. Then he let the goblet float down the stream to the next poet. After they had all drunk their *sake* and recited their poems, the Emperor picked the best one, and then they all had more *sake* and maybe some:

FISHY EGG ROLL

[MAKES ABOUT TEN]

½ pound fish (white meat)
½ teaspoon salt
1 tablespoon sugar
6 eggs
2 tablespoons soy sauce
3 tablespoons sake or sherry
3 tablespoons water
1 tablespoon salad oil

Skin, bone the fish, and chop it fine. Now add salt and sugar to the fish. Beat up the eggs, soy, wine, and water and combine with the fish. Heat half the oil in a large pan, put half the fish-and-egg mixture in it, and fry until it is brown; then turn it and brown the other side. Turn it out on a napkin or towel and roll it up in cloth, fastening ends with toothpicks. Now do the same with the other half of the fish-and-egg mixture, using remaining salad oil. Refrigerate for hours, remove wrapping, and slice into 2-inch pieces. Lovely with *sake*, sherry, gin, beer, or whatever. Serve on pumpernickel rounds, which the Japanese never had.

The boy walked into the grocery store. "My ma says she wants one pound of Gorgonzola cheese," he said. The storekeeper got the cheese, wrapped it up, and handed it to the boy. "My ma says you should charge it," he said. "Okay," said the storekeeper, "what's your name?"

"Papadoupolis," said the boy.

"Listen, kid," said the storekeeper, "take the cheese and tell your ma it won't cost her a cent. You think that in one day I'm going to write 'Gorgonzola' and 'Papadoupolis'?" It is much easier to make:

FRIED MOZZARELLA CHEESE

1 pound Mozzarella cheese	3 eggs, beaten
½ cup flour	1 cup bread crumbs
½ teaspoon salt	½ cup olive oil

Slice the cheese into 1-inch cubes. Sift the flour and salt together. Coat the cheese cubes with flour, dip them in beaten eggs, then in bread crumbs, back into the eggs, and then give them a final coating of bread crumbs. Heat the oil and fry the cheese cubes until they are golden brown.

Soups

SOUPS

Do you have a warm feeling of kinship for the citizens of our sister state, Massachusetts? If you do, perhaps you would like to memorialize a day famous in that Commonwealth's glorious history by making a dish which has great significance on August the Fourth.

MUTTON AND MUTTON SOUP

[SERVES FOUR TO SIX]

3 pounds mutton (adult lamb)	1 parsnip
	1 turnip
1 teaspoon salt	3 small onions
3 quarts cold water	

Salt mutton, place in kettle, and let stand for half an hour to bring out flavor. Pour in cold water to cover, let stand for 1 more hour. Bring to boil, then simmer 3 hours. Blot up excess fat with paper napkin. Add vegetables; simmer for additional hour. Taste for flavor, add seasoning to taste. Cool and then refrigerate overnight. Anybody who likes mutton soup likes it hot. On the morning of August 4th, 1892, in Fall River, Mass., Mrs. Borden served this meat and soup to her stepdaughter, Lizzie Borden. Mrs. Borden and her husband were found later that day, axed unto death. She had served the mutton soup cold, with a side dish of bananas. For breakfast.

Lizzie was acquitted by a jury, and if you had been on that jury undoubtedly you also would have voted to free her. My goodness! Cold mutton soup! For breakfast, yet! Fortunately, these days it is extremely difficult to find a place which sells mutton, so we don't think anyone will be making soup from it. Even if you can find mutton, don't. But here now are some soups that will cause people to take flowers to you, not an axe.

When he speaks of chicken, Brillat-Savarin, that wise and funny French gastronomical philosopher, says: ". . . we shall find food that is both light and savory, and agrees as well with invalids as with the man whose health is most robust; for who among us, after faring by command of the doctor like a very desert father, has not revelled in a well-done wing of chicken, the herald of his recall to social life?"

There was this woman in the Bronx who bought two live chickens and kept them on her fire escape to fatten them up. Sadly, one of the birds became indisposed. So she killed the healthy chicken to make soup to bring the one that was ill back to health. Here's her recipe for:

CHICKEN-IN-THE-POT

[SERVES FOUR TO SIX]

1 3-pound chicken, cut up
1 tablespoon salt
3 quarts cold water
vegetables (onions, carrots, celery stalks, bunches of soup greens, anything that you like, or that's available; parsley, turnips, even parsnips will do.)

Salt the chicken, let it stand in kettle one hour. This brings out flavorful juices. Add water and allow to stand for another half-hour. Bring water to boiling point, then simmer, covered, for three hours. You like clear soup? If you do, remove stuff that has come to surface of kettle. If you want the soup to be nutritious, leave it alone. Add vegetables, at least two cupfuls, but as much as you like and whatever kind you like. Cover and simmer for another hour (that makes four hours altogether). Strain, chill, remove the surface fat. (A paper napkin will blot up excess fat.) Throw the vegetables away; all the good that was in them is now in the soup. After four hours of cooking you will have 1½ quarts of soup. Reheat soup, taste it for flavor, add salt and pepper if required. Hot soup should be hot. Cold soup should be cold. Lukewarm soup is an abomination. Do you like matzo balls with your chicken-in-the-pot? ☞

MATZO BALLS (KNAIDLACH)

2 eggs	½ teaspoon salt
¼ cup butter, or, preferably, chicken fat, melted	1 cup matzo meal
	⅓ cup cold water

Beat together eggs, fat, and salt. Stir in matzo meal slowly. Add water as needed. Keep stirring until mixture is stiff and resists fork. Form into ball and chill for two hours in refrigerator. Tear off pieces and form into size of golf balls. Cook in soup for 30 minutes.

In Scotland the first Monday in January is called Handsel Monday. "Handsel" means a gift given by hand. And in olden times on this day, farmers used to give the men who worked for them a great breakfast of a large variety of roasted meats, all washed down with ale and whiskey, and then everybody spent the day visiting their friends, who probably gave them more roasted meats and ale and booze. How nice! If any friends visit you on this night, give them:

COCKALEEKIE

[SERVES FIVE TO SIX]

1 4½- to 5-pound chicken, cut up	1½ cups rice
2 teaspoons salt	12 leeks, white parts only, sliced; or 2 medium onions, sliced
½ teaspoon pepper	

The name of this soup—delicious versions can be found in cans—comes from the fact that it is generally made with a tough old rooster, or cock, see?

Dissect the chicken, put it in a pot, cover the chicken with water, bring it to a boil, and then simmer gently until it is tender, about 2 hours. At end of first hour, add the salt and pepper. Now take the chicken out of the pot and put in the rice and the sliced white parts of the leeks or onions, and cook the broth for another 20 to 25 minutes. While this is going on, take the meat off the chicken and add it to the soup (you throw the bones away). Cook it for another 10 minutes and what have you got? Scottish chicken-in-the-pot, that's what.

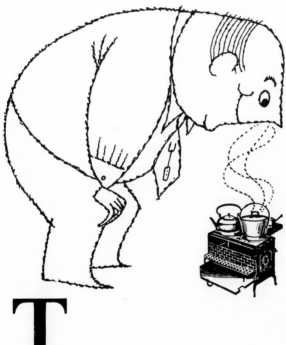

The husband of a friend of ours is a very nice man with but one fault. He is a terrible glutton. He is very fat, but still he keeps eating everything he shouldn't, which, of course, makes him all the fatter. One day, our friend told us, her husband waddled into the kitchen where she was cooking a delicious-smelling soup. "My," he said, "that smells delicious." She didn't answer him, but only sobbed quietly, because she knew what was on his mind. "I'm going to take a little nap now," said her husband. "Will you please wake me up when I am hungry?" This was not what she expected. "What in the world do you mean?" she cried out. "How can I tell when you are hungry?" He stared at her disdainfully. "Don't be silly," he said. "Whenever you wake me I'll be hungry." What she was cooking was:

TURKEY SOUP

[SERVES FOUR TO SIX]

turkey carcass	½ cup chopped onion
water to cover	¼ cup parsley
¾ cup chopped carrots	1 cup tomatoes
1 cup chopped celery	½ teaspoon salt
(leave on leaves)	¼ teaspoon pepper

You know how many people just throw out the bones of a turkey after Thanksgiving. Thousands! Maybe millions! It is a terrible waste, because turkey soup is so wonderful, and so full of nourishment. What wasteful people we Americans are! Don't you be one of them, hear? Cut, tear, chop up the carcass after first seeing to it that there are no bits of dressing clinging to the inside of the body cavity. Bring the water to a boil, add the turkey bones, cover the pot, and simmer for one hour. Now add all the other ingredients—you can toss in whatever vegetables you have around the house; you don't have to stick to just the ones we listed, you know. If you have any leftover vegetables that have been cooked already, add them to the soup about 5 minutes before you reheat and serve the soup. Now, after you have added the uncooked vegetables, simmer, covered, for another hour. Then let it cool, chill it, skim off the fat, reheat the soup (this is the time to add cooked vegetables). And serve it real hot. Hot soup should be hot, we always say, cold soup should be cold, but lukewarm soup is pheh.

January 28th is the birthday of Charlemagne, King of the Franks and Emperor of the West, who lived from 742 to the year 814. Charlemagne is credited with many, many accomplishments, but we like him best for two things he is said to have done. He is supposed to have founded the University of Paris, but maybe an even greater achievement was to stop the peasants of what is now France from trampling grapes, when they made wine, with their bare feet. This, he said, was unsanitary! Can you imagine? In the eighth century, to be aware of sanitation? *Incroyable!*

In France, for a long time, on Charlemagne's Day, the heads of universities and their faculties used to give a great breakfast with champagne, and the guests of honor were the students with the highest standing. Charlemagne himself was said to have been a moderate eater for royalty in those days; for breakfast, merely a joint of venison and a whole cheese, and no more than three glasses of wine.

He was pretty moderate in other ways, too. He never had more than a couple of wives and a small gaggle of concubines at one time. As far as anyone knows, what has always been a great national dish, and one which Charlemagne may have eaten, is:

ONION SOUP

[SERVES SIX]

1½ pounds onions, sliced
⅓ cup butter
3 cans concentrated
    beef consommé
2 cans water

6 slices toast
½ pound Gruyère,
    Swiss, or Cheddar
    cheese, grated
pepper

Slice the onions very thin, separate the rings. Melt all but 2 tablespoons of the butter and sauté the onions, stirring, until they are well browned. In a separate saucepan combine the consommé with the water, hot it up and pour it into the pan with the onions and let it simmer, covered, for 30 minutes over low heat. Now get hold of a large baking dish or casserole and put in 3 of the slices of toast. Pour half the soup on the toast, and then pour on that, lavishly, half the cheese. Add rest of the soup. Now put the other toast slices into the soup, pour on the rest of the cheese, dot it all with the remaining butter and add pepper. Put the dish into a hot oven and bake it until the cheese on top melts. This is great for an evening meal, but it is especially good for a late Saturday or Sunday breakfast. And if you want to drink champagne with it, who's going to stop you? What was good enough for Charlemagne is none too good for us Americans.

December 10th is Human Rights Day, because on that day in 1948 the United Nations adopted the Universal Declaration of Human Rights, and its anniversary is celebrated in almost every country in the world—maybe, ironically, behind the Iron Curtain, too. We think that one of the fundamental rights of all humans is to be able to eat well, and so they will, if you give your family:

BRANDIED ONION SOUP

[SERVES FOUR TO FIVE]

½ cup butter
2 tablespoons olive oil
2 pounds onions, sliced
6 cups beef bouillon
1 teaspoon sugar

salt and pepper to taste
5 tablespoons brandy
French bread (or Italian)
grated Parmesan cheese

Melt butter over low heat, stir in olive oil, and fry the onions until they are quite brown. But don't burn them. Add the bouillon, sugar, salt, and pepper, cover the pan, and let it all simmer over very low heat for about 1 hour. Ten minutes before the hour is up, add the brandy and stir everything around. During the last 10 minutes, toast bread slices, put them in soup plates, and sprinkle with grated Parmesan cheese. Be lavish with the cheese. Now, when the hour is ended, pour the soup into the plates. The bread slices will float to the top. You know, don't you, that when you cook with brandy, wine, or beer, the heat makes the alcohol evaporate in seconds? But the flavor of the liquor or wine adds zest to the dish! Of course, if you are leary about the kiddies, you can always put aside portions for them before you add the brandy.

A little boy we know asked his mother one day what she was cooking. "Macaroni," she snapped lovingly. The little boy pondered this. "But why is it called macaroni, Mommy?" he asked. His mother glared at him adoringly. "Because," she yelled affectionately, "that's the only name it could have. It looks like macaroni, it feels like macaroni, and it tastes like macaroni, so that's why they call it macaroni!" What she didn't tell the little boy is that when you cook it with beans it is called:

PASTA FAZOOLA

[SERVES SIX]

1 pound kidney beans	½ cup chopped celery
1 can whole tomatoes	½ pound elbow macaroni
1 clove garlic, minced	5 tablespoons olive oil
1 carrot, chopped	½ cup grated Parmesan
salt and pepper	cheese
1 onion, chopped	

Soak the beans overnight. Drain and cover them with fresh water, add salt, cover pot, and bring the water to boiling point and then simmer for an hour. Add everything except the macaroni, olive oil, and cheese, and simmer for another hour.

Now get another pot, put in enough water to cover the macaroni, add salt, bring the water to boil, and add the macaroni. Stir it from time to time, and cook from 8 to 10 minutes, depending on how you like your macaroni: if you like it chewy, or *al dente*, which is Italian meaning "for the teeth," cook it no more than 8 minutes. When the macaroni is as you like it, drain it and add to the beans.

Add the oil and stir it all around gently, and pour it all into a huge serving dish and spill the grated cheese all over it. (The way Italians spell this dish is *"Pasta e Fagioli."* But it is always called "Pasta Fazoola," and what it is, is pasta and kidney bean soup and is it good!) With plenty of Italian or French bread, this is a complete meal.

*t*he Russian couldn't be convinced that in the United States there was more freedom of speech than in his own country. "Listen," said the American, thoroughly exasperated, "if I wanted to, right now, I could fly to Washington, go to the White

House, and walk right into the President's office and tell him personally that I think he's a terrible man."

The Russian sneered. "So what?" he asked. "If I wanted to, I could fly to the Kremlin, walk right into Chairman Khrushchev's office and tell him right to his face that I think the President of the United States is a terrible man, too." Ivan the Terrible was a terrible man, but he loved good food and maybe he even ate:

HOT MEAT BORSCHT

[SERVES SIX TO EIGHT]

8 beets
3 quarts water, boiling
2 medium onions, minced
2 cloves garlic, minced
2 pounds short ribs
marrow bone
½ head of cabbage, shredded

salt and pepper to taste
4 tablespoons sugar, maybe a little more
¼ cup lemon juice, maybe more
2 eggs, beaten

Scrape all the beets; grate 4 of them and cut the others into 1-inch slices. Into the boiling water put all the beets, onions, garlic, meat, and bone. When the water comes to a boil again, cover the pot and simmer it for 1½ hours. After 30 minutes, skim off the top, re-cover the pot. When the soup has cooked for 1½ hours, add the cabbage, stir it all around, and add a little salt and pepper. Cook it uncovered for another 30 minutes, and then add the sugar and lemon juice, and cook for another 30 minutes. In a bowl, add some hot soup to the beaten eggs, beat it all up well, and then add this to the pot, stirring it around. Now taste the soup; it should be sweet and sour, so add sugar or lemon juice, whichever it requires. When you serve it, put some of the cut-up meat into each plate. Throw the bone away. Well, you don't *really* have to throw it away; do whatever you do with used-up old bones. And for when it gets warm, we have for you (see index) a cold, meatless borscht with sour cream and a hot potato.

St. Barbara's father, who was, alas, a pagan, was very cruel to the young girl and waxed particularly angry always because she used to feed the poor people. We know a girl whose maiden name was Joan O'Sullivan, a newspaper colleague of ours, who was brought up on corned beef and cabbage, Irish stew, and Irish coffee, and other such Gaelic delights until, one day, she went to a party, spoke to a stranger and, not long after that, fell in love with him and married him. This fellow's name is Archie Vassiliadis, a Greek-American artist, and now they have produced two little daughters and a book for teenagers called *100 Ways to Popularity*. Now the former Joan O'Sullivan has all but forgotten her Irish upbringing on Irish stew and Irish coffee, and on St. Barbara's Day she always feeds her husband:

FASSOULADA (Greek bean soup)

[SERVES SIX]

1 pound dried beans (Yankee, lima, or chick peas)	1 cup chopped carrots
	2 tablespoons parsley flakes
	3 tablespoons tomato paste
2 quarts water	½ cup olive oil
1 cup chopped celery	salt and pepper to taste
2 large onions, chopped	

Soak the beans overnight. Next day drain them, rinse them, and then cover with fresh water. Bring to a boil, then simmer for about 2 hours, or until the beans are tender. Taste one, that's how you'll know if they are tender. When they are tender, but not mushy, add all the other ingredients, stir the mixture around a couple of times, and let it simmer for about another half hour. DON'T let the beans get mushy, hear?

he boy was home from college for a vacation and his father fearfully asked him how he stood in his class. "I've got the second-highest standing in my whole class of 1,500," the boy said proudly. "Why aren't you at the top of your class?" asked the father, who was always griping about how expensive it was to put a boy through college. Because, the boy told him, a girl was at the top of the class, that's why he wasn't at the top.

"A girl?" cried out Daddy. "You mean to say you're going to let a mere girl beat you out in scholastic standing?" The boy smiled patronizingly. "Things have changed, old Daddy-o," he said politely. "It's not like it used to be in the old days when you were a boy. Chicks aren't very mere these days, you see."

Chick peas are known in almost every part of the world, and they have all kinds of names, like *homos* in the Middle East; *garbanzos* is what the Spanish-speaking people call them; Jews call them *nahit;* and the Greeks call chick peas *revithia.* Whatever they are called, they are especially good in:

CHICK PEA SOUP

[SERVES SIX]

1 pound dried chick peas	2 medium onions, chopped
2 quarts water	2 teaspoons salt
2 pounds beef	½ teaspoon pepper
1 marrow bone, cracked	
½ pound bacon, or ½ pound sausage	

Cover the chick peas with water and soak them overnight. Drain and rinse them just before you start cooking, which will take about 3 hours. (Don't be alarmed. You don't have to stand over the hot stove all this time; there are several intermissions from a half to a whole hour when you go your own jolly way. Okay?) You see those 2 quarts of water up there? Boil it. Put in the chick peas and bring the water to a boil again. Now reduce the heat, cover the pot, and let it simmer for 30 minutes. Add the beef and the cracked marrow bone. While this is cooking for another 30 minutes, prepare the bacon or sausage—or both, if you like. Half cook the bacon or sausage, cut it up, and add it to the pot. Cover it—you should have a tight cover—and simmer it on lowest possible heat for 1 hour more. Now add the onions and salt and pepper, and cook for 1 hour more. Cut up the beef into bite-size pieces, serve the soup with equal portions of each ingredient in each plate. This should be a full meal for 6 people, who won't need anything else but a salad or a dessert.

One of Fred Dickenson's three daughters, home from college for the weekend, was describing with great enthusiasm something she had learned in school the week before. "Look, Daddy!" she cried out with girlish joy in her voice. "Just imagine that I am holding a wand in my two hands. Now, in order to round out my upper arms and firm up certain of my muscles, all I have to do is hold it vertically in front of me in this fashion and rapidly move the lower end with great vigor!"

Fred, who is a world-renowned authority on the blending of malts and hops, listened to the pretty child with an expression of mingled pride, love, and astonishment. "My, my," he said admiringly, "isn't higher education marvelous!" And then, "If you had a bunch of straw tied to the lower end of that wand, you'd be sweeping," he adding sneeringly.

You can sweep your house while you cook:

BEEF SOUP WITH RICE OR NOODLES

[SERVES FIVE TO SIX]

beef shank	1 number 2½ can tomatoes
2 onions, chopped	¾ cup rice (or egg
1 cup chopped celery	noodles)
3 tablespoons butter	salt and pepper to taste

In a large pot, cover beef shank with water and bring it to a boil. While you are waiting for the water to boil, chop up the onions and celery and sauté them in butter for about 10 minutes. When the water comes to a boil, add the tomatoes and then add the sautéed vegetables, bring to a boil again, lower the heat and simmer, covered, until the meat is tender, about 2 hours. Remove the bone, cut off meat, and put bone back in pot; set aside meat. Remove the vegetables, put them through a sieve, and set aside. Add the rice or noodles and cook until they are tender. Before serving, correct seasoning, cut up meat in small pieces, and put it into soup with strained vegetables. This is a rich, thick soup and should make a complete meal for 5 or 6 people.

*t*he day before, the family had eaten roast beef. This day they were having hash. And when the head of the house bowed his head to say grace, the young son was heard to mutter. "And what's the matter with you?" asked the father. "Well, I don't see why we have to give thanks," the lad mumbled sweetly, "because we did it last night, and it's the same old stuff all over again." No one will mutter about your left-over dishes if you give them what the Chinese call:

YATKA MEIN

[SERVES SIX]

1 pound thin noodles	salt and pepper
2 cans consommé	3 hard-boiled eggs, halved
2½ cans water	6 tablespoons scallions,
1 to 2 cups meat, cooked	minced
and shredded (beef,	1 tablespoon parsley
pork, chicken, fish,	1 teaspoon soy sauce
anything)	

Boil the noodles in salted water for no more than 8 to 10 minutes. Mix the consommé and water and bring to boiling point and then lower heat so that it simmers. Drain the cooked noodles, add them to the consommé, drop the shredded meat into the pot, stir it all around for a minute or two. Correct seasoning. (The meat is already cooked, so it just has to be hotted up.) Now distribute the soup, noodles, and meat among 6 bowls, add half a hard-boiled egg to each one, share out the chopped scallions, sprinkle with parsley, and add soy sauce.

*T*his man had been making himself obnoxious to the Chinese laundry man for all the years he had been taking his clothes there, and the Chinese had taken it all calmly and with infuriating blandness. But one day, it became too much to bear. The boor pointed to the Chinese writing on his package of clothes and said, sneeringly, "That's my name in Chinese, I suppose?" The Chinese smiled. "No sir, suppose wrong. That descliption. Say, 'Big, fat Melican man, sroppy crothes, frat feet, stupid sense of humor.'"

Every Chinese restaurateur has told us that when their customers ask a question, generally they ask: "But what do you Chinese people have for breakfast—egg foo young, or chop suey, or what?" And generally the Chinese gentleman will say that he eats ham and eggs, just as everyone else does. But a traditional Chinese dish, which we've never seen on any menu, is eaten not only for breakfast, but at any other time of day, with variations, and it is called:

CONGEE (or JOOK)

[SERVES SIX]

¼ cup rice
2 quarts water
1 tablespoon dried shrimp

1 tablespoon grated tangerine or orange peel

The dried shrimp is an ingredient which can be bought only in Chinese or Japanese grocery stores, but almost every large city—and many small ones—in the country has at least one such store which can be found in the classified telephone directory. All you do is bring the water to a boil, add the rice, dried shrimp, and grated peel, bring to a boil again, and then simmer for 2½ hours. This is a fine gruel, and, incidentally, it is probably the best cure known to man for what the commercials on television call "dietary indiscretion," or hangover. There are many variations of *congee*, with beef, chicken, fish, and many other ingredients, which make a heartier meal than is generally wanted for breakfast, and one of these is chicken *congee*, called:

GAI JOOK

[SERVES FOUR TO SIX]

½ pound cooked chicken, cut into bite-size pieces
1 teaspoon vegetable oil
¼ teaspoon salt

1 teaspoon light soy sauce
⅛ teaspoon pepper
½ teaspoon sugar
1 tablespoon sherry

Stir all these ingredients together, pour into the basic *congee* (see previous recipe), bring to a boil, and simmer for about 5 minutes. This is wonderful served with chopped scallions. For beef *congee*, or *ngow yuk jook*, just substitute cubed cooked beef for the chicken. Same for *yu jook*, which is fish *congee*.

march 18th is the Fiesta of St. Joseph, the patron saint of Sicilian homes, and in every village it is celebrated with a feast given by the richest inhabitant. An old man, a pretty girl, and a child are chosen from among the villagers to represent the Holy Family, and they are served first. When they have finished the sumptuous, multi-course meal, open house is declared and then the other villagers take their turns at the table. This goes on all day long, and nobody keeps track of the repeaters. No matter what else is served, there is always a delicious, nourishing:

MINESTRONE

[SERVES SIX]

2 tablespoons olive oil
2 tablespoons butter
1 large onion, minced
2 cloves garlic, minced
1 teaspoon chopped
    parsley

1 tablespoon tomato paste
1½ quarts water, boiling
2 stalks celery, chopped
2 cups peas
salt and pepper to taste
1 cup elbow macaroni

Hot up the oil and butter in a large pot and then sauté the minced onion and garlic, then add the parsley. Dissolve the tomato paste in one cup of the boiling water, add it to the pot and let it cook for 5 minutes. Now add the celery and the peas and the boiling water and cook, covered, over low heat, for 45 minutes. Now add the seasoning and macaroni and cook for another 10 minutes. Have lots of any kind of grated cheese you like on the table so everyone can take as much as he wants of it to sprinkle on the soup.

What better way to celebrate George Washington's birthday can there be than to cook a dish which, though he didn't invent it, was inspired by him at Valley Forge during that terrible winter when it looked as though the infant nation would die of malnutrition, cold, and despair.

General Washington, it is said, called in the cook and begged him to cook something splendid for the grumbling, starving, rapidly deserting army. All he had in the mess, the cook said, was some tripe which a local butcher had donated, some bones, and scraps of meat, and a few peppercorns. "Do the best you can," said General Washington, so the cook, a Pennsylvania Dutchman, invented a soup which has been famous to this day as:

PHILADELPHIA PEPPER POT

[SERVES SIX]

1 pound honeycomb tripe	1 cup carrots, diced
1 2-pound veal knuckle	⅓ cup celery, diced
3 quarts cold water	½ cup sliced green pepper
½ teaspoon peppercorns	3 tablespoons parsley,
2 teaspoons salt	chopped
⅛ teaspoon thyme	1 tablespoon flour
1 tablespoon fat	¼ cup elbow macaroni
1 large onion, sliced	

Unfortunately, we don't know the name of George Washington's cook, or we might honor him, too. An old Pennsylvania Dutch recipe calls for cooking the tripe for 8 hours the day before making the soup, but this really isn't necessary. First cut the tripe up—after washing it, of course—into ½-inch pieces. Wipe the veal knuckle with a damp cloth, put it and the cut-up tripe into a large pot with the 3 quarts of water. Bring it to a boil and remove the scum that rises to the top. Add the peppercorns, salt, and thyme, reduce the heat, and cover the pot and let it simmer slowly for three hours.

Now strain the soup, discarding the peppercorns, and pour it back into the pot with the tripe and veal knuckle. Bring the soup to a boil, and let it cook uncovered, until the soup is reduced to about 2 quarts. Melt the fat, and sauté all the vegetables until they are soft. Now add the flour, stir it all around and add it all to the soup pot. Add the macaroni and cook it until the macaroni is tender, about 8 to 10 minutes. Now take out 'the veal knuckle and cut off the meat and put it into the soup (throw the bone away). Taste the soup and correct the seasoning; if you want it more peppery, add pepper, no?

The story goes that when the soldiers at Valley Forge smelled and ate this soup, they were so happy, they shouted, "Bring on the Redcoats!" But we have eaten with soldiers, and somehow, we doubt that that shout ever got shouted, no matter how good that soup was.

In the old days in China, the Feast of the Winter Solstice was celebrated every December. The whole family would gather in the kitchen, and when the Chinese say the whole family they mean the whole family—all the sons and their wives and children and all the daughters and their husbands and children, and the grandchildren, with their wives and husbands and great-grandchildren. It got pretty crowded.

They would make an offering to their ancestors, and then the newest bride would make a great lump of dough, and all the members of the family would take hunks and roll out pieces which they would fill with pork. On the next morning, they would be rolled in flour, then in brown sugar and sesame seeds, and cooked. Sounds something like piroshki, doesn't it? But we've told you about piroshki so this time we'll tell you about:

EGG CUBE SOUP

[SERVES FOUR TO SIX]

6 cups chicken stock or consommé
3 eggs
1 scallion
½ teaspoon salt

¼ teaspoon pepper
1 tablespoon corn oil
1 teaspoon sugar
2 teaspoons soy sauce

Heat the stock or consommé, and while it is heating, beat the eggs lightly. Chop up the scallion, using the green part as well as the white. Stir together the eggs, the cut-up scallion, and the salt and pepper.

Now heat up the tablespoon of corn oil in a frying pan and fry the egg-scallion mixture in it. When the omelet is set on the bottom, turn it with a spatula and fry the other side. Remove it to a plate, let it cool, and cut the omelet up into cubes. Bring the stock, or consommé, to a boil, stir in the sugar and soy sauce, get the sugar thoroughly dissolved, toss in the cubed omelet, stir that around just until it is thoroughly heated and serve immediately. This delicious concoction we learned from our old friend Sou Chan, an Oriental philanthropist who has a store on 52nd Street in Manhattan, which he operates only in order to wear out his old clothes.

The man in the restaurant was angry. He called the waiter to him. "What is this?" he barked, pointing at the plate in front of him. The waiter looked at the plate he had brought out of the kitchen only a minute before. "Why, sir," he said, "that's bean soup." The angry customer sneered. "I don't care what it has *been*," he snarled. "I want to know what it is NOW!" Nobody will say that if you make:

BLACK BEAN SOUP

[SERVES SIX]

1½ cups black beans	1 large onion
ham bone (or 2 pounds plate flank and some beef bones if you are kosher)	2 cloves
	1 stalk celery
	1 bay leaf
	½ cup tomato purée
2 quarts water	

NOTE: If you don't use ham bone, add 1 tablespoon salt

Soak the beans in water to cover overnight. Put the ham bone—or plate flank and beef bones—into a large pot along with 2 quarts of water, the onion—do we have to tell you to peel it?—the cloves, celery, and bay leaf. Bring it to a boil, then lower the heat and simmer, covered, until the beans are quite soft.

Now take out the ham bone—or meat and beef bones—and put the beans through a sieve. Better yet, purée them in a blender if you have such a thing. Put the puréed beans back in the soup, add the tomato purée, and cut up the flank meat—or cut the meat from the ham bone—add that to soup, and reheat. Toss a shot of sherry into each adult's plate just before serving, and be careful which portions you serve the kiddies. We don't want any fussing around with the Society for Prevention of Cruelty to Children. With pumpernickel or rye bread this soup is a full meal in itself for many people. But if it isn't, give them a:

CORNED BEEF AND HORSERADISH SANDWICH

1 cup chopped cooked
    corned beef
1 tablespoon prepared
    horseradish

3 tablespoons mayonnaise
dry mustard (if you like it
    hot—maybe ⅛ to ¼
    teaspoon)

Mix it all up and spread on pumpernickel or rye bread. (Actually, we think it's pretty silly writing recipes for sandwiches. Listen, you want a sandwich, look in the refrigerator, on your shelves, use any kind of combination of any kind of food you like—if you think they'll go together—and slap them between two pieces of whatever kind of bread you like.)

HE: "What are those marks on the bridge of your nose caused by?"

SHE: "They are made by glasses."

HE: "By glasses! My goodness! What you should learn to do is tilt your head back, then the booze would flow easier."

Here is an easy-flowing way to cook an easy-flowing:

SPLIT PEA SOUP

[SERVES SIX]

2 cups split peas	1 carrot, grated
2½ quarts water	1 stalk celery
1 pound flank beef (or ham bone with some meat left on it)	3 sprigs parsley
	2 teaspoons salt (none, if you use ham bone)
beef bones (if you don't use ham bone)	1 teaspoon pepper
	2 potatoes, peeled and sliced raw
2 onions, chopped	

If you aren't using pre-soaked peas, put them in water to cover and let them soak overnight. Get hold of a nice pot and in it put the water, the peas, beef and beef bones (or the ham bone), the onions, carrot, celery, and parsley. Cover the pot and cook it over low heat for 1½ hours. Now add the salt, pepper, and the potatoes. (We know it's silly to tell you to peel the potatoes first, but do you know, if we don't say that, sometimes some people will write and ask, "Should I peel the potatoes?" Yes, we tell them, peel the potatoes. Oh, well.) Cook it for about another 45 minutes, when the peas should be nice and soft. Now take out the meat and set it aside. If you are using a ham bone, cut off what meat is on it, save the meat, and throw the bone away. Force the soup through a food mill, or better yet, agitate the devil out of it in an electric blender if you have one. Now taste the soup. If it is too thick, add a little boiling water. Now let it cool and refrigerate it. We like to leave it in the frig overnight, because soup tastes better the second day. Spoon off excess fat from top of soup with a paper towel, cut up the pieces of meat, reheat the soup, correct seasoning if necessary, and serve real hot and steamy. This is a nice hearty lunch, served with rye or pumpernickel bread. If you have it for dinner, make your next course a lighter one than usual.

e heard of a fellow who, sadly, was much given to strong waters. One night his wife sent their young son to the friendly corner tavern to fetch him home. The lad walked in and found his daddy hanging on to the bar with both hands. "Hello son!" the awful but happy fellow cried out when he saw his son. "Come and have a drink with me!" The young lad shuddered. "Oh, no, Daddy," he whined, "to me it smells and tastes terrible." His daddy glared at him angrily. "Why you stupid young fool," he said, "do you think it smells and tastes good to me?" You know what will smell and taste good? This will smell and taste good:

LENTIL SOUP WITH FRANKS

[SERVES SIX]

2 cups dried lentils	1 tablespoon butter
3 quarts bouillon or stock	1 teaspoon flour
½ pound salt pork, or ham bone with some meat on it	3 diced potatoes
	3 boiled frankfurters

Wash and drain the lentils, cover them with cold water and let them soak overnight. Next day, drain them again and cover with fresh cold water (my, this gets pretty monotonous, doesn't it?) and bring it to a boil. Let it boil for 10 minutes and then we drain the little things again. Now add the bouillon —or stock—to the pot with the lentils, put in the salt pork or the ham bone, bring the pot to a boil again, reduce the heat and let it simmer, covered, for about 3 hours. Half an hour before the 3 hours are ended, discard salt pork or ham bone, stir the butter and flour into the soup, and add the diced potatoes. Cut the frankfurters into 1-inch pieces, and distribute them between 6 soup plates and pour the lentil soup into the plates.

The lady on the bus, her arms full of bundles, was counting out pennies. "Twelve, thirteen, fourteen, fifteen," she said, and tried not to drop her bundles as she handed the pennies to the driver. "Nah," he snarled politely, "I can't take them." The lady glared at him disdainfully. "Well, if you can't take them," she said so loudly that the bus driver was abashed, "why don't you try giving them to the company?" Why don't you try giving your company:

CLAM CHOWDER

[SERVES SIX]

2 dozen clams	⅛ teaspoon pepper
3 cups water	¼ teaspoon thyme
3 strips bacon	1 pint milk or cream or
1 onion, chopped	half-and-half
2 large potatoes, diced	1 tablespoon parsley,
½ teaspoon salt	chopped

Scrub the clams under running cold water with stiff brush and then put them into a deep pot. Pour in 3 cups of water, cover pot tightly, and steam the clams until they are all opened. Drain them, saving the liquor, and let the clams cool so you can handle them. Strain the clam broth carefully and hold on to it. When the clams are cool, take them out of the shells, cut away and discard all the dark parts, and cut the clams up in pieces that are not too small.

Cook the bacon in another kettle and when it is crisp, remove from pot and save for use later. Fry the chopped onion in bacon fat until it is soft, add clam broth, the diced potatoes, salt, pepper, and thyme. Cover the pot and let it simmer for 10 minutes. Now add the cut-up clams and the milk or cream, bring it almost, but not quite, to the boiling point. This will serve 6, so distribute the chowder between 6 soup plates, sprinkle each with a little parsley. As we've said before, hot soup should be hot; cold soup should be cold, but lukewarm soup is awful.

he clean but threadbare panhandler walked forthrightly up to the matron who was walking down the street and, raising his hat, he accosted her. "Madame," he said, not at all servilely, but rather with a note of pride in his voice, "I have seen better days." The matron drew herself haughtily to her full height, looked him right in the eye, and sneered. "So have I," she said snappishly, "but if you think I am going to stand here in the street talking to an absolute stranger about the weather, you are mistaken." If hot weather is getting you down, try to revive your spirits with some cold soups, like:

WINE SOUP

[SERVES SIX]

2 quarts water
1 small stick cinnamon
peel of half a lemon
4 tablespoons minute
    tapioca

3 egg yolks
¾ cup of sugar
1¼ cups dry white wine

First bring the water to a boil, put in the cinnamon and lemon peel, and boil for 5 minutes. Strain, and remove the cinnamon stick and throw away the lemon rind. Stir the tapioca into the cinnamony water, bring it to a boil again, and cook it for about 20 minutes, or until the tapioca is clear. Combine the egg yolks and sugar and beat mixture strenuously until it is yellow and frothy. Then mix it into the hot, tapioca-cinnamony-lemony water, stirring. Add the wine, stir it all around, let it cool, and refrigerate it for several hours.

>>>> It was quite warm when the young woman went to her doctor for her first pre-natal examination, and later, when they sat in his office, the doctor gave her his instructions. "You are in wonderful condition, my dear," he said. "All I have to tell you is to take several baths a day, so you will be refreshed at all times; get a lot of fresh air, and wear light, loose clothing."

That evening when her husband came home from work, he asked her what the doctor had said. "The doctor said," she said, her bright eyes gleaming with anticipated pleasure, "that I must go to the beach for one month, then I must go to the mountains for another month, and that I have to get a complete outfit of summer clothes." The doctor might also have told her to eat plenty of cold, nourishing soups like:

JELLIED TOMATO SOUP

[SERVES FOUR]

1 cup tomato juice	1 cup chicken consommé
1 celery stalk, chopped fine	or beef bouillon
	½ cup tomato paste
1 tablespoon onion, chopped	⅛ teaspoon thyme
	1 tablespoon gelatine
¼ teaspoon lemon rind, grated	¼ cup cold water
	1 tablespoon lemon juice

Put into a saucepan the tomato juice, chopped celery, chopped onion, lemon rind, and the consommé—or beef bouillon—and bring it to a boil. Stir in the tomato paste and stir it to dissolve it thoroughly. Add the thyme. While this is coming to a boil, soak the gelatine in the cold water, and when the mixture comes to a boil, pour the gelatine into the soup and stir it until it is dissolved. Put the soup through a fine strainer, let it cool, add lemon juice—you might want more or less than 1 tablespoon—according to your taste. Now wet a mold, pour the soup into it, and refrigerate it for hours and hours. When you serve it, garnish it with chopped hardboiled egg yolks, chives, or whatever your fancy leads you to choose. This should serve four, unless they are all eating for two.

he had been doing extremely well in business—well, actually he had become rich—and his wife had been doing her best to make their way of life keep pace with his accumulating wealth. This gave him great pleasure, for he loved his wife dearly, and his greatest joy was to make her happy. Also, he figured that spending money lavishly helped to make more, because it impressed his business associates. So he did not object when his wife told him that it was about time they got rid of their old cook and hired a chef, instead. But he was curious. "What is the difference," he inquired, "between a cook and a chef, my love?" His wife smiled smugly. "A chef," she said, "is a cook who can cook a month's supply of soup and every day for a month can give it a different name." Unless you are a Norwegian, you probably never have heard of a fruit soup called:

BLABAER SUPPE

[SERVES SIX TO EIGHT]

1½ quarts blueberries	½ cup sugar
water to cover	½ cup port wine
3½ tablespoons cornstarch	

Put the berries—picked over and washed—into water that covers them, bring to a boil, then reduce the heat and let simmer, covered, until the berries are quite mushy. Put it all through a fine strainer and discard the debris. Dissolve the cornstarch in some cold water and stir it into the soup. Add the sugar, stir it like mad, and bring it to a boil. Let it boil for about 5 minutes, remove it from the heat, add the wine, and let it cool. When it is quite cool refrigerate it for many hours. The colder the better. The Swedes have a blueberry soup, too, but they call it *blåbärsoppa* with an umlaut over the second "a" and a little circle (we never did know what those little circles are called) over the first "a." There's nothing over the third "a." Isn't it amazing, when you think of it, how the Swedes and the Norwegians have words that sound so much like English words for the same thing? Like, for instance, *blabar*, and *blabaer* for our blueberry. And the Swedes have a tomato soup and you know what they call it? They call it *tomatsoppa*, that's what they call it!

The young fellow asked his girl to marry him. "Can my mother live with us?" she asked.

"Of course, my love," said he. Then she asked if he would give her as much money each week as she wanted, and he agreed enthusiastically. "Will you stop smoking?" she then inquired. "Oh, of course, darling, if you want me to." And how about drinking? Would he stop drinking? "I'll never take another drink as long as I live!" he cried out. And how about giving up bowling and pool with his friends? "I'll never again go out with the boys!" he promised. "And will you let me buy all your clothes?" she asked. "Of course, my dearest," he whispered.

"Listen," she said sweetly, "do you think I'd ever marry an idiot like you?" Maybe he was willing to give all that up because she made such wonderful:

VICHYSSOISE

[SERVES FOUR TO SIX]

3 tablespoons butter	2½ cups chicken consommé
4 leeks (white parts only), chopped	1 teaspoon salt
1 small onion, minced	1 cup cream
4 medium potatoes, diced	chives, chopped

Hot up the butter and fry the chopped leeks and onion until they are golden brown. Add the potatoes and consommé to the pot, salt it, stir, and bring it to a boil. Let it simmer until potatoes, onion, and leeks are quite soft. Take the vegetables out of the soup and put them through a sieve, or purée them in a blender. Return the puréed vegetables to the soup, let it cool, then refrigerate it for hours and hours. Just before serving, blend in the cream, which should be quite cold also, and garnish each plateful—there should be 4-6 servings—with chives, lots of chives. Very few people these days make handmade soup at home, and small wonder, because it really is hard to beat some of the commercial soup makers. An easy way to make vichyssoise from cans is to take:

1 10¼-ounce can frozen condensed cream of potato soup, partly thawed	2 ice cubes, smashed ½ cup of heavy cream chopped chives
1 10¼-ounce can condensed onion soup	

Put everything except the cream and chives into a blender, with the smashed ice cubes, run on high for about 15 seconds. Add the cream to blender, run for 2 seconds and empty contents into soup plates. Sprinkle with chopped chives. Try vichyssoise both ways, see which you like best.

Louis XIV, King of France, was one great royal glutton, and at dinner time he would have four different kinds of soup, a pheasant, a partridge, ham, mutton, salads, several desserts, fruits, and much champagne. He demanded far more of his many concubines than most rulers did; Louis' had to be great cooks, also. The *Cordon Bleu* school of cooking was founded by one of his women, Madame de Maintenon, who also invented several epicurean delights for her royal lover. His wife, Maria Theresa of Spain, although he thought her a great big bore, taught his chefs many Spanish recipes, some of which are still used not only in France, but in Spain, too, of course. Every American tourist who has been to Spain knows:

GAZPACHO

[SERVES THREE TO FOUR]

1 onion, chopped	salt and pepper
2 green peppers, chopped	3 tablespoons olive oil
1 cucumber, chopped	2 teaspoons lemon juice
3 tomatoes, chopped	1 cup ice water
2 cloves garlic, minced	

Stir together the chopped onion, peppers, cucumber, tomatoes, and garlic, and force the mixture all through a fine sieve, or, better, put it all into an electric blender and purée it. Add the salt and pepper. In a glass or wooden bowl, add the olive oil, drop by drop, agitating it severely all the while. Add the lemon juice and ice water, stirring vigorously. Now put it away in the refrigerator and let it get real cold. (You can cut the chilling time drastically by putting it into the freezing compartment, but for goodness sake, don't forget about it and let it freeze!) When you serve the *gazpacho*, be sure to have on the table plates of:

chopped tomato	chopped green pepper
chopped cucumber	bread cubes fried in garlic
chopped onion	butter, cold

Everyone can help himself to whatever he wants of this stuff to add to the *gazpacho*. As we said, every American tourist who has been to Spain knows *gazpacho*, but nobody knows if this is a soupy salad or a thick soup, not even the Spaniards, who use it for one, one time, and for the other, another time. In all other respects, Spaniards are all too scrutable.

Fish

The bridegroom looked rapturously at his brand-new wife as she danced joyously around the stateroom of the ship which was their secret honeymoon hideaway. "At last," said the happy young man, "we are alone, and now we are not two, but one, just as the Justice of the Peace said." The bride stopped dancing and smiled fondly at her husband. "Ah, yes, darling," she said, "but we must be practical, so when you ring for the steward, order dinner for two." This is what the steward brought for them:

BAKED SALMON STEAK

[SERVES SIX]

6 salmon steaks	½ teaspoon salt
1 tablespoon Worcester- shire sauce	dash of pepper
⅓ cup butter, melted	1 tablespoon parsley, chopped

Get hold of a baking pan and grease it. Brush steaks with mixture of Worcestershire, butter, salt and pepper, and place them in pan. Bake for 30 minutes in an oven preheated to 350 degrees, basting with melted butter. About 5 minutes before removing from oven, sprinkle parsley over the steaks; makes them look pretty and parsley is tasty, too. (We know a beautiful sexy girl in Hollywood who says she eats a pound of the stuff every day and that's why she's beautiful and sexy, but somehow we doubt all that.)

January 13th used to be celebrated in Scotland because, centuries ago, the prior of a monastery near Glasgow, named St. Kintegern, performed a miracle on that date. It seems the queen fell in love with a soldier in the army of her husband, Roderick, and she gave him a ring which the king had given her.

When the king saw the ring on the soldier's finger, he waxed wroth, grabbed the ring, and threw it into the River Clyde. Well, sir, then that sneaky king asked his wife one day, "Dearie, where's that ring I gave you?" The queen, very troubled, went to see St. Kintegern and told him the whole sordid story. St. Kintegern went to the Clyde, caught a salmon, cut it open, and there was the ring in the salmon's belly! The queen showed it to her husband, and the silly man apologized for suspecting her! You don't have to apologize for serving:

BAKED SALMON

[SERVES THREE TO FOUR]

1 cup bread crumbs	1 teaspoon salt
½ cup hot milk	¼ teaspoon pepper
2 tablespoons minced onion	⅛ teaspoon paprika
2 tablespoons butter or margarine	1 cup canned salmon, drained
	2 eggs, separated

Soak the bread crumbs in the milk, squeeze them as dry as you can. Now sauté the onion in 1 tablespoon of the butter—or margarine—until it is soft. Mix together the bread crumbs, onion, salt, pepper, paprika, the salmon, and egg yolks. Beat the egg whites stiff and fold them in with this mixture. Grease a baking pan with the remaining tablespoon of butter, put the entire mixture into it. Now get hold of a larger pan, put in some hot water, place the pan with the salmon in it, and bake it for 30 minutes in an oven preheated to 350 degrees. Maybe your husband will give you a ring after eating this, but don't count on it.

Right after Easter in Egypt, there comes a period called *Khum'a'ses'n,* and during that time there is a day, observed by everyone, which has no religious connotations. It is called "Smell the Breezes Day." And you know how the day is supposed to start out? You are supposed to break an onion and smell it. This is supposed to bring good luck, and, as an added boon, clear the sinuses. Then everyone dresses up and goes out to the country for a picnic.

In our neighborhood there is a lot of picnicking going on all the time, right in the backyards, only they call what they do "cookouts," which is a word we deplore, although we like outdoor cookery. Sometimes. Another word we abhor is "brunch," meaning a combination breakfast-lunch. But what we love, when the shad are running, for a late combination breakfast-lunch is:

PAN-BROILED SHAD ROE

[SERVES TWO, MAYBE FOUR]

2 pairs shad roe   salt and pepper
flour   lemon wedges
lots of butter

If we had 2 pairs of shad roe, we would eat them all by ourself, but most people consider 1 pair sufficient for 1 person, and we know some people who think 2 pairs of shad roe are enough for 4 people! It takes, a learned friend used to say, all kinds. Well, anyway, what you do is dip the roes—split them apart first—into some flour, hot up the butter—you should be lavish with the butter—and put the roes in the pan, turning them, so they get heavily coated. Now season them. Cover the pan and cook the roes over low heat—very low heat—for about 15 minutes, turning them 2 or 3 times. Serve them with wedges of lemon, and the plate looks nice with a garniture of parsley, which is also good to eat with the roe. Another good thing with shad roe is crisp bacon. Oh yes, when you serve the roe, pour all the hot butter in the pan all over the roe. There can't be too much butter. And for a heartier meal, what could be better than pan-broiled shad along with the roe? The shad, which your fishmonger will sell you already boned, because it takes a professional to bone this fish, should be done precisely the same way as the roe, except that it will take a little longer. But always remember—fish are such delicate creatures that overcooking will make them tough.

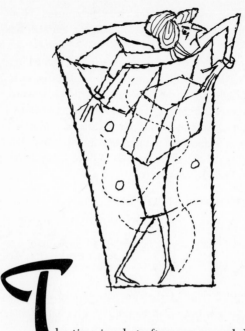

*T*he time is a hot afternoon several decades ago. The scene is a fashionable, but very warm, drinking place in New York City—you see, air conditioning still had to be invented—and at the long, highly polished bar stood Wilson Mizner. Mr. Mizner was a fabulous man whose wit and immense charm made him a legend in his own lifetime, though he was a known gambler and a rogue who would not cavil at the commission of any form of chicanery and whose peculiar attitude towards life made even his few legitimate endeavors, such as writing movie scenarios, seem highly dishonest.

Into the bar walked a stranger, panting and all but expiring from the heat. The only vacant space at the bar was next to Mr. Mizner, who was having refreshments with a friend. The stranger caught the barman's eye and said: "Bartender, I would like to have something long, frigid, and full of gin."

Mr. Mizner turned to face the perspiring stranger. He drew himself up to his full, imposing height. "Sir," he snarled, "you are speaking of my wife!" This is how the sorely tried Mrs. Mizner cooked fish in gin, a wonderful trick she learned from Harry

Lee of the Peking Restaurant in New York City, famous among connoisseurs of Chinese cookery, for it is one of the rare places which specializes in the North Chinese cuisine:

HUNG SHAO

[SERVES FOUR TO SIX]

1 yellow pike (3-4 pounds)
5 ounces corn oil
½ teaspoon salt
1 cup water
1½ ounces gin
1 ounce soy sauce
6 scallions
½ cup shredded bamboo shoots
½ ounce shredded ginger root
½ chopped green pepper
2 tablespoons chopped parsley
1 teaspoon cornstarch

Have the fish cleaned and scaled, but ask your fishmonger to leave on the head and tail, only because it looks so much prettier that way. Use a turkey roaster or fish broiler with a removable tray. Take the tray out, pour the corn oil into the roaster and get it quite hot, but do not let it smoke. Pour in the salt, stir it around, lower the heat, and sauté the fish 5 minutes on each side. Remove fish—using extreme care not to break it—and place it on the tray, which you have greased lightly with corn oil. Put the tray into the roaster, pour over the fish first the water, then the gin and soy sauce, and steam the fish over low heat for 20 minutes with the roaster, of course, covered tightly.

Cut the scallions into 2-inch pieces; after 20 minutes put the pieces on top of the fish, add to the roaster all the other ingredients except the cornstarch, and steam for another 5 minutes.

Now remove the fish to a hot serving platter. Add the cornstarch to the sauce in roaster, stir it until it thickens, and pour the sauce over the fish. This, says Harry Lee, is the way the northern Chinese Mandarins loved to have fish cooked, except that some Mandarins like to have more than 1½ ounces of gin used by their cooks. (The Chinese word for "gin," says Harry Lee, is *gin*. He seems to think the Chinese invented gin, as well as gunpowder.)

Two door-to-door salesmen, one young and the other an older man, met in our neighborhood, which is infested by these bell-ringers, and they got to talking. "What I don't like about door-to-door selling," said the younger man, "is that I keep getting insulted."

The older man looked at him in astonishment. "Insulted?" he cried out. "Why, I've been a salesman for 35 years, man and boy, and I've had doors slammed in my face! I've been kicked down flights of stairs! And I've been punched in the nose and laughed at! But never have I ever been insulted!"

Nor will you be if you serve your family and guests:

CHIVEY BROILED SCROD

[SERVES THREE TO FOUR]

1 2-to 2½- pound scrod	1 teaspoon lemon juice
⅓ cup butter	1 teaspoon parsley,
salt and pepper to taste	minced
2 tablespoons chives, chopped	

You know what a scrod is? A scrod is a young cod. Why don't they just call it a young cod? Who knows? Have the fish split and the backbone removed. Now take ⅓ of the ⅓ cup of butter and melt it. Preheat your broiler to 350 degrees, put the fish in pan, and pour over it the melted butter, and sprinkle with salt and pepper.

Let some of the melted butter run under the scrod fillets. Have the fish two inches from source of heat and broil the fillets until the top is nice and brown. Baste it at least once with the butter in the pan. Don't let it get dry, don't overcook it. Now make:

CHIVEY SAUCE

Cream the butter remaining and combine it with the chives, lemon juice, parsley. Heat it in a small pan, and let everyone pour as much as he likes on the fish at the table. Maybe sometime you would like to try this cold on hot fish. If you would, make the sauce hours before you cook the fish, so it will get real chilled. It's great that way, but you'll have to soften it up.

eskimos are very nice people and they have some wonderful traits and beliefs. One is that animals have souls and that the Eskimos have to explain to the souls of the departed animals—and fish —why it was necessary to kill them for food. So every year on December 9th—which is called "December Moon"—the Eskimos have a festival to pay their respects to the whales they killed and ate during the preceding year. Isn't that nice?

It is possible to buy whale steaks in a couple of places in New York, but swordfish steaks are easier to find anywhere, and we have a lovely recipe for them, given to us by a lovely young actress named Julienne Marie.

SWORDFISH JULIENNE MARIE

[SERVES FOUR]

2 4½-ounce bottles
    pimiento-stuffed
    green olives
¼ pound butter, maybe a
    little more
2 2-pound swordfish
    steaks, cut 1¼ inches
    thick

¼ teaspoon salt
¼ teaspoon coarsely
    ground pepper
2 cups heavy cream

Drain the olives and chop them up pretty fine. Melt the butter in a large frying pan, get it nice and hot, but don't let it start smoking. Fry the two swordfish steaks over moderate heat until they start browning slightly, which should take about 10 minutes.

While they are still in the pan, cut each steak in two, and turn them over carefully with a spatula. Sprinkle the fish with the salt and pepper. Let them cook on this side for about 10 minutes, until they get browned lightly. About this time, you may have to add some butter to the pan to prevent the fish from sticking.

Turn the fish steaks once more and fry for another 5 minutes. Put the fish on a very hot serving plate and keep it all warm.

Add the chopped olives to the juice in the pan, scrape the pan, and then stir in one cup of the heavy cream. Heat it almost to boiling point, stirring all the time, but DON'T let it boil. Now add the second cup of cream, stir, stir, stir, stir, heat it up good, and pour it all over the fish, and serve it all IMMEDIATELY—with boiled potatoes, Julienne Marie says. And with wine, we say.

A friend of ours was in the hospital, so we paid her a visit. Well, she told us all about her illness, and we had a grand time. She said the doctor said to her: "You know, my dear, the treatment I gave you didn't do you any harm, of course, but what really pulled you through is your remarkably strong constitution." Our friend, who, we must say, has a pretty nimble wit, said the doctor blushed when she replied. "Well, if that's the case, you just see to it, young man, that you remember my strong constitution when you make out my bill." Your bill will be small if you cook:

POACHED SEA BASS

[SERVES FOUR TO FIVE]

1 3-pound sea bass (trout or any kind of fish will work just as well)
1 wedge of ginger (about the size of a quarter)
3 tablespoons shredded ginger
3 scallions, chopped fine
3 tablespoons vegetable oil
2 teaspoons salt
¼ teaspoon pepper
2 tablespoons light soy sauce

Put the fish in a large pan for which you have a cover. Pour in water until the fish is covered and floats. Now take the fish out and put it aside. Boil the water, and while you are waiting, crush the wedge of ginger. Reduce the heat so the water just simmers, pour in the mashed-up ginger, and put the fish into the simmering water. Now increase the heat a bit, but don't let it boil, and bring it down to simmering again.

After about 15 minutes, turn the fish; test with a fork 10 minutes later. When it flakes easily it is done. Remove from heat. In a small saucepan, sauté the shredded ginger and scallions in the vegetable oil until brown. Arrange the fish on a serving dish and sprinkle it with the salt, pepper, soy sauce, and finally with the sautéed scallions and shredded ginger.

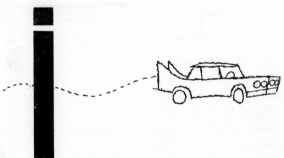

"I was driving home after sitting up with a sick friend," the defendant said, "when suddenly this car came down the wrong side of the road, with no lights, and crashed into me. I was all cut up around the head, and my car was wrecked, and the fellow in the other car apologized for what he had done, and he said to me, 'You look all shaken up. Would you like a drink of booze to settle your nerves?' So I said yes, it would do me good, because I was shaking from fright. So then he gave me four more drinks. And then I asked him, 'Aren't you going to have a drink yourself?' He answered with

a sneer, 'No, I'll wait until after the cops get here.' "
Did you ever have:

POACHED FISH IN COURT BOUILLON?

[½ POUND OF FISH PER SERVING]

2 pounds fish heads and bones	3 cloves
½ cup celery, chopped	6 peppercorns
½ cup onions, chopped	1 teaspoon salt
2 sprigs parsley	1 cup dry white wine
	1½ quarts water

Have your fishmonger give you the fishheads and bones. And when we say "Give," we mean "Give." If he charges you anything for fishheads and some old bones, he is not the sort of fishmonger we want to have anything to do with. Wipe trimmings with damp cloth and get hold of a large pot and put everything into it and bring it to a boil, then lower the heat and simmer for 30 minutes. Strain, throw away bones and heads.

POACHED FISH

Any whole fish (have it weighed)	2 tablespoons lemon juice
	1 teaspoon salt

Have the fishmonger clean fish. Douse with lemon juice, rub in salt. Use enough of the court bouillon to cover the fish, bring it to a boil, lower the fish into the boiling liquid gently, lower heat, and let it simmer gently for about 12 minutes to the pound. Serve it with:

CAPER SAUCE

3 tablespoons butter	2 egg yolks, beaten
3 tablespoons flour	¼ cup caper juice
1½ cups strained court bouillon	2 tablespoons capers, chopped

Melt butter, stir in flour gradually, then slowly add court bouillon. Bring it to a boil. Beat up the egg yolks in a bowl, pour the boiling sauce over them, and pour everything back into the pan. Over low heat, stir it all until it thickens. Now pour in the caper juice and capers. Stir and correct seasoning.

The poor, but honest young fellow was madly in love with a beauty. But there was a hindrance to his desire to marry her. She was very rich, and though he knew that she was fond of him, he was sure that she didn't love him enough to marry him. "You are very rich," he murmured one night as they sat in the cheapest seats in a neighborhood movie house. "Yes," she whispered back. "Will you marry me?" he asked. "No," she replied. "I was sure you wouldn't," he said sadly. "But if you were sure, then why did you ask me?" she asked. The young fellow sighed. "I wanted to see," he said, "how it would feel to lose a million dollars." You don't lose a thing if you propose to make:

CHOWDER POACHED FILLETS

[SERVES FOUR]

4 fish fillets (flounder, fluke, any kind you like)
1 can Manhattan clam chowder
juice of half a lemon

⅛ teaspoon paprika
3 tablespoons Parmesan cheese, grated
2 teaspoons parsley, chopped

Wipe your fillets with a damp cloth. Cook the clam chowder according to the directions on can. Put the fish fillets in a baking dish and sprinkle with the lemon juice. Add the paprika, grated cheese, and parsley to the soup and pour it all over the fish. Bake for 20 minutes in your oven, which you have preheated to 350 degrees. Serve this real hot with garlic bread and a green salad.

There were two men fishing from opposite banks of a river separating West Berlin and East Berlin. The man fishing on the Western side kept catching fish after fish all afternoon, but the man on

the Communist side of the river didn't even get a bite all day. They didn't talk to each other until the man on the Western side of the river started to leave. The Communist German asked him how many fish he had caught. "Twenty," said the West German. "So how come," the Communist German asked, "that I didn't even get one bite?" The West German smiled. "On this side of the river," he said, "the fish aren't afraid to open their mouths." Everyone will be open-mouthed with astonishment and pleasure if you make:

FRIED FISH WITH PUERTO RICAN SAUCE

[SERVES SIX TO EIGHT]

2½ pounds onions, sliced thin
1½ cups olive oil
1½ cups water
24 green olives, pitted
2 tablespoons capers
1 4-ounce can pimientos, sliced

2 8-ounce cans tomato sauce
2 tablespoons vinegar
1½ tablespoons salt
2 bay leaves
1 clove garlic, chopped
4 pounds fish, cut in 1-inch slices

First, make the sauce, like this: mix together the onions, ½ cup olive oil, the water, olives, capers, pimientos, tomato sauce, vinegar, 1 tablespoon salt and the 2 bay leaves. Cook it over moderate heat for one hour, stirring occasionally. When the sauce is almost ready, discard bay leaves, rub rest of salt into the fish. You have one cup of olive oil left, right? In a separate pan—a large one—heat the oil and brown the garlic in it. Now fry all the fish pieces on each side until they are cooked, about 7 minutes altogether, turning pieces once. When they are all fried, put them on a heated serving platter, douse all with the sauce. *Arriba!* We learned this way of fish frying from a Puerto Rican lady named Señora Valldejuli, a cousin of José Ferrer, who wrote a wonderful book called "Caribbean Cookery."

T

he salesman called on a prospect and found him too distracted to listen to a sales pitch. "Is something wrong?" asked the salesman. The man said he was upset because he had promised to bring home to his wife an ocelot for her birthday and the cheapest he could get one was $300, which he thought was too steep a price.

"You bet it's too steep!" cried the brash salesman. "Why, I've got one I'll let you have for $150!" The man was delighted and said he would take it at that price. "Just a minute," said the salesman, "I gotta call my office." So he called his boss and said, "Hey, boss, I just sold a guy an ocelot for $150. What the dickens is an ocelot?" Do you know what is a:

MUCHLI PAAL KARI?

[SERVES SIX]

4 tablespoons coconut flakes	2 teaspoons coriander, ground
2 cups milk	½ teaspoon turmeric, ground
4 tablespoons shortening	
6 flounder fillets	½ teaspoon cayenne
1 cup scallions (white part only), chopped	1 teaspoon ginger, ground
	1 onion, sliced

Put the 4 tablespoons of flaked coconut into the two cups of milk and let it soak to make coconut milk while you do the rest of the recipe. (Of course, you got coconuts, you can get milk out of them.) So first you hot up the shortening and fry the fish fillets. Take them out of the pan, and hold on to them because without these fish, you got nothing, much less a *muchli paal kari*. Now stir-fry the scallions until they are soft. (Some cookery writers say "cook onions"—or scallions—"until they are transparent," and now there are even some who say onions should be cooked until they are "translucent." Beats us why they say such things. We have tried looking through fried onions, and couldn't see anything, not even light.) Anyway, after you've got the scallions soft—soft, you hear?—put the fish back in the pan. Now make a paste out of the coriander, turmeric, cayenne, ginger and onion slices by putting them all into an electric blender, or through a grinder.

Let's get back to the coconut flakes and milk—you remember the coconut flakes and milk? Squeeze the flakes, throw them away, and pour the coconutty milk into a bowl, if it isn't already there. Add the paste you made out of the spices and onion to the milk, stir it all around violently, and spread some of this stuff on each flounder fillet. Cover the pan and let it simmer for 5 minutes. Turn the fish over, cover the pan again, and simmer for an additional 5 minutes, and what you've got is *muchli paal kari*. What does it mean? Who knows? We got this from a book called "The Art of India's Cookery," and we tried this recipe and it's what some cookery writers call "scrumptious." But not us.

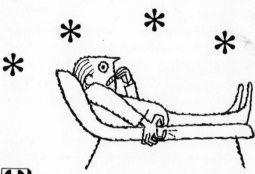

he three mothers were talking about their sons. My son," said the first one, "sends me to Florida for a month every winter." The other two ladies nodded. "Yes, that's nice," said number two mama. "My son sends me to Florida in the winter too, but he also buys me a new fur coat every year." The third lady said, "They are very nice. But you know, my son not only sends me to Florida and buys me minks, but five days a week he goes to a psychiatrist, and he lies down on a couch, and you know, he only talks about me!" Your family will say nice things right to your face if you give them:

WINEY FLOUNDER FILLET

[SERVES THREE TO FOUR]

6 tablespoons butter	2 cups dry red wine
2 pounds flounder fillets, or sole	½ pound sliced mushrooms
	salt and pepper

Let us not kid ourselves, nor should we let our fishmongers kid us either. Sole is exceedingly difficult to come by; only a very few of the best seafood restaurants ever have the real article. What the retail fishmen and most restaurants sell as sole is really nothing but flounder. So ask for flounder instead of sole, and save money. And flounder is good even though it isn't called sole.

Melt 4 tablespoons of the butter, sauté the fish gently on both sides, then add the wine. Cover the pan, and cook until the fillets are done—flake one with a fork, to test—and then remove the fish from the pan. Leave the cover off the pan and cook until the sauce is reduced to half the original quantity.

While this is going on, in another pan sauté the sliced mushrooms in the remaining 2 tablespoons of butter, add salt and pepper to taste. Now pour the butter into the pan with the winey sauce, pour it all over the flounder fillets, and place the sautéed mushrooms on top of the fish.

a Hungarian woman friend told us a story about a sad little fish dealer, whose wife was a high-born lady, in Budapest. Ah, dear old Buda, and darling Pest across the river! Shlomo the fish dealer decided to improve business, so he put up a sign, reading, "FRESH FISH SOLD HERE" in his window. One of his wise-guy friends pointed out that the word "HERE" was unnecessary, because where else would he be selling his stupid fish? So Shlomo painted out the word "HERE."

Another of his smart-alecky buddies came along and said, "Why say 'FRESH'? Would you be selling stale fish?" So Shlomo deleted "FRESH." Sure enough, Sally-Ann, his snobbish, well-born fishwife who never let anyone forget that hers was an ancient, noble Hungarian family, distantly related to the G*b*rs, came in and sneered her famous sneer. "IS SOLD," she said. "What else? Would you be giving it away for free?" Unhappy Shlomo! He crossed out "IS SOLD."

Of course one of his stuss-playing pals, who operated a clandestine *shtrudel* joint, stuck his foolish head in the doorway and bellowed, "Why do you say 'FISH'? For a mile around, everyone knows you got fish here!" So Shlomo crossed out "FISH," and who can find it in his heart to condemn him for taking to drink? Shlomo liked:

BAKED FISH — HULA STYLE

[SERVES SIX]

1½ cups cream (heavy)
2 cups coconut flakes
2 teaspoons salt (you like more salt, okay, use more salt)

6 slices white-meat fish (sea bass, snapper, etc.)
butter or margarine

With much excitement, stir up cream and coconut flakes in a saucepan, where else? Bring the stuff to a boil, turn off heat, go for a walk, read a book (we recommend something light and funny by Kafka, a real swinging kid who loved this fish dish), take a shower, have a beer, or whatever you like—only leave the stuff alone to soak for half an hour. When you come back to it, squeeze all the liquid out in a cheesecloth, and throw the pulpy stuff as far as you can. You say we didn't tell you to clean the fish, or wash or dry it? Well, now we're telling you. Sprinkle salt all over the fish. Place the fish pieces tenderly in a baking dish which you have buttered or margarined. Spill the coconut-cream stuff all over the fish, heedlessly, and bake in a preheated oven at 350 degrees for 10 minutes less than an hour. How did all these Hungarians get to like a South Seas fish dish like this? They are great travelers, these Hungarians, that's how.

An English magazine called *John Bull* had this charming little story several years ago, when they were all delighted by the official word that Queen Elizabeth was going to have a baby: "Mummy," asked a 10-year-old girl, "how did the Queen know she was going to have a baby?"

Her younger sister, aged five, thought this was a pretty silly question. "How did she know?" the five-year-old said, scornfully. "Well, the Queen can read, can't she? It was in all the papers." What you will rarely see in the papers is:

CARP IN CHICKEN FAT

[SERVES FOUR TO FIVE]

1 2- to 2½-pound carp	2 tablespoons soy sauce
⅓ cup chicken fat	2 tablespoons sherry
2 scallions	¾ cup hot water

Your mother never cooked carp this way and neither did your grandmother, unless they happened to be Chinese. Have your fish cleaned and scaled. Melt the chicken fat in a skillet large enough to hold the fish. Cut the scallions into ½-inch pieces, including the green. Over high heat, brown the fish on both sides—about 3 minutes for each side. Okay, you got both sides browned, so now pour the soy sauce over it, and then the sherry. Lower the heat to moderate, let the fish cook like this for 3 minutes, then add the ¾ cup of hot water to skillet. Toss in the cut-up scallions and cook for another 20 minutes, turning the fish once. Our Chinese friends tell us this is an old Mandarin recipe, and you can take it from us, those old Mandarins knew how to live.

*B*ack in colonial days, on November 30th the Scots who lived in Virginia used to celebrate St. Andrew's Day—he is the patron saint of Scotland— in a fashion that had nothing to do with religion but seemed to have been a lot of fun, in some ways. They raced horses, they had cudgel matches, in which the young men fought with clubs, and the winner, apparently the last man to stay on his feet, won a hat. They also had beauty contests for the girls, with the winner getting a prize of a pair of silk stockings. Singing contests were held, with all the singers being given "liquor sufficient to clear their windpipes." Doesn't that sound jolly? And it may be that they ate:

FISH PIE

[SERVES TWO TO FOUR]

1 pound filleted fish (any kind you like)
6 anchovy fillets (optional)
¼ teaspoon salt (if no anchovies)
¼ teaspoon pepper
2 eggs
1 cup milk
1 tablespoon parsley, chopped

Cut the fish fillets into bite-size pieces. Grease a baking dish or casserole, arrange the fish pieces in dish, and—if you aren't using anchovies, which you don't have to if you don't like anchovies—sprinkle the fish with ¼ teaspoon salt, as well as the pepper. Now beat up the eggs with the milk, stir in the parsley, and pour this mixture over the fish pieces. If you are using the anchovies—they add zest to this dish—cut them up and distribute them over the fish-milk-egg mixture. Bake this for 45 minutes in oven preheated to 325 degrees. In the old days in Scotland, Saint Andrew's Day used to be celebrated by cooking a sheep's head, which we don't think many people would want to do these days, though we *can* give you a recipe for a boiled one, if you like.

a young father was telling a friend of his, an older man, about the trouble he was having with his children. They were insolent, disobedient, and rowdy, he said sadly, and the only way he could control them was by chastising them regularly. "Oh, that's too bad," said the friend. "I never had any trouble with my four sons. The only times I ever raised my hand to them was in self defense." You won't have to defend yourself if you give your family:

KEDGEREE

[SERVES FOUR]

2 cups fish, cooked (fresh or canned)
4 tablespoons butter
1 teaspoon curry powder (or dry mustard)
1 cup rice, cooked (⅓ cup uncooked)

3 eggs, hard boiled
salt and pepper
1 tablespoon parsley, chopped

Flake the fish, removing all skin and bones. Melt the butter in a saucepan, mix in the curry powder (or mustard), add the flaked fish, rice, and cook over low heat. Chop up whites of eggs, add that to the mixture in the saucepan. Add salt and pepper to taste, and when the *kedgeree* is sufficiently hotted up, put it into four serving dishes and sprinkle with chopped-up egg yolks and then the chopped parsley. *Kedgeree* comes from India and it means "a crazy, mixed-up fish dish." It is good to have with *kedgeree* an assortment of condiments like flaked coconut, cashews, chutney, chopped scallions, peanuts, raisins, and pimiento.

When we were covering Criminal Courts as a young newspaper reporter, we attended a trial where a witness soon had the District Attorney who was handling the case whimpering for mercy.

"Do you know the defendant?" the D. A.'s man asked.

"How should I know him?" replied the witness.

"Did you ever talk to him?"

Answer: "Why should I talk to him?"

Q. "Did you ever meet him?"

A. "How could I meet him?"

Q. "Why do you answer every question with a question?"

A. "Why not?"

Well, why not make:

BAKED SMOKED WHITEFISH?

[SERVES SIX TO EIGHT]

3 pounds smoked whitefish	heavy cream
butter for greasing dish	3 tablespoons bread crumbs
⅛ teaspoon pepper	2 tablespoons butter

Skin the smoked whitefish, remove the bones, and try to keep the fillets as large as possible, without breaking them up, see? Now grease a shallow baking dish with the greasing butter, put the fish fillets into the dish, sprinkle them with pepper—you don't need salt because smoked whitefish are salty enough—and pour heavy cream over the fish. The fish shouldn't be covered with the cream; just get the cream as high as the fish in the dish, okay? Now sprinkle it all with the bread crumbs and put little dollops of butter all over it. Preheat your oven to 425 degrees and bake fish until the tops are a pretty gold color, about 10 minutes. You know what the Norwegians in our neighborhood call this? They call it *fiskgratin*, that's what they call it. The Danes have a baked fish dish they call *fisk gratin*, which is much fancier, and sometime, maybe, we'll give it to you. The Swedes call baked fish *ugnstekt fisk*, and the Finns have a baked fish dish they call *kalakukko*, and another one with baked herring, they call *silakkalaatikko*. How do we know all this? Well, where we live in Brooklyn, it is the capital of Scandinavia, and there are more Swedes, Finns, Danes, and Norwegians here than in most of the big cities in Sweden, Finland, Denmark, and Norway, and they are all great fish eaters. To them, *gefilte* fish (see index) is very exotic.

We know a man who says he read somewhere that the art of conversation has died completely since TV was inflicted upon the suffering world, so he tried to do something about it and found that it was hopeless. After dinner one night, he tells us, he remarked, as his wife was washing and drying the dishes, that he remembered learning as a boy that each year 5,000 elephants were used to make keys for pianos. "Isn't it amazing," his wife exclaimed, "how they can teach those animals to do almost anything!" Now, he says, he sits in the living room and reads about the Mets not only while his wife does the dishes, but also while she cooks:

SHRIMP-STUFFED RED SNAPPER

[SERVES FOUR]

1 red snapper, 2 pounds or more	2 teaspoons salt
	2 tablespoons butter

Tell your fishman to leave the head and tail on when he dresses your fish because it looks so pretty. When you get home, wash the fish inside and out with cold water, and dry it. Rub salt into fish inside and out and then fill it with:

SHRIMP STUFFING

3 tablespoons onion, chopped	2 slices bacon, cooked and crumbled
¼ cup celery, chopped	salt and pepper to taste
4 tablespoons butter (or margarine)	1 cup bread crumbs
½ cup shrimp, cooked and chopped	1 egg, beaten

Sauté the onion and celery in a pan with 4 table-spoons of butter, but don't brown them. You've got all the other ingredients—except the fish—in a bowl, yes? Okay. Pour the sautéed onion and celery and melted butter into the bowl and stir it up good. Now let's get back to the fish. Take the stuffing and stuff the fish with it; then sew it up or use skewers to hold the stuffing in. (Sewing is better.) Melt the remaining 2 tablespoons of butter and rub it all over the fish. Now put the fat little fish into a greased baking pan, put the pan into the oven pre-heated to 350 degrees, and bake it until the fish flakes easily when stuck with a fork—about 40 min-utes.

We have a friend who is a remittance man. He lives in Spain, and he is very happy. His son, a rich and famous surgeon, sends him a large check each month on condition that he stay out of this country. Our friend firmly believes that nature is a better healer than any doctor, and he used to hang around his son's office and tell the surgeon's pa-tients that his son was a quack. Isn't that terrible?

Our friend, in a recent letter, wrote that every day for a long time he used to buy two oranges from a peasant lady who never had more than a dozen oranges on her little stand near his home. One day he wanted to buy the entire lot. "No, no," yelled the peasant lady furiously, "you may have only two oranges! What would I do all day if I sold you all of them?" In Spain, he wrote, they cook:

SHRIMP IN SHERRY SAUCE

[SERVES FOUR TO SIX]

¼ cup olive oil
1½ pounds large shrimp
1 onion, chopped
1 4-ounce can pimientos, drained and diced
1 garlic clove, crushed
¾ teaspoon salt
2 tablespoons parsley, minced
½ cup dry sherry
½ cup water
1 tablespoon soft bread crumbs

Iot up the oil, fry the shrimp, and when they are golden brown take them out of pan. Now lower the meat, and put into the pan the chopped onion, the drained and diced pimientos, garlic, and salt. Cook until the onion is soft. Now add all the remaining ingredients—except the shrimp—and simmer it, stirring until the sauce thickens. This should take about 5 minutes. Now put the shrimp back into the pan, cook it for another 2 minutes, and then pour it all on a nice bed of rice.

◆◆◆ e had dinner one night at the lovely, lavish apartment of Carroll Baker, the lavishly lovely young actress, who entertained us with droll stories and fed us both on a lovely, lavish dinner of scampi, which she cooked herself.

"I know an actress," Carroll Baker said, "who went to a head doctor because she suspected that all was not well with her. 'I'm an actress,' this actress said to the doc, 'but I'm in bad trouble on account of I can't act, and what else I can't do is sing or dance.' She also told the doctor that she didn't know anything she could do in show biz, like which there is no biz, as you might have heard."

Laughing gaily, Carroll continued: "The doctor told this actress that what she should do is get out of show biz and into some other. But the actress got angry. 'How can I get out of show biz, you silly man? I'm a star!'" Here's Carroll Baker's recipe for:

CAMPI

[SERVES FOUR TO FIVE]

pounds shrimp (large)	1 teaspoon dry mustard
½ cup corn oil	2 teaspoons salt
tablespoons parsley flakes, dried	¼ teaspoon pepper
tablespoons fresh parsley, chopped fine	garlic (Carroll used 4 cloves which she pressed with much affection)
tablespoons lemon juice	

Must we keep telling you to clean and devein shrimp if they are fresh? Well, all right, clean and devein them, will you? But leave a piece of shell at

the tail. Split the shrimp, but be careful, don't cu
them in half, see? Stir up all those other ingredient
up there, vigorously, and dump the shrimp into th
mixture, agitating the shrimp around the bow
Now cover the bowl and let them marinate. Just g
away and do something else, will you, like talkin
to your husband, maybe, but just let the shrim
marinate. For 2 hours.

Preheat broiler to 500 degrees, put shrimp wit
marinade—in a pan, what else?—4 inches fror
source of heat for about 10 minutes, turning onc

his man never wanted to do anythin
around the house, so his wife finally nagged hi
into going to the doctor. "I'm always tired," th
man told the doctor. "I don't seem to have an
energy or drive when I get home." The doctor ex
amined him thoroughly and kept shaking his hea
all the time. When the examination was over, th
man said, "Listen, Doc, give it to me straight.
can take it, tell me in plain, simple English, jus
what's the matter with me."

The doctor said, "Well, in plain, simple Englis
there's nothing the matter except that you're lazy
The man beamed. "That's fine, Doc," he said, "no
give me a fancy medical term for it, so I can te
my wife." Try pepping up YOUR husband with:

CURRIED SHRIMP

[SERVES TWO TO THREE]

¾ cup flour
½ cup milk
2 eggs
½ teaspoon salt
1½ teaspoons curry
    powder

deep fat
1 pound shrimp (shell
    and devein if fresh,
    thaw if frozen)

Make a batter by mixing together thoroughly flou
milk, eggs, salt, and curry powder. Get your fat ho
dip the shrimp in the batter and fry them until the
are golden. Drain on paper towel and serve he
with chutney, which is pretty hot, too.

A handsome young Italian-American fellow we know was courting a lovely young lady rather strenuously, and his campaign seemed to be a winning one. As the final battle in this war of love, he took her to dinner at Brione's Restaurant, a fine Italian eating place in Bay Ridge, Brooklyn, and plied her with cocktails, a splendid dinner with wine, and after-dinner liqueurs. The conversation was as sparkling as the wine they drank, the young lady sparkled and giggled happily and looked tempting and appetizing, and bestowed fond glances on our young friend all through the meal.

But then, after the final liqueur had been drunk, the young lady sighed happily and said, "That was wonderful. Now, will you please put me in a taxi because I have to go home and wash my hair."

Our friend was angered almost to the point of frenzy, but he restrained himself. He told the waiter he would be right back, took the girl out, got her a cab, then came back into the restaurant. He stalked over to the table he had occupied, picked up the check, and tore it up. "I am not paying," he said, "because this meal and the drinks got me no place at all." You'll get anywhere you want if you cook:

SHRIMP FRA DIAVALO
(Brother Devil, excuse the expression)

[SERVES FOUR TO SIX]

2 pounds shrimp
2 cloves garlic, chopped
4 ounces olive oil
1 1-pound can whole
    peeled tomatoes,
    crushed with fork
½ teaspoon pepper
1 teaspoon hot red
    pepper flakes

¼ teaspoon oregano
1 teaspoon salt
1 teaspoon parsley,
    chopped
2 basil leaves

Sauté shrimp and garlic in hot olive oil. Add tomatoes, pepper, red pepper flakes, oregano, salt, parsley, basil, and cook over low heat until sauce is thickened (about 10 minutes). Serve real hot.

Uanuary 25th is the Feast of St. Paul the Apostle. In the old days, people used to recite on this feast day this poem:

"If St. Paul's Day be fair and clear,
  It doth betide a happy year,
  But if by chance it then should rain,
  It will make dear all kinds of grain,
  And if the clouds make dark the sky,
  Then meat and fowl this year shall die;
  If blustering winds do blow aloft,
  Then wars shall trouble the realm full oft."

There doesn't seem to be any special food connected with this saint's day, but we have a friend named Paul—poor devil has an ulcer—who always eats bacon and tomato sandwiches on special occasions. If it rains on this day, or if it doesn't, it would be nice consolation—or celebration—to eat:

BAKED LEMON OYSTERS

[SERVES TWO TO FOUR]

1 clove garlic
1 tablespoon butter
½ teaspoon parsley,
   chopped

3 tablespoons lemon juice
2 tablespoons dry white
   wine
1 dozen oysters

Preheat oven to 400 degrees and make sauce. First, put the garlic through a press, melt the butter, put in the garlic and all the other ingredients (except the oysters) and let it cook uncovered over low heat. Don't let it boil. Put the oysters, on the half-shell, on an oven-proof serving plate and bake for 4 minutes. Pour the sauce, which you have stirred vigorously, over the oysters and serve to 2, 3, but not more than 4 people as a first course.

*T*he old man sitting on a park bench one Sunday afternoon listened smilingly as a chance acquaintance bragged about his children and his grandchildren. When the braggart paused for breath, the old man said, "I am very proud of my children also. One of my sons is a novelist, another is an actor, and the third is a newspaper reporter."

The new acquaintance beamed and asked, "And what do you do?" The old man shrugged his shoulders deprecatingly and replied, "Oh, I? I have a candy store. It isn't a very big candy store, but I manage to support all my sons and their families."

Your family will say you support them like a millionaire if you give them:

OYSTERS ROCKEFELLER

[SERVES NINE]

¼ pound butter
½ cup raw spinach, chopped
½ cup bread crumbs
1 onion, minced
¼ cup Parmesan cheese, grated

1 teaspoon Worcester-
shire sauce
½ teaspoon salt
3 dozen oysters

Some fishmongers who sell oysters will be happy to open them for you, and it isn't just because they think they might find a pearl in one of them, as an untrue folk tale has it. For oysters Rockefeller, you need the oysters in the bottom, rounded shell. You don't need the top shell.

Melt the butter, then stir every other ingredient except oysters into the pan with the butter and make a sort of paste out of it. Now preheat your oven to 400 degrees, put the oysters on a pan, and bake them for about 3 minutes until the edges will begin to frizzle. Take the oysters out of the oven, cover each one with some of the mixture, and put the pan back into the oven until the tops are browned. Four oysters like these should be enough for one person. Serve with lemon wedges.

A silly young fellow who had been boring Buddy Hackett, the formerly fat comedian, tried to ingratiate himself by saying, "Hey, Buddy, you know on my way to New York this morning, I passed by your house?" Buddy sneered. "Is that really so?" he inquired in his charming, snarling way. "Thank you very much." No one at your table will snarl if you pass them this:

SCALLOPED OYSTERS

[SERVES THREE TO FOUR]

2 tablespoons butter	1 teaspoon Worcestershire
1 pint oysters	sauce
2½ cups cracker crumbs	⅓ cup butter, melted
¼ cup oyster liquid	½ teaspoon salt
¾ cup light cream	⅛ teaspoon pepper

Butter a shallow 1-quart baking dish, put in half the oysters, then a layer of half the crumbs, and then the rest of the oysters. Mix together the oyster liquid, cream, Worcestershire sauce, melted butter, and salt and pepper. Pour the mixture over the oysters. Cover with remaining crumbs, dot with butter, and bake for 45 minutes in an oven preheated to 350 degrees.

THE politician was proudly telling his cohorts about the wonderful reception he had received from his constituents everywhere he went on his campaign tour through the city. "Why," he said grandiloquently, "when I spoke before the great crowd gathered in the meeting hall of the Free and Independent Order of Part-time Abstainers, that huge multitude sat there listening to my recital of my record with open mouths, every last one of them."

One of his more dubious followers demurred. "Aw, gowan, now," the fellow said, "they never all yawn at the same time." Nobody at your table will be bored with:

FRIED OYSTERS

[SERVES SIX TO EIGHT]

2 eggs, beaten
½ cup flour
salt and pepper to taste

4 dozen oysters
½ cup cracker crumbs
4 ounces butter (1 stick)

Have your fishmonger open the oysters, and if he gives you any guff about it, find a more obliging fishmonger, see? Beat up the eggs, then sift the flour with seasoning. Now dip the oysters first in eggs, then in flour, back in the eggs, and then in cracker crumbs. Now put all the breaded oysters in the refrigerator for a couple of hours. This makes the breading stick to the oysters. Melt the butter in skillet, and get it hot, but don't let it smoke. Fry the oysters until they are a delicate brown, not more than 2 minutes on each side. Over-frying makes them tough.

September has an "r," and what have we got? Oysters, that's what we've got, and we wait for them a long, long time. As the waiter put down the bowl before the famished customer, he remarked pleasantly enough, "It's a great adventure eating oyster stew, isn't it?" The man, a grumpy type, looked up and growled, "Why?"

The waiter beamed. "You never know," he said, "when you'll find a pearl with the oysters, that's why." The man lifted his head from the bowl, which he had been stirring suspiciously. "I'm not looking for pearls," he snarled. "What I'm trying to find is an oyster." You'll never have that problem with this:

OYSTER STEW

[SERVES THREE TO FOUR]

1 quart milk	1 teaspoon salt
1 cup heavy cream	¼ teaspoon pepper
(optional)	1 pint oysters
2 tablespoons butter	½ teaspoon paprika

Scald the milk and cream (if you use cream, which makes it richer, subtract 1 cup milk). Melt half the butter over boiling water, add milk and cream, and keep stirring until it reaches boiling point. Now stir in salt and pepper and take away from heat. Drain the oysters, pour liquor into double boiler, and cook the mixture for 15 minutes. Add oysters and cook until the edges of oysters get curly. Distribute remaining butter among soup bowls, serve stew, and sprinkle with paprika. Some like a dash of Worcestershire sauce.

The maid was telling the gardener all about the dinner party their employers had given the night before, and he was open-mouthed with astonishment by the magnificence of it all. "First," she said, "they had cocktails with caviar and then they went in to dinner, and they had oysters, then turtle soup, then lobster, and all through the dinner they drank champagne, and oh! it was just so grand!"

"And what did they talk about?" asked the gardener. The maid replied proudly, "Us!" Here are a couple of seafood dishes we have had at home, following recipes we got from the Mediterranée, a wonderful seafood restaurant where we first ate:

OYSTERS VÉNITIENNE

[SERVES FOUR]

⅛ pound prosciutto
(Italian ham) or
thinly sliced boiled
ham
½ green pepper
3 slices pimiento

2 dozen oysters on half
shell
2 tablespoons butter,
salted
2 tablespoons grated
Parmesan cheese

Chop the ham, green pepper, and pimiento. Distribute some of each on the oysters, dot them with butter, sprinkle Parmesan cheese over all. Broil 3 inches from source of heat until the edges of oysters curl and cheese is melted. This is a great prelude for four people to:

LOBSTER ARCHDUC

4 small lobsters
1 black truffle
½ cup butter
1½ tablespoons flour
1 cup milk

½ teaspoon salt
¼ teaspoon pepper
1 tablespoon dry
mustard
2 tablespoons sherry

If your lobsters are live, and that's the best way to get them, put them head first into a pot of boiling water to cover for 10 minutes. Isn't that a lovely pink they turn? Well, so would you if you were put head first in boiling water, heavens forfend! Some fishmongers are happy to kill your lobsters for you and to clean them too—you know, take out the back vein that runs from the head to the tail and the sack in back of the creature's head, if you ask them nicely. Let the beasts cool so you can handle them, then drain them, cut them open, and remove all the meat. Keep the shells as intact as you can, because you are going to need them. Now, chop up the lobster meat, slice the truffle thin, and mix up the lobster meat and sliced truffle. If your lobsters have coral (pink) and tomally (green), you have an added boon: use them too. Now, stuff all this back into the shells. Melt the butter, stir in the flour, and add milk and all the other ingredients. Cook over low heat, stirring all the while until the sauce thickens, and then pour it all heedlessly over the stuffed lobster. Preheat your oven to 425 degrees and bake the lobsters for 10 minutes, or until they are good and hot. And don't talk about the servant problem while you are eating this; the servants might not like it.

A friend of ours wrote a book, and really it was a terrible book, and we would have felt sorry for him, except that he was quite obnoxious about it; he just wouldn't stop talking about it. One day at lunch with several people, he was complaining bitterly because his book hadn't yet been reviewed.

"I can't understand those stupid reviewers," he said. "I really think there is a conspiracy of silence about it. What would you advise me to do?" There was a silence which was broken by another friend of ours.

"My advice," said Debs Myers, "would be to join it." Everybody will join in your praise if you give them:

NUTTY LOBSTER OR SHRIMP

[SERVES FOUR TO SIX]

1 cup almonds, blanched
  and slivered
½ cup butter
1 pound cooked lobster
  meat, or cooked
  shrimp

½ teaspoon salt
dash of pepper
1 teaspoon parsley,
  chopped

Fry the almonds in melted butter, stirring so they are lightly browned all over. Take them out of pan and put in the lobster meat—or shrimp—and fry it until that's all lightly browned, too. Sprinkle with salt, pepper, and parsley, stirring it all up well in the pan. Add the almonds. On toast, this is great. It will give you 4 generous portions or 6 smaller ones.

T he teacher had been having a terrible lot of trouble with this one boy in her class. It wasn't that he carried a switchblade knife; and he had never smoked a reefer in class, or anything like that; but he was terribly lazy, though obviously very bright, and he just wouldn't do any work at all, in or out of the classroom.

One day, while all the other high school students were busily writing a composition, this young lout kept staring dreamily out the window, doing nothing except scratching once in awhile. Finally, the teacher became more exasperated than usual. "Listen, Wilfred," she said to the young fellow, "don't you know you are supposed to be writing a composition on the subject, 'What I Would Do if I Had a Million Dollars'?"

The boy yawned and put his feet up on the desk. "But teach," the youthful wise-guy said, "this is just what I'd do if I had a million dollars!" Even if you had a million you couldn't buy a better:

FRIED SOFT-SHELLED CRAB

[SERVES SIX]

2 eggs, beaten	6 pieces white toast
3 tablespoons milk	salt and pepper
12 soft-shelled crabs	parsley, chopped
flour	tartar sauce
bread crumbs	
deep fat for frying (peanut oil is real good)	

Most fishmongers will dress your crabs for you, but if you happen to have an old, crabby fishmonger, here's how to do it: Jab each crab between the eyes with a sharp knife. Now fold back the soft points of the shell and remove the gills, which are spongy portions right there under the points. Now put the crab on its back and, with scissors, snip off the small piece at the lower part of the shell which ends in a point.

Okay, that's over, thank goodness. But do try to get your fishmonger to do it, even though it's not difficult, once you have practice. Now beat the eggs with the milk. Dip each crab first in the eggs, then in the flour, back in the eggs, then in the bread crumbs. When you've got them all coated, it's good to refrigerate them before frying; the breading sticks better that way, and that's the secret all restaurants use in frying breaded foods. Hot up your fat—we say peanut oil is best—and fry the crabs until they are a deep golden-brown all over. Turn them while they are frying. Take them out with a perforated spoon, drain them on paper towels, season them with salt and pepper, and put one crab on each piece of toast, cut in half triangularly. To each customer, 2 crabs. Garnish with chopped parsley and have tartar sauce—icy cold—at the table. You know, don't you, that you eat everything on a soft-shelled crab, legs and all? It's a lovely time of the year when the soft-shelled crabs are around.

April 13th is the birthday of Thomas Jefferson, third President of the United States, author of the Declaration of Independence, founder of the University of Virginia, and a staunch champion of religious freedom and many other great causes. He could read Latin and Greek, he played the violin, he studied law and architecture, he was a splendid horseman and gardener, and when the British burned the Library of Congress, he sold his great library to the United States for a piddling sum of money!

But you know what else Thomas Jefferson did? When he was Secretary of State, he sent at his expense a man all the way to Italy to learn how to make macaroni! And he was the first man to serve spaghetti in this country! He also introduced French-fried potatoes to this country! He was the second U. S. president to live in the White House, and whenever he gave a dinner party he and his French chef would go to the market early in the morning to buy supplies! What a man! In his honor, let us have a variation of a splendid dish he loved, which is called:

CRAB PELAU

[SERVES FOUR]

1 cup coconut flakes
1 cup milk
3 tablespoons oil
1 medium onion, chopped
1 tablespoon flour
1 1-pound can whole, peeled tomatoes

2 tablespoons tomato paste
salt and pepper
¼ teaspoon curry powder
1 cup brandy
1 cup rice
2 cups crab meat

First, put the coconut flakes in the milk and let it soak for awhile. While it's soaking, hot up the oil, fry the onions, and stir in the flour. Put the tomatoes through a sieve, mix in the tomato paste, and add this to the fried onion in the pan. Now strain the coconut. Save the milk, but throw away the coconut flakes after squeezing milk out. Put the coconut milk, salt and pepper, and curry powder into the pan with the onion and tomatoes. Stir it all around, add the brandy and rice, cover the pan after stirring the contents, and cook it over low heat for about 30 minutes. Add the crab meat 10 minutes before the time is up. They do a dish like this in Spain and in South America, where they call it *centolla con tomates salsa de coñac*. And there is a quaint Spanish folk saying which quaint Spanish folk say: *"Tengo una hambre que parecen dos,"* which means "I am so hungry that I feel like twins."

A friend of ours took a tour through the South last summer and, because he is a Civil War buff, went on a bus trip around a couple of the old battlefields. The driver of the bus, who had a set spiel, kept talking about all the glorious victories won by the Confederate Army, and it finally irked our friend, who said during a pause in the bus driver's monologue, "Didn't the northern armies ever win a battle?"

The driver glared at him with snaggle-toothed venom. "Nosirree," he snarled, "and they ain't GONNA win any, long as I'm the driver of this here old bus!" You know what day January 19th is? It's the birthday of General Robert E. Lee, that's what it is, and if you feel like celebrating it, why don't you cook some:

MARYLAND CRAB CAKES

[SERVES THREE TO FOUR]

1 pound crab meat,
    flaked
1 egg, beaten
salt and pepper
1 tablespoon Worcester-
    shire sauce

1 teaspoon dry mustard
1 teaspoon lemon juice
4 tablespoons butter
bread crumbs

Mix everything together—except 3 tablespoons of the butter and the bread crumbs. Now, when you've got it all thoroughly combined, shape the stuff into cakes and coat them with the bread crumbs. Hot up the butter and fry the cakes on both sides until they are a delicious-looking golden brown, like Diahann Carroll.

This newly rich woman drove up to the hotel in the mountains and handed the car keys to the bellhop. "All my luggage is in the trunk," she said. "Will you please get it out and bring it to my suite?" The bellhop struggled up with six large, heavy bags, and then the befurred lady gave him a brilliant smile and said, "Now go back to the car, and in the back you will find a 14-year-old boy. Please carry him up here, too."

The bellhop, exhausted, objected. "Gee whillikers, lady," he said. "What's the matter, can't he walk?" The lady drew herself up haughtily. "Of course he can walk," she said frostily, "but thank goodness, he doesn't have to any more!" You don't have to be Spanish to like *Almejas a la Marinera,* which is what Spanish people call:

MUSSELS À LA MARINERA

[SERVES TWO TO FOUR]

4 dozen mussels	2 teaspoons parsley,
1 tablespoon olive oil	chopped
1 medium onion, chopped	1 teaspoon salt
2 cloves garlic, minced	½ teaspoon pepper
2 tablespoons lemon juice	1 cup dry white wine
2 teaspoons bread crumbs	

Scrub the mussels well with a stiff brush under cold, running water. Put about 1 inch of water into a large pot, add the cleaned mussels, and over high heat steam the mussels for about 3 to 5 minutes, until the shells open. Drain the mussels, save the liquid, and let them cool so you can handle them. While the mussels are cooling, strain the broth. Remove the beards from the mussels, and put them back into the pot along with the strained broth and everything else except the white wine. Simmer it for about 10 minutes covered. Taste the liquid and correct the seasoning, if necessary. Add the white wine and cook over low heat for an additional 5 minutes. Serve this with French or Italian bread to sop up with gravy. Most people allow a dozen mussels for each person; we like more than a dozen. Mussels can be bought in cans as well as live.

March 12th is the Day of St. Gregory, the great sixth-century Pope who revised the chant which has since been called by his name. St. Gregory was the son of a wealthy Roman senator who left him a great fortune, half of which he gave away to the poor; the other half he spent building a number of monasteries, one of which he entered. He did much good for the poor and he was a man of great learning; therefore, he is known as St. Gregory the Great. For some reason or other, the children of Belgium for a long time believed that it was St. Gregory who freed frogs from the winter's ice, and they made a school holiday of his day, chanting songs in his honor, and marching through the streets collecting presents. So on this day, why not have:

FRIED FROG LEGS

[SERVES SIX]

1 dozen frog legs
½ cup dry white wine
2 tablespoons lemon juice
3 cloves garlic, minced
2 tablespoons chives.
    minced

1 tablespoon parsley,
    chopped
flour
⅓ cup butter
salt and pepper
2 ounces brandy

Wash and dry the frog legs, then marinate them for an hour or two in mixture of wine, lemon juice, garlic, chives, and parsley. Dredge the frog legs in flour, melt the butter, and brown the legs and season them. Pour the marinade into the pan, cook-stir, turning the legs, and empty the pan into a serving platter. Now heat the brandy and pour it, flaming, into the platter at the table. This will serve six, two legs per person, as a main course with crusty French or Italian bread to sop up the delicious sauce. With this what's good is:

CREAMED MUSHROOMS-ONIONS-PEAS

1 10½-ounce can
    condensed cream of
    mushroom soup
⅓ cup milk
1 10-ounce package
    frozen peas, cooked

1 dozen small white
    onions, cooked
1 teaspoon soy sauce

Combine the soup and milk over low heat, Drain and add the peas and onions; stir in the soy sauce. Keep stirring as you cook.

Meats

When we were much younger, the dish that was most often mentioned as the height of gastronomical splendor—next to lobster—was a steak smothered in onions. Nobody we knew broiled steaks indoors or outdoors, over or under direct heat—steaks were always pan-broiled or fried, and smothered, as we said, with onions. Which reminds us of a steak-smothered-in-onions story.

The customer in the restaurant called the waiter. "How was this steak cooked?" asked the customer. "It was smothered in onions," said the waiter. "Hmph," hmphed the customer, "it died a hard death, didn't it?" In the Caribbean, they have a dish called *Carne Frita con Cebollas*, which means:

STEAK SMOTHERED IN ONIONS

[SERVES THREE TO FOUR]

2 pounds fillet of beef	1 teaspoon pepper
3 tablespoons vinegar	fat
3 cloves garlic, pressed	4 large onions, sliced
2 tablespoons salt	

Wipe meat with a damp cloth and dry it. (Most times, home economists who write about food say, "wipe meat with a CLEAN damp cloth. . . ." well, WE'RE not going to insult your intelligence.) Now cut the meat into thin slices, maybe ¼ inch thick. Most markets sell individual steaks that are good for this dish.

Rub into each piece of meat the vinegar, pressed garlic, and salt and pepper. (You can use garlic flakes if you first let them soak in a teaspoon of water.) Hot up your fat, brown the onions slowly over low heat, and when they are thoroughly browned, but not burned, remove them from pan, and hold on to them for use later. Now fry the steaks over high heat for a short time on each side, if you like them rare. When you are doing the last of the steaks, put the onions back into the pan to hot them up and then spread the onions over the steaks. Put some hot water—maybe 3 or 4 tablespoons—into the pan, scrape the pan to get the good stuff in it, and pour it over the steaks and onions.

(We like it better with a little red wine, instead of water, but we don't want you to start thinking we're a wino or anything like that, for goodness' sake.)

During the next-to-last unpleasantness, an American correspondent, assigned to our former glorious ally, Russia, visited for the second time a small village near Pinsk, which, contrary to popular opinion, is nowhere near Minsk. "Why," the nosey correspondent asked a wily peasant, "is there only one windmill in this town, when last year, when I was here, there were two windmills? Why was the second windmill torn down?" The aforementioned wily peasant smiled wilily. "Because," he said with a snaggle-toothed grin, "we had only enough wind for one windmill." This is how they cooked steak in that village, when they had:

STEAK

[SERVES THREE TO FOUR]

2 pounds roundsteak or chuck
flour
salt and pepper to taste
2 cups onion, sliced

4 tablespoons butter or fat
1 cup water
1 cup sour cream

Bludgeon the steak with a blunt instrument, pound in the flour, salt and pepper, and cut the meat up into 3-inch squares. Sauté the onion until soft, take it out, and brown the meat. When the meat is browned, return the onion to pan, add water and sour cream, cover, and cook over low heat for about 1½ hours. (Taste a piece after 1½ hours; if its tender, it's finished, see?)

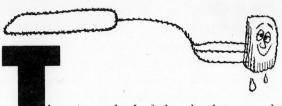

here is a school of thought that a good steak doesn't need anything except fire, and then some salt and pepper and maybe a little butter, and in general, I subscribe to that theory. But once in a while, merely for the sake of variety and piquancy, and to startle my guests, I like to serve with a fine steak a boozy sauce. And here's how I do a:

STEAK IN RYE

[SERVES SIX TO EIGHT]

1 stick of butter
4½ pounds sirloin
3 tablespoons flour
8 scallions or 1 small
    onion
½ cup rye whiskey
1 tablespoon beef
    extract
juice of 1 lemon
salt and pepper to taste

Melt the butter in a large pan. Wipe meat with a damp cloth, dry it and then coat with the flour. Over high heat—being careful not to let the butter smoke—sauté the steaks on both sides, according to how rare or well-done you like your meat. (If you think that pan-frying a steak is far from gourmet cooking, regard for yourself the great French chefs who think that broiling a steak on coals is barbaric and that pan-frying is the only way to treat a fine steak.)

When you have the steak done as you like, take it out of the pan, put it on a heated platter to keep it warm and make the sauce. Mince the scallions or onion, cook in the pan until golden, add the rye, beef extract, lemon, and salt and pepper. Now heat it, stirring, until the liquid is reduced to half its original quantity. Put the steak into the pan for just one minute to get it good and hot, turning once, and remove to a serving platter, pour the boozy sauce all over it and serve.

When Asparagus Week comes around, it's because the asparagus growers have a lot of asparagus, that's why. And that's why it is a good idea to use this darling vegetable in your menus, because when stuff is in large supply, it is at its best and cheapest.

Which reminds us about an inept city gardener we know who was once planting asparagus seeds in his back yard. His small son was watching him and the boy asked, "Hey, Pop, why do they have such pretty pictures on seed packages?" The unhappy fellow stood up, stretched his tired back, and in a discouraged voice said, "Because they'd at least like the people who plant the seeds to know what they'd look like if they ever came up." You won't be discouraged if you cook:

ASPARAGUSY STEAK

[SERVES THREE TO FOUR]

2 1-pound pieces round steak
3 tablespoons flour
1½ cups asparagus spears, uncooked
⅛ teaspoon oregano

salt and pepper to taste
1 cup canned whole tomatoes
4 potatoes, peeled and sliced
2 onions, sliced

Smash the devil out of the steaks with anything you've got handy—a baseball bat will do fine. Now dredge them in flour. Put one of them in a roasting pan or Dutch oven, cover it with the asparagus spears, dust it all with the oregano and seasoning, and put the other steak on top of the first one. Now mash up the tomatoes good and pour them on the meat. In your oven, which you have preheated to 350 degrees, bake it for 1½ hours. Take a peek once in awhile, baste it, and, if it is too dry, add a little hot water.

After a half-hour, add the sliced potatoes and the onions. Isn't it silly to have to tell you to peel the potatoes? But if we don't, somebody is sure to call up and ask, "Should I peel the potatoes?" So we tell them, yes, and peel the onions, too, dear.

Do people keep asking you, "What's cooking?" Well, they keep asking us, and it gets pretty tiresome, let us tell you. Let's just see you stop us from telling you. Anyway, someone we know was asked that dopey question the other day, and she said, "Nothing, except my Uncle Pincus has just invented a musical stove. When it cooks *lasagna,* it plays 'Return to Sorrento.' When it cooks *gefilte* fish, it plays, 'Oy, Der Rebitzen,' and when it cooks *paella,* it plays 'Granada.'" What's the point of all that? she was asked, and she replied: "Nothing, except that it stops dopes from asking, 'What's cooking?'" Did you ever cook:

STEAK WITH BLUE CHEESE

[SERVES THREE TO FOUR]

3-pound porterhouse steak	2 tablespoons onion, minced
½ cup blue cheese, crumbled	1 tablespoon soy sauce
	¼ teaspoon pepper

Broil the steak on both sides however you like it—rare, medium etc.—and meanwhile combine all other ingredients. When steak is done the way you like it, spread the cheese mixture on top, put it back under the broiler until the cheese is melted, and maybe your stove won't sing, but your family will.

On a bus the other day, we overheard a couple of young women, both of them obviously new brides, discussing family budgets. One was particularly morose. She and her husband were having trouble keeping up the payments on their car; the TV set had to be paid for every week, and, in addition, the TV repairman was a steady visitor at their house. They hadn't realized that a home-owner had to be a plumber, electrician, carpenter, painter, and landscape designer, and so they had to have these characters at their home all the time.

"Yes, yes," said the other young woman, "it's the same way with us. But you know? We don't want to be rich; we just want to be able to afford to live just like we're living right now, that's all." You will be living well if you fry a:

PICKLED STEAK

[SERVES TWO TO FOUR]

2 pounds round steak
1 teaspoon salt
¼ teaspoon pepper

2 tablespoons wine
    vinegar
butter, or fat as needed
3 tablespoons (hot) water

The steak should be cut about 1½ inches thick. Beat the steak with a blunt instrument, then, take a knife and gash it unmercifully on both sides. Now stir the salt and pepper into the vinegar and rub this mixture all over the steak and let it stand—read a book, have a drink, go for a walk—for an hour.

Now get hold of a good heavy pan, melt the butter (but don't let it smoke) and fry the steak on both sides, not more than 2 minutes for each side if you like steak rare, more if you like it more well-done. When you have got them fried to your taste—just slice, but not all the way through, to see how the color is—remove to a hot platter and pour the hot water into the pan.

Scrape up the delicious stuff in the steak pan and raise heat to high. When the water and butter boils, you've got a great gravy. This is good for one glutton, two good eaters, or four dainty ones.

We are old enough, it makes us sad to say, to remember many of the stories they used to tell when Calvin Coolidge was in the White House. One of the best of them was about a dinner guest who watched with astonishment as the President of the United States poured some of the coffee in his cup into his saucer, then added a little sugar and some cream. The guest was horrified, but he figured that if the President of the United States drank his coffee like that, the least he could do was to follow his example. So he poured coffee into his own saucer, then some sugar, and then some cream. And he almost fell through the floor when he saw Coolidge calmly pick up the creamed-sugared coffee he had prepared so carefully and put it on the floor for the White House cat, who lapped it up with delight. Your family will do the same if you cook:

WINO-COFFEE STEAK

[SERVES FIVE TO SIX]

3 pounds round steak, 1-inch thick
¼ cup flour
salt and pepper to taste
⅓ cup olive oil
2 onions, sliced thin
2 pounds mushrooms, whole

1 dash of tabasco
1 teaspoon sugar
1 tablespoon Worcestershire sauce
½ cup dry red wine
¾ cup strong black coffee
½ cup of water
1 pint sour cream

Cut the beef into bite-size pieces, season the flour, and dredge the meat well in the seasoned flour. Hot up the oil, brown the meat in it and then add the onions and mushrooms and cook until they're soft. Add everything else—EXCEPT the sour cream—cover the pan and simmer over low heat for an hour, or until the meat is nice and tender. Pour it all into a heated serving dish and pour all the sour cream over it.

A high school boy we know told his father, a highly successful businessman, that he was planning to become a writer instead of joining him in his firm. "If you become a writer," said the father, "you will be ill-clad, ill-fed, and ill-housed until you are 50 years old." The young man looked puzzled.

"And what will happen when I am 50 years old, Daddy?" he asked. The father smiled benignly. "Ah, my son, by the time you are 50, you will be accustomed to it." Your family will be happy if you become accustomed to making:

WINEY FILET MIGNON

[SERVES THREE TO FOUR]

2 tablespoons butter
2 tablespoons minced onion
2 pounds filet mignon, 1½-inches thick

salt and pepper
⅛ pound butter (½ stick)
½ cup sweet sherry

In 2 tablespoons butter, brown the minced onion. Remove onions and brown the filet on all sides over high heat, about 5 minutes on each side. Lower the heat, season according to taste with salt and pepper, and continue cooking for another 5 minutes, turning the meat once. In a separate pan, melt the ⅛ pound butter, adding the wine, pour it over the meat, and let it simmer for about 2 minutes. This will be fairly rare if your filet is cut 1½ inches thick. If you like it more well done, let it simmer longer.

The poor but shifty-eyed young man had told the millionaire father of a girl that he wanted to marry her, and the rich man was cross-examining him. He had asked all the usual questions—about schools the young man had gone to, his salary, his prospects for the future, his family history back four generations, and all that jazz. And then he asked, "If I were a poor man, would you still want to marry my daughter?" The young man nodded eagerly. "Why, yes sir," he cried enthusiastically, "I certainly would!" The rich man's face grew purple with rage. "Get out of here!" he shouted.

"You think I'm going to let my daughter marry a cretinous fool?" You'd be smart if you tried:

MUSHROOM-STUFFED STEAK

[SERVES THREE TO FOUR]

2 pounds fillet of beef
3 slices bacon
1 onion, chopped
½ pound mushrooms, sliced
1 teaspoon parsley, chopped

½ teaspoon salt
¼ teaspoon pepper
¼ teaspoon basil
1 egg
2 tablespoons cream
oil

Have your butcher cut the fillet into four or five slices—or do it yourself if he is the surly type—and have him beat on them and flatten them down to about half their former thickness. If you are doing it yourself, put the meat between two pieces of waxed paper or an old rag and beat on it with anything handy—the flat of an ax, a beer can, baseball bat, whatever you like. Now fry the bacon, leave the drippings in pan, and remove the bacon and crumble it. Sauté the onion, mushrooms, and parsley, and add the salt, pepper, and basil. Take it away from the heat. Beat up the egg with the cream and add this to the other mixture. Spread all this over the meat slices, roll them up, and fasten them with skewers or toothpicks, or tie them up with kitchen twine. Now brown them thoroughly in hot oil, then cover, lower heat, and cook, turning frequently, for another few minutes, according to how rare or well-done you like your steaks.

*T*his suburban friend tells us that she isn't speaking to her husband this week because he remembered their wedding anniversary. Seems in previous years, he did forget the date of their wedding and then would be so contrite that his gift would be much more generous than it would have been ordinarily.

But this evening when he got off the train, he was carrying a large carton and was beaming. "See," he said, as he got into the car, "I didn't forget this year. I bought you a mink coat." His wife said, "But you know I wanted a new car; you promised me a car, not a mink." "Yes, dear, I know," he said, "but I couldn't find anyone who sold imitation cars." You've probably heard about this phony dish all your life, but did you ever try:

MOCK DUCK?

[SERVES THREE TO FOUR]

2 tablespoons onion, chopped
¼ cup butter (or fat)
1 cup bread crumbs
1 egg, beaten
¼ teaspoon salt
¼ teaspoon pepper

2 rump steaks, 1 pound each
3 tablespoons fat
2 cups boiling stock (or bouillon)
flour

Sauté onion in melted butter or fat—mix together bread crumbs, egg, and salt and pepper, and add to onions in pan. Stir vigorously. Spread dressing over one of the rump steaks, put the other on top of it, and sew edges together. Now put 3 tablespoons fat in skillet, heat it good, and brown both sides of the sewed-together steaks. Pour in the boiling stock, cover skillet, and lower heat. Let simmer for about 2 hours until tender. Now cut the thread off meat. Add just enough flour to the drippings to thicken. Place meat on hot serving platter, and pour gravy over meat. Garnish with parsley, and line edge of platter with mashed potatoes.

If you think this tastes like duck, you couldn't be more wrong. Then why do they call it "mock duck?" Beats us. If YOU know, let us know, will you?

A very cheap fellow we knew was told by

his doctor that he had to go to a specialist for treatment, and the cheapskate was appalled when he was told that this medical man was so eminent he charged $50 for the first visit and $25 for each one after that. But this fellow thought he was just as smart as he was cheap, so when he came into the specialist's office, he said, heartily, "Here I am again, Doc!" He certainly got foxed, because the doc was no dope. "Well," said the specialist, "just follow the course of treatment I gave you before, and that'll be $25, please." A fairly cheap meal to make is:

SWISS STEAK

[SERVES THREE TO FOUR]

½ cup flour
1 teaspoon salt
½ teaspoon pepper
3 tablespoons fat
2 pounds round or chuck
    steak

1 medium onion,
    chopped
1 cup tomatoes, mashed
3 carrots, sliced
    lengthwise

Mix flour, salt, and pepper and pound mixture into the steak. In hot fat, brown the meat and onion. Then pour tomatoes all over it, cover, and cook in oven preheated to 350 degrees for 1½ hours. Half an hour before it is done, put sliced carrots into pan. All that meat and no:

POTATOES?

⅔ cup oil (olive or salad)
5 potatoes, peeled and
    sliced about ¼-inch
    thick

salt and pepper to taste

Pour oil into large baking pan or pie plate; coat both sides of potato slices in oil and don't pile them one on top of another—spread them out, you hear? Salt and pepper them. Put the potatoes in 350-degree oven in which you're cooking that lovely Swiss steak, for 45 minutes. The beauty part of this way of making French fries is that you don't have to keep turning them, see? Just go away and read a good book, or something, while it's all cooking.

*T*here have been judges in our criminal courts who have become pretty callous about the feelings of the defendants who come before them for sentencing, and, indeed, it is understandable that this should occasionally happen, exposed as they are every day to tales of crime and brutality. Most of them, however, do try to avoid undue harshness and some of them even attempt to put themselves in the place of the prisoners. (Which wouldn't be such a bad idea, in one or two cases we've been familiar with.)

Anyway, there was the judge who asked a prisoner if he'd ever been in jail before. "No, never," the man replied, bursting into tears. "Now, now," said the kindly judge, "don't cry, you poor fellow. You'll be there soon." No one will cry if you give them:

BAKED FLANK STEAK

[SERVES SIX]

juice of ½ lemon
3 pounds flank steak
1 teaspoon salt
⅛ teaspoon pepper
¼ cup flour
1½ tablespoons fat or butter
1 large or 2 small onions, minced
2 tablespoons green pepper, minced
2 tablespoons celery, minced
2 tablespoons carrot, minced
¼ cup catsup
2 cups water, boiling

Rub the lemon juice into both sides of the meat; then add salt and pepper to the flour and rub that into the meat. In a large pan, melt the fat and sear the meat on both sides. All the vegetables should be minced. Mix them together with catsup and place them on the meat. Now pour the hot water around the meat in the pan and cook it for 2½ hours in a slow oven, 200 degrees. Every once in awhile, baste the meat with the liquid in the pan, which will make a nice gravy, which will make 6 people happy.

A girl we know was a witness to an accident, and the policeman collecting the names of the people who saw it finally came to her. "And what is your name?" he asked. Our friend, a very pretty girl, smiled and said, "Julie Jones." The policeman snorted in derision. "Who do you think you're kidding? Come on, now, what's your name?" Julie Jones, who is accustomed to people doubting her, smiled again, and replied, "Charlotte Brontë." The cop leered at Julie. "Did you think you could get away with giving me that phony Jones stuff?" There's nothing phony about:

BEEF STEW

[SERVES FOUR TO FIVE]

2½ pounds round steak
pieces of beef suet
¼ cup of flour
3 cups beef broth
2 carrots, cut in 1-inch
    slices

6 small white onions
¼ teaspoon thyme
1 tablespoon parsley,
    chopped
juice of ½ lemon
1 cup dry red wine

Cut the meat into bite-size pieces, removing any suet on it. Hot up the suet until you have about 4 tablespoons of melted fat, discard the rest of the suet. Now add the meat, brown the pieces on all sides, and sprinkle with the flour. Heat the broth in separate pan and add it slowly to the meat. Cover the pan and simmer over low heat for 2 hours. Cut carrots into 1-inch pieces, add them and all the remaining ingredients to pan and cook for another 30 minutes.

a neighbor of ours had as a dinner guest one night a small girl, friend of her own small girl. She noticed that the child was having trouble handling her knife and fork, so she kindly offered to cut up the meat on the little girl's plate. "Oh, that's all right," the little dear said. "I can do it all right.

Sometimes at home we have tough meat, too." The way to avoid such embarrassments is to serve little girls—and little boys, too—

NORWEGIAN MEATBALLS

[SERVES FOUR TO SIX]

2 pounds boneless sirloin
1½ teaspoons salt
½ teaspoon pepper
½ teaspoon ground
    ginger

2 cups beef stock
4 tablespoons flour
4 tablespoons butter or
    chicken fat

Grind the meat fine, mix in the seasonings. (It's the ground ginger that makes a Norwegian meatball different from a Danish, Swedish, or any other kind of meatball.) Using a small amount of the beef stock at a time, moisten the meat until it can hold its shape in small balls, bigger than a marble, but smaller than a ping pong ball. You probably won't need all of the beef stock to do this. (You can make the stock by simmering two bouillon cubes in two cups of water.) Roll the balls in the flour. Melt whatever fat you are using and brown the balls well, all over. Add some of the stock you have left over just short of covering the meatballs, cover the pan, and simmer over low heat for 15-20 minutes. The Norwegians call them *kjölttboller;* the Swedes call them *köttbullar,* and the Danes call them *frikadeller.* But we like the Norwegian kind best, because they don't use bread, cracker crumbs, or cereals to adulterate them. We like them on noodles.

The young man looked sad and pale and deeply troubled. So one of his friends asked him, "Why do you look so sad and pale and deeply troubled?" The fellow sighed. "Because," he said unhappily, "the most wonderful girl in the world turned me down when I asked her to marry me." His friend laughed.

"Why, you dope," said the friend, "don't you know that when a woman says 'no,' she almost always means 'yes'?"

"Oh, yes," said the disappointed lover, "but this girl didn't say 'no.' What she said was 'yerch.'" No one will ever say that if you cook:

BEEF AND BEANS

[SERVES SIX TO EIGHT]

2 cups navy beans	1 tablespoon salt
fat	½ teaspoon pepper
3 pounds chuck	1¼ teaspoons prepared
2 onions, chopped	mustard
2 tablespoons honey	

Soak the beans overnight after washing them. Next day, simmer the beans for 20 minutes in the water in which they soaked. Now drain the beans and save the water. (You'll need most of it later.) In a Dutch oven, hot up a little fat and brown the meat all over. Take the meat out. (Don't throw this away either.) Now toss into the Dutch oven half the chopped onions and half of the cooked beans, put the meat on top of this, and cover it with the remaining beans and onions. Mix up the honey, salt, pepper, and mustard with 3 cups of the beany water and pour it over all. Simmer this for hours and hour and hours over a very slow fire. From time to time, you'll find things getting dry, so, when necessary, add some beany water, hotted up. This is obviously not for the woman who works; it takes too long, but is it ever good!

With this serve a green salad with any kind of dressing you like. We like a garlicky oil-and-vinegar one; but you do as you like.

Larry Penates, a writer friend of ours who bears watching—just watching, not reading—was complaining to his wife—not a bad whiner herself —about their son-in-law who had just left their home with their daughter. They had had a delicious dinner of beef *à la mode,* one of Mrs. Penates' specialties.

"Our son-in-law is a great big cretinous oaf," exclaimed Larry Penates as he slammed the front door on the young couple. "He doesn't know beans about horses and booze!" When his wife said she thought that was admirable, Larry snorted in derision. "You fool," he said affectionately to his dear wife, "you would be right, except that our son-in-law, not knowing anything about race horses, bets on them, anyway. And with no understanding at all of alcoholic beverages, he drinks copiously, nevertheless." Here is how Mrs. Penates makes:

BEEF À LA MODE

[SERVES FIVE TO SIX]

3 pounds eye round	½ cup celery, diced
salt and pepper	8 small carrots
1 cup water, boiling	½ cup peas
1 bay leaf	

Ask your butcher to lard the beef with ¼-inch strips of salt pork. (Maybe you remember how arrogant butchers were during the next-to-the-last unpleasantness? Larding, of course, means running strips of salt pork or bacon through lean meat, which makes it juicier and tastier. If your butcher won't take the trouble to lard the beef, curse him roundly, leave, and find a butcher-fellow who will.) Salt and pepper the meat according to your taste, brown it all over in a Dutch oven or heavy pot, and add boiling water and bay leaf. Cover and simmer 3½ hours. Add vegetables and simmer another half hour.

A friend of ours took his wife to the theater and then she didn't speak to him for weeks. What happened was that one of those charming old crones who infest the theatrical district confronted him as he was guiding his wife through the crowds and whined, "Buy a corsage for your lady?" He shook his head negatively. "Buy one," she demanded with a leer, "for the woman you love!"

The man stopped. "I can't buy a corsage," he said, "for the woman I love because I'm a married man, and my wife won't let me." If your husband makes terrible jokes like that, he'll be sorry if you cook:

SOUR-CREAM POT ROAST

[SERVES THREE TO FOUR]

2 pounds chuck	⅓ cup shortening
⅓ cup flour	5 onions, sliced
½ tablespoon salt	½ pint sour cream
½ teaspoon pepper	5 tablespoons milk

Cut the meat up into bite-size pieces. (Your bite-size may be bigger or smaller than ours, who knows?) Dredge meat in seasoned flour, get the shortening hotted up, and brown the meat all over. Cover the meat with the onion slices and pour in the sour cream. Let it simmer covered for 1½ hours, when the meat should be tender. Take the meat out and keep it on a warmed platter. You are bound to have some flour left over from the stuff you used to coat the meat. Okay. Mix the leftover flour with the 5 tablespoons of milk, add to the liquid in the pan, stir it all around over low heat until it thickens, and pour it over the meat.

Grace Downs, who operates a school for girls who want to become airline hostesses, was taken to a restaurant by a friend who was pleased when she asked the waiter if she could give her compliments to the chef. The chef was honored. Grace was led into the kitchen and came back to the table waving a little card on which was written the recipe for the dish she had just eaten. "I told the chef I didn't have paper or anything to write down the recipe," she whispered to her friend, "so he let me borrow this card from his recipe file.

I figured if I got it away from him he would never again be able to cook and serve that terrible dish I just ate." This is NOT what Grace ate:

HUNGARIAN GOULASH

[SERVES SIX]

3 pounds chuck beef
2 teaspoons salt
½ teaspoon pepper
2 tablespoons paprika
6 tablespoons butter or fat

5 medium onions, chopped
1 can tomato sauce
1 clove garlic
½ cup sour cream

Cut meat into bite-size pieces. Mix together salt, pepper, and paprika, and roll the meat in seasonings until all pieces are coated. Melt half the butter or fat in large frying pan, sauté the onions, stirring constantly, and when it is all soft, take the onions out of the pan. Now melt rest of the butter and brown the meat on all sides. Put the onions back into the pan, add the tomato sauce and garlic, and mix it all up thoroughly in the pan. Cover the pan and simmer over low heat for 3 hours. Once in awhile, give it all a stirring. Just before you are ready to serve, pour in the sour cream and stir that around for a minute or so. Serve this on:

BROAD NOODLES

1 8-ounce package broad noodles
3 quarts water
1½ teaspoons salt

Bring the water to a boil, pour in salt, add the noodles. Start timing when water comes back to boil, keep stirring, and let them cook for 10 to 15 minutes, depending on consistency you like. Drain thoroughly.

A friend of ours was walking down the street one day recently when someone came up behind him and gave him a terrific slap on the shoulder.

Our friend turned around to see an utter stranger, who, on seeing our friend's face, exclaimed, "Holy mackerel, mister, excuse me. I'm sorry. I thought you were my friend, Joe Mitnick."

Our friend rubbed his hurting shoulder. "And suppose I was Joe Mitnick," he said, "do you think that's a nice thing to do to a friend of yours, hitting him like that?" The stranger grew angry. "Listen, buddy," he said, "what difference does it make to you what I do to Joe Mitnick? You don't even know him!" Your family will know you're a good cook if you give them:

KRAUTY BEEF

[SERVES SIX TO EIGHT]

3 pounds chuck beef	1 teaspoon paprika
2 large onions (or 3 small ones)	1½ pounds sauerkraut, drained
2 tablespoons fat (chicken fat is best)	1 cup water, boiling
1 tablespoon salt	½ bay leaf
¼ teaspoon pepper	

Cut the beef into bite-size pieces. Fry the onions until they are soft and then brown the meat on all sides. Season the meat with salt, pepper, and paprika, cover the pan, and cook it over low heat for 30 minutes, stirring occasionally. Now add the sauerkraut to the meat and onions and cook it all for 10 minutes. Add the boiling water and the bay leaf, cover the pan again, and cook it for 1½ hours longer over low heat. When you are ready to dish it out, remove the bay leaf.

The famous surgeon had performed a difficult, delicate operation on the man, who asked him, several days later, what was his fee. "$500," replied the surgeon. "$500!" the man exclaimed.

"Who has $500?" The surgeon replied, "Well, if that's too steep for you, how about $350?" The man shook his head negatively. "Who," he said, "has $350?" The surgeon was getting irked. "Well, how about $250?" he asked. "Who," the man asked sadly, "has $250?" The surgeon angrily asked, "Well, how much have you got?" The patient smiled sadly. "Nothing," he said. "I got nothing."

The surgeon strode up and down the room, muttering. Then he said, "If you haven't any money, how did you have the gall to come to an expensive surgeon for your operation, instead of going to a clinic?" The man raised his head from the pillow. "Doctor," he said proudly, "where my health is concerned, nothing is too expensive."

It is not expensive to make:

ESSIG FLAISH

[SERVES SIX TO EIGHT]

4 pounds beef (brisket, chuck, or plate flank)
5 onions, chopped
1 teaspoon salt

3 cups water, boiling
4 tablespoons lemon juice
3 tablespoons brown sugar

That exotic name for the dish up there means "sweet and sour meat." Use a heavy skillet or Dutch oven, get it hotted up, and brown the meat all over in it. If it is very lean meat, use a little fat. After you've got the meat browned, add the onions and brown them. Now toss in the salt and the boiling water, cover the thing, lower the heat, and cook it for 2 hours. Then pour in the lemon juice and the sugar, stir it all around, and cook it for another half hour. Take the meat out, slice it, but not too thin, and return to utensil to cook for another 20 minutes. Taste the gravy and add more sugar or more lemon, according to your idea of what "sweet and sour" means. We know what we like. Who knows what you like?

The young man was very sad because his girl had just broken off their engagement, and his best buddy was trying to console him. After telling him that time heals all wounds and other frighteningly original thoughts, the buddy said, "You'll meet another girl soon, and then you'll forget all about that chick Zenobia." The sad young man shook his head sorrowfully. "Oh, no," he moaned piteously, "I won't forget Zenobia for at least ten years, because that's how long it will take me to finish the installment payments on the mink coat I bought her." Here's a delicious meat dish you can put in the oven and forget until it is ready:

POT ROAST

[SERVES SIX TO EIGHT]

4 pounds rump beef
1½-ounce package onion soup mix

1 can condensed tomato soup

In a Dutch oven, sear the meat on all sides, pour over it the onion soup mix and then the condensed tomato soup. Cover the Dutch oven, and put it in oven at 325 degrees. Go to the movies, play bridge, canasta, or whatever you like for three hours, and when you come back to the oven, the pot roast will be ready. The gravy this makes will go good with:

FRIED MASHED POTATOES

4 medium potatoes
2 eggs
1 teaspoon baking powder

¼ teaspoon salt
⅛ teaspoon pepper
deep fat

Boil, peel, and mash the potatoes. Beat up eggs with baking powder, salt, and pepper; then combine thoroughly with the potatoes. Get your fat real hot, and drop the potato mixture into it from a spoon. When the potato cakes are browned, they are finished, so take them out, drain them on a paper napkin, and serve hot.

The pretty little teenage graduate of a secretarial school was applying for a job in a Manhattan advertising office. She had passed her spelling test—she was asked to spell her name—and her typing test—she identified the typewriter—and her shorthand—she took down the words of the first stanza of the "Star Spangled Banner," which the waggish fellow testing her had sung slowly and fervently, and then she was given an application to fill out.

She sailed through the application rapidly, but hesitated when she got to the line which read "Sex —." Then she straightened her shoulders and proudly wrote: "Never!" And she stalked out of the office never again to be seen. Your guests will come back again and again if you give them:

BEEF STROGANOFF

[SERVES FOUR]

1½ pounds tenderloin of beef, cubed
salt and pepper to taste
1 tablespoon flour
2 tablespoons butter
2 cups beef stock or bouillon

1 4-ounce can mushrooms (or ½ pound fresh mushrooms, cut not too fine)
1 tablespoon tomato paste
1 small onion, chopped
1 cup sour cream

Season meat with salt and pepper according to taste; let it stand for a couple of hours. Brown the flour in one tablespoon butter, work it to a smooth paste, and add stock slowly, stirring all the while. Bring it to a boil, add mushrooms, and stir in tomato paste. In another frying pan sear meat in remaining butter, then brown the chopped onion. When the onions are browned and meat seared all ver, put meat and onions in the other pan with auce, and simmer it over low heat for about five ninutes. Now add the sour cream, stir for three ninutes, and serve.

A very rich man was being buried and there vas one man at the services who stood out, because is lamentation was louder than that of anyone else, specially of the relatives of the deceased. One of he dead man's sons sidled over to the stranger. Why do you weep so bitterly?" the son asked. You weren't related to my father, were you?" The nan's sobs became louder. "No, I wasn't related," e cried out miserably. "That's why I am weeping!" Jo one will weep if you give them:

BEERY BEEF

[SERVES SIX TO EIGHT]

4 pound butter or fat	1 tablespoon cider vinegar
sliced onions	2 teaspoons salt
pounds round steak	½ teaspoon pepper
tablespoons flour	½ teaspoon sugar
cup boiling water	¼ cup parsley, minced
can beer	½ teaspoon thyme
bay leaf, crumbled	

Use a big, heavy frying pan with a cover, or a Dutch oven, and hot up the butter or fat in it—never let butter smoke—and fry the onion slices until they are soft, and then take them out and hold on to them. Now brown the meat all over, take it out, and hold on to it, too. Put the flour into the pan, Dutch oven, whatever you are using, stir it around until everything is smooth, add the boiling water, and stir it all around again. Now put the meat and onions back in the pan, pour in the beer and all the other ingredients. Cover, and let it simmer (turning the meat occasionally) over low heat for 2½ hours when it should be nice and tender. If it needs more liquid during cooking, add more beer. When you serve this, pour the sauce over the meat slices. Even non-beer drinkers like it!

We heard about a small boy in the suburbs
oh, he's about three or four years old, who was al-
lowed to have dinner one night with the family
when his grandparents were there. He was very
happy on this auspicious occasion, so he felt he had
to help make conversation, and everyone thought
this was real cute.

At one point, he said, "Mommy, you know
Willie's nose?" Everyone laughed. "I know Willie,"
said his mother, "so I suppose I know his nose.
What about his nose?" Everyone stopped laughing
and rushed out of the house when the little boy said
calmly, "Well, just before dinner, he fell into the
lake up to it." Some day when you feel up to it,
why don't you try:

YANKEE POT ROAST

[SERVES SIX TO EIGHT]

1 cup dry red wine
2 tablespoons lemon juice
2 peppercorns, crushed
1 bay leaf
1 clove garlic, crushed
¼ teaspoon thyme
4 pounds boneless brisket,
    chuck, or round
¼ cup shortening

2 cups tomatoes, peeled
    and mashed
2 tablespoons tomato paste
1 cup beef bouillon
1 teaspoon salt
small potatoes, sliced car-
    rots and peas, all
    cooked
parsley, chopped

Make a marinade of the wine, lemon juice, peppercorns, bay leaf, garlic, and thyme, and let the
meat stand in this overnight in the refrigerator,
turning it from time to time. This is a fine dish for
company, because most of the work is done before
they arrive, and you can schmooze with them, booze
with them, or whatever, and not be all pooped from
being over a hot stove when they arrive, see? Next

day, sear the meat in a large pot in the hot shortening, turning it to brown all over. Take it out of the pot, add the marinade to the pot along with the tomatoes, which should be mashed, the tomato paste, and the bouillon. Stir it all around and bring it to a boil. Put the meat back into the pot, add salt, cover it, and reduce the heat so the sauce simmers. Cook it for about 3 hours, turning it in the pot every hour. If you think the pot needs more liquid, add bouillon, wine, or a combination of both, and correct seasoning of gravy, if necessary, according to your taste. The meat should be served sliced, thin. Bring it to the table with enough slices cut to make one serving for each person, and have all the meat on the platter surrounded by the cooked potatoes, carrots, and peas. Have the gravy in a gravy-boat (what a silly word that is, "boat" for a serving dish) so everyone can use as much or as little as he wants. Sprinkle parsley over the meat and vegetables. Have hard rolls or crusty French or Italian bread to sop up the gravy.

April 19th in Maine and Massachusetts is a holiday—Patriots' Day—and even if you live in the Bronx or Brooklyn you can celebrate it by eating this Yankee pot roast. Why is it Yankee pot roast? Who knows? Put oregano in it, it'll be Italian pot roast. If you put oregano in anything, it smells and tastes deliciously Italian, even *gefilte* fish, probably.

a very pretty lady (How do we know she's pretty? Because she sent along her picture, that's how.) forwarded us this story about her ancestors, as well as a recipe, both handed down through the matriarchs of her family for countless generations:

SHE: "What did Eve do when Adam came home late every night for two whole weeks?"

HE: "I don't know. What DID Eve do when Adam came home late every night for two whole weeks?"

SHE: "Eve counted Adam's ribs, that's what, stupid."

Here's how to have:

BRAISED RIBS

[SERVES THREE TO FOUR]

3 pounds short ribs
2 teaspoons salt
dash of pepper (lots of dashes if you like it hot)
1 teaspoon paprika
1 teaspoon dry mustard
1 tablespoon sugar

1 tablespoon Worcestershire sauce
½ cup catsup
¼ cup water
¼ cup cider vinegar
½ cup onion, chopped
garlic, as much as you like

Brown the ribs, pour off the fat, combine all ingredients and pour over ribs. Cover and bake for 2 hours in oven preheated to 350 degrees. Remove cover during last half hour.

On the first Sunday in Advent, preparations begin for the celebration of the birth of Jesus. That day also marks the birthdate of the Prophet Mohammed, which is celebrated by Moslems everywhere. Shops are closed in Cairo, and the streets are crowded with people, among whom go wandering dervishes, magicians, fakirs, and buffoons. And the mosques are crowded with believers who all day recite passages from the Koran, and sing songs in praise of Allah. Your family and guests will sing your praises if you give them:

EGYPTIAN HAMBURGERS

1 pound beef, chopped
1 pound lamb, chopped
2 eggs, beaten
1 onion, chopped
¼ cup cold water
2½ tablespoons parsley, chopped
1 teaspoon salt
¼ teaspoon cayenne pepper
1½ cups bread crumbs
¼ pound butter (you want to make Kosher Egyptian hamburgers, then use chicken fat instead of butter)

Mix up the beef, lamb, eggs, onion, water, parsley, salt, and cayenne with one cup of the bread crumbs. Form them into hamburger-shaped hamburgers and then roll them in the ½ cup of bread crumbs you have left over. Melt the fat as you require it, and fry the hamburgers over low heat until they are done the way you like them—well-done, medium, or rare.

The eighth day of the Chinese New Year is called The Birthday of Mankind. If the weather on this day was good, the old-fashioned Chinese believed it meant that many children would be born during the year and that animals and plants, as well as people, born on this day would flourish. But if the weather was rotten, they believed everybody and everything born on this day would have rotten luck. Let us hope it is a nice day and let us all have:

BEEF AND RICE

[SERVES TWO TO THREE]

3 tablespoons vegetable oil
1 clove garlic, pressed
½ teaspoon salt
¼ teaspoon pepper
1 pound beef, ground
3 tablespoons soy sauce
1 cup water, boiling
3 scallions, cut in ½-inch pieces
2 teaspoons cornstarch
4 tablespoons cold water
3 cups rice, cooked

Heat the oil, fry the garlic lightly, add salt and pepper to pan, and fry the meat, stirring constantly, for 5 minutes. Add the soy sauce, boiling water, and the scallions. Bring to boil and stir for 3 minutes. Mix the cornstarch with the cold water, and add it to the pan, and cook, stirring steadily, until the sauce is thick. This should be ready at the same time as the rice has finished cooking, for it should be hot, of course. Put the rice in a large serving platter, pour the meat and the sauce over it. This is called, in Chinese, *ngow yuk fun*, and it can be even more fun to eat—if you like—by adding 1 tablespoon of curry to the meat when you are stir-frying it, and then placing 4 poached eggs on top of the meat after you have put the meat and its sauce on the rice. This will make a hearty meal for 2 to 3 people.

Texas celebrates San Jacinto Day on April 21st to commemorate the battle between the Mexican Army and the Texans in 1836 in which the Mexican Army was defeated, giving the territory its freedom. The scene of the battle, 22 miles east of

Houston, is a state park in which there is a monument 570 feet high and a museum full of letters and diaries of Texan patriots, including Sam Houston.

Most stories about Texas and Texans we don't think are very funny, but we do like the one about the real estate man in Texas who was trying to sell an Easterner some land. "All we need here in West Texas," he said, "to become the garden spot of the world, is some good people and water." The Easterner snorted. "Well, that's all," he said, "that hell needs." In Texas they love Mexican food, especially:

CHILI CON CARNE

[SERVES FOUR TO FIVE]

2 tablespoons fat
½ cup onion, chopped
1 pound ground beef
1 1-pound can kidney beans
1 1-pound can whole, peeled tomatoes
1 tablespoon (or more) chili powder

1 teaspoon salt
⅛ teaspoon pepper
⅛ teaspoon cayenne
½ teaspoon monosodium glutamate
red pepper flakes, maybe

Hot up the fat and sauté the onion until it's soft. Now add the ground beef and stir-fry it, browning it well and breaking it all up. Drain the can of kidney beans and slowly add the beans to the pan. Drain the tomatoes and mash them—hold on to the tomato liquid—and add them to the pan. Stir it well so that everything is combined, cover the pan, and cook for 30 minutes. After 30 minutes add all the other ingredients, stirring once more. Chili con carne should be rather liquid, not quite like soup, but almost. So add some of the tomato liquid to the pan. Simmer for another 30 minutes. If it looks too dry, add some tomato juice if you've used up all the liquid from the can of tomatoes.

We like chili real hot, so we add some chopped red pepper flakes when we make chili. But you've got to be careful with these pepper flakes—they really are hot, hot, hot.

All the waitresses in the restaurant were called together by the manager before the lunch crowd started coming into the place, and he lectured them earnestly about their appearance. "Today," he said sternly, "I want you all to be looking your best and I want you to be very nice to the customers. Very friendly. Try to walk like Charlene Holt or Kim Novak. I want all the customers to notice you today."

The waitresses heard him out with great interest, and then the youngest and prettiest one there asked eagerly, "Why? Who's coming? Some big shot? Some talent scout?"

"No," said the manager, "nobody special is coming. It's just that the meat is tough." You have undoubtedly noticed that when your meat is tough, there is quite a good deal left over. When that happens the thing to do is:

BAKED HASH

[SERVES FOUR TO FIVE]

3 cups cooked meat
1 onion (or more), sliced
3 tablespoons butter or fat
2 cups potatoes, boiled and diced
2 carrots, cooked and diced

½ cup peas, cooked
2 tablespoons flour
½ cup consommé or beef broth
¼ teaspoon thyme
salt and pepper to taste
bread crumbs

Cut the meat into bite-size pieces. Sauté the onion in 1 tablespoon butter or fat and brown it well. Now grease a casserole, pour everything in except the bread crumbs, and stir it all around. Sprinkle the top with bread crumbs, dot with butter or fat, and bake it in an oven preheated to 400 degrees until the bread crumbs are browned, which should take about 20 minutes. Everything in it is cooked, so all it needs is a good hotting. Serve this with hot biscuits on which you can pile the hash.

and now here's how to load meat balls with an extra wallop:

LOADED MEAT BALLS

[SERVES THREE TO FOUR]

1½ pounds chuck steak, chopped
1 egg, beaten
1 teaspoon salt

1 tablespoon catsup
¼ cup water
1 slice white bread, crumbed

SAUCE

2 tablespoons olive oil
1 small onion, minced
1 clove garlic, crushed
¼ teaspoon salt
2 dashes Angostura bitters
1 beef bouillon cube

1 teaspoon dry mustard
1 teaspoon flour
1 cup water
½ cup bourbon
¼ cup sweet vermouth
¼ teaspoon oregano

Mix together the meat, egg, salt, catsup, water, and soft bread crumbs. Now form them into small, bite-size balls. Get the olive oil good and hot in a frying pan and then fry the meat balls, shaking the pan over the heat, until they are well-browned all over. When they get to a nice mahogany color, take them out of the pan. Now, fry the onion, which you have minced, and the garlic, which you have crushed in a garlic press or mashed with a blunt instrument, until they are soft, but not browned.

Add all the remaining sauce ingredients to the pan and bring to a boil. Cook over high heat, stirring steadily, until the liquid is reduced and the sauce is thickened and the bouillon cube is thoroughly dissolved. Now put the meat balls back into the pan, cover, reduce the heat, and simmer it for 5 minutes. This can be served immediately, of course, but it tastes better if you cook it the day before serving, letting it cool and then refrigerating for a whole day. If you do that, you reheat it, of course, before serving.

The successful man was showing his unsuccessful fraternity brother all over his magnificent apartment on Central Park South, filled with not-too-old antiques and hand-painted oil paintings and all such things. Every time his host asked him how he liked something, he just grunted. He was not happy, you see?

Finally they came to the long, broad terrace which afforded a breath-taking view of Central Park, filled with trees flamed with the beautiful colors of autumn, skulking footpads, and molesters of all sorts. "And what do you say about this?" the host asked proudly. His guest shrugged. "Yerch," he said. "You take away Central Park, and what have you got?"

Take the wine away from this and you just have:

VEAL SCALOPPINE

[SERVES THREE TO FOUR]

1 pound thin veal cutlets (Italian style)	1 clove garlic (optional, shmoptional)
½ cup flour	½ cup sweet sherry
¼ pound butter or fat	1 lemon, sliced

Cut veal into 4-inch pieces, put them in paper bag with flour, bounce bag around until veal pieces are thoroughly coated. Melt butter in skillet, but don't let it smoke. Brown garlic! Brown meat on both sides, then add the wine. Cover the skillet and simmer over low heat until meat is tender—taste a piece, that's how you'll know. Let everybody use salt and pepper to his own taste, at the table. Garnish with lemon.

American Education Week is much more important, don't you think, than National Pretzel Week, National Sauerkraut Week, or any of those other sennightly commercial celebrations, because it is sponsored by the U.S. Office of Education, the National Education Association, the American Legion, and the National Congress of Parents and Teachers to promote increased interest in public schools.

Which reminds us about the high-school girl who was sent to the principal's office. "I don't like the way you've been acting," said that pompous gentleman, "so, Jenny, you will have to stay with me for an hour after school today." Jenny, a pretty, pert little thing, shrugged her shoulders. "I don't mind," she said smiling sweetly. "If it's okay with your wife, it's okay with me, too." Let us teach you how to make:

SHEPHERD'S PIE

[SERVES FOUR TO SIX]

½ cup celery, sliced	salt and pepper to taste
3 tablespoons onion, minced	¼ cup parsley, chopped
1 clove garlic, minced	2 cups carrots or peas (leftovers), cooked
3 or 4 tablespoons butter (be lavish)	3 cups gravy or canned chicken broth
3 cups beef or lamb, etc. (leftovers), cubed	3 egg yolks, beaten
	3 cups potatoes, mashed

Brown celery, onion, and garlic in one tablespoon of butter. Now add the meat, salt and pepper, parsley, and stir around wildly. Turn off heat and add cooked vegetables to saucepan. Stir in gravy or chicken broth. Mix the egg yolks into the mashed potatoes, and then line a casserole with some of the potatoes, leaving plenty for the topping. Pour everything into casserole and then top it with the rest of the mashed potatoes. Dot it with rest of the butter. In oven preheated to 375 degrees, bake it for 30 minutes, or until the potatoes are well browned.

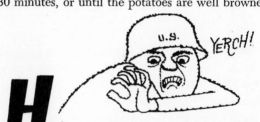

Here's a variation on a famous dish to which all servicemen have always reacted with a great deal of emotion, and which they did *not* call:

CREAMED CHIPPED BEEF ON TOAST

[SERVES TWO]

3 tablespoons onion, minced	3 tablespoons flour
2 tablespoons green pepper, chopped	2 cups milk
3 tablespoons butter	10 ounces chipped beef
	½ cup cognac
	¼ teaspoon paprika

Fry the onion and green pepper in the melted butter until they are a light brown. Sprinkle the flour into pan and then add the milk and then the meat, stirring it like crazy all the time it simmers until the mixture gets thickened. (Lay off the cognac until we tell you to use it, or you'll get pretty thick yourself.) When the mixture is thick, add the cognac, let it all simmer for another 5 minutes, stirring all the time, take it away from the heat, dust with the paprika, and pour this stuff on pieces of toast. The cooks in the Army, Navy, Air Force, and Marines didn't use cognac when they made this dish, so maybe that's why the servicemen called it what they did.

Ronnie Drinkhouse watched with pleasure as one of his friends had two martinis, an order of *paté de foie gras,* a delicious rare sirloin steak, and a baked potato topped with sour cream and chives, all of which he washed down with a lovely bottle of *rosé* wine. "You eat pretty good," said Ronnie admiringly. "Yes," replied the friend, "but if my doctor should see me eating like this, he'd bawl me out something terrible." Ronnie clucked sympathetically. "You're supposed to be on a diet?" he asked.

"No," said the friend, "I still owe him $500 for my operation." No matter how much you owe him, your doc couldn't get mad if he saw you eating:

BARBECUED VEAL STEAK WITH MARINADE AND SERVING SAUCE

[SERVES SIX]

4 tablespoons lemon juice	¼ cup honey
2 teaspoons salt	4 veal steaks, each ¾ to
2 tablespoons dry	1 pound
mustard	

Stir together all sauce ingredients with great vigor, and then marinate the veal steaks for at least a couple of hours, stirring the steaks around so they all get equally soaked in the sauce. Now take out the veal, put it on the grill—or in the broiler—three inches from source of heat for about 15 minutes, turning once, and basting two or three times. Pour remaining sauce, if any, on meat just before serving.

One of the more annoying aspects of being a famous singer is that you are always being forced to listen to a lot of performances by young hopefuls whose parents think they have bred a virtuoso. A friend of a friend once induced Lena Horne to listen to a young lady, accompanied by her mother at the piano.

The mother played, the young girl sang, and Miss Horne suffered intense pain. When the tenth song was ended, the mother turned and brightly asked, "Well, what do you think? What should she do now?" Lena replied, "Find her a nice young man and let her get married." Your daughter will have no trouble getting married if she knows how to make:

STUFFED BREAST OF VEAL

[SERVES EIGHT]

5 pounds breast of veal
    (have the butcher
    make a pocket in
    the veal)
2 teaspoons salt

½ teaspoon pepper
1 teaspoon paprika
2 cloves garlic, minced
3 tablespoons fat

Rub salt, pepper, paprika, and garlic into the meat. Now make the:

POTATO STUFFING

2 cups potato, grated
    and drained
½ cup onion, chopped
4 tablespoons potato flour

1 egg
1 teaspoon salt
¼ teaspoon pepper

Mix up all this stuff and stuff into the pocket in the veal. Now sew up the pocket. Get hold of a nice roasting pan, melt the fat in it, and put the meat in. Preheat your oven to 325 degrees and roast the veal for three hours. Keep basting the meat, adding water if the pan gets too dry. If you like wine, try basting it with a dry red wine.

We hear that there are some people who don't like garlic! Incredible! Well, try this trick, which was taught us by a nice lady cookery writer in California. When you've minced, chopped, or whatever you do to your garlic, mix it up with the salt you are going to use, and let it stand for awhile. That cookery writer lady in California told us it would take the curse off the garlic, if that's what you think of garlic, but the good of the garlic would still be there. We tried this trick and it doesn't work. But since we happen to love the dear little thing, we don't use this sneaky trick to deflower our garlic. What have we come to? Even on our foods must we use deodorizers?

the pretty young girl was asking for a job as a reporter on a New York newspaper, and the city editor asked her if she had ever written anything. "Yes," she said, "last year I wrote a story for a confession magazine published here in New York." "And did the magazine buy the story?" asked the city editor. "Well, no," the girl said, "but the editor came all the way to Seattle to see me." People will come long distances if you will cook for them:

VEAL PARMIGIANA

[SERVES THREE]

1 pound veal cutlets	1 small can tomato paste
flour	1 bay leaf
salt and pepper	olive oil
grated Parmesan cheese	garlic
2 eggs, beaten	½ pound Mozzarella
bread crumbs	cheese
1-pound can peeled,	
whole tomatoes	

The veal cutlets should be Italian style, beaten thin, almost thin enough to be able to read a newspaper through them. (We've worked for newspapers that seemed as though we were reading them through veal cutlets.) If you can't buy the thin boughten kind, beat them thin yourself, putting them between sheets of waxed paper or an old towel and bludgeoning them with a blunt instrument. Dip each cutlet first in the flour mixed with salt, pepper, and one tablespoon Parmesan, then in the beaten egg, back into the flour again, once more in the beaten egg and then in the bread crumbs. Get a large platter, put the cutlets on it, and put them away in the refrigerator for a couple of hours. This helps keep the breading on the meat when you fry it later. If you've got more than one layer of breaded cutlets, separate them with waxed paper.

While this is chilling, make the sauce. Put the tomatoes into a pan, through a sieve, mix in the tomato paste, put in the bay leaf and simmer over low heat, covered, stirring it occasionally. After the cutlets are thoroughly chilled—a couple of hours, at least—get hold of a large skillet and hot up some olive oil, maybe 2 tablespoons. Slice the garlic into the oil and brown it. Fry the cutlets, browning each side. Add oil to the pan as you need it. You notice we didn't say how much garlic to use? Well, we're mad, mad, mad about garlic, and the amount we use would probably appall you; use as much as you like.

Now get a large baking pan, grease it lightly and put the fried veal cutlets in, side by side. Sprinkle them lavishly with grated Parmesan cheese, remove the bay leaf, and pour the tomato sauce over the cutlets. Finally, put sliced Mozzarella cheese on each cutlet, sprinkle with some more Parmesan. Bake in oven preheated to 350 degrees until the cheese is melted and bubbly—about 15-20 minutes. Serve spaghetti with a butter sauce with this. Just cook spaghetti—about 8 minutes, if you like it chewy—put a large lump of butter into the bowl and toss the spaghetti so it gets all coated with butter. Have plenty of grated Parmesan at the table. Also plenty of red wine to go with it all.

Y ou know when Columbus Day was first celebrated in America? It was on October 15th, 1792, in New York City, and it was the Society of Tammany (what we now know as Tammany Hall) which did the celebrating, because New York didn't have a very large Italian population in those days.

Let us honor Columbus by making:

VITELLO TONNATO
(Veal with tuna fish sauce)

[SERVES SIX TO EIGHT]

3 pounds leg of veal	2½ teaspoons salt
1 large onion	2 7-ounce cans of tuna
1 clove	fish
1 bay leaf	8 anchovy fillets
4 sprigs parsley	2 tablespoons lemon juice
2 ribs celery	1 cup olive oil
6 whole peppercorns	2½ teaspoons capers

In a large saucepan, cover the veal with water, put in all the vegetables and the peppercorns and salt. Cover the pan and cook over medium heat until the meat is tender, about 1¾ hours. Throw everything away except the veal and put it in a large bowl. To make the sauce, drain the tuna and the anchovies and put them through a sieve. Mix them up well, adding the lemon juice, and then add the olive oil slowly, beating it viciously all the while. When you've got this stuff thoroughly subdued, toss in the capers and stir them up until they are thoroughly and evenly distributed. Now pour it all over the veal in that large bowl, cover the bowl, and let it marinate in the refrigerator overnight. Every once in awhile, turn the veal. (Once when we mentioned this in a recipe, a lady sent us a telegram asking how many times she should get up during the night to turn the meat. Listen, DON'T get up in the night unless you have to; just turn the meat once in awhile whenever you think of it.) Just before you are ready to serve, take the veal out of the bowl and cut slices as thin as you can. Spread the sauce over the veal and serve. Columbus never had it so good, and neither did Isabella!

This friend of ours had the misfortune to ride in the subway during the height of the rush hour, but she counted herself fortunate because she was able to get a strap to hold on to. At each station, she told us, people got in and out of the car she was in, and she kept getting buffeted about, though she was able to maintain her grip on the strap.

Directly in front of her was a large, loutish man, seated in revolting comfort, reading the racing chart in his newspaper. She knew that she stepped on his foot once or twice, as people pushed and shoved her, and each time she did, he glared at her. Finally, he put down his paper and said in a loud, swinish tone of voice, "Lady, why don't you put your foot where it belongs?" Our friend says she told him, and everyone within hearing laughed when they heard her, "Oh, how I wish I could!" You could, if you wished, cook:

SCHNITZEL HOLSTEIN

[SERVES SIX]

½ cup flour
1½ teaspoons salt
½ teaspoon pepper
3 pounds veal steak (6 pieces)
2 eggs, beaten
1 cup bread crumbs
¼ pound butter (or olive oil)

3 tablespoons lemon juice
3 tablespoons parsley, chopped
6 anchovy fillets (optional)
6 eggs, fried

Agitate the flour, salt, and pepper. Dip veal slices in this mixture, then into beaten eggs, and then into bread crumbs. Now put the breaded veal into the refrigerator for a couple of hours. This will make the breading stick when you fry the veal steaks. Get a large frying pan, melt half the butter—or heat the oil—and fry the veal, over low heat, turning once, for about 15 minutes. When all the veal slices are well-browned and tender, remove them to a hot serving platter. Now melt the remaining butter—or heat the remaining oil—and add the lemon juice and parsley. Put one anchovy fillet—if you are using them—on each veal steak, top with a fried egg, and pour over it all the butter-lemon-juice-parsley you've got all hotted up. The veal steaks should be very thin.

A lawyer friend of ours tells us he was horrified one day when an old lady, a very nice old lady who told him proudly that she was 92, said she wanted to divorce the husband to whom she had been married for 71 years. "You want to divorce this man to whom you've been married for 71 years?" he says he asked her. "Why do you want to break up a marriage that has lasted so long?" The old lady drew herself up, he says, with pride and much strength and replied firmly, "Because enough is enough." Your family will never, never say that if you serve them:

VEAL PAPRIKA

[SERVES FOUR TO EIGHT]

2 pounds veal, cubed	1½ teaspoons salt
¼ cup of flour	½ teaspoon pepper
¼ cup butter or margarine	2 tablespoons paprika
2 medium onions, chopped	¼ teaspoon thyme, ground
2 cups water	1 cup sour cream
	1 teaspoon lemon juice
	shredded wheat wafers

Dredge veal in flour (put the flour in a paper bag, drop in the cubed veal, and bounce the stuff around, and this they call dredging, see?), then brown the veal in the butter or margarine. Toss the chopped onion into the pan and when the onion is soft, but before it is browned, add the water, salt, pepper, paprika, and thyme. Cover the pan and cook it all for about an hour, when the veal should be as tender as a mother's lullaby. Take the pan away from the heat and just before you serve the delicious dish to your ravenous family, pour in the sour cream and the lemon juice and stir it all around wildly. Put shredded wheat wafers into the plates (makes four servings for gluttons or 8 servings for dainty eaters like you and me) and pour the Hungarian delight over all.

On St. **P**atrick's Day, unless some lepre-
chauns come out with paint brushes, there won't be
a green line down the middle of Fifth Avenue, because of the big fuss when an Italian group wanted
to have a purple line painted for them on Columbus
Day. You remember? Traffic Commissioner Barnes,
who is almost as irascible as Bob Moses, drew the
line at drawing lines down New York's Fifth
Avenue.

Many years ago, we asked a departed colleague
named Basil Dickinson Gallagher, who was widely
known as "Red," the meaning of the expression
"lace-curtain Irish." "Well," said Red Gallagher,
"lace-curtain Irish are people who have fruit in the
house, even if there's nobody in the family who is
sick." What the Irish very often have in their
homes, especially on such festive occasions as St.
Patrick's Day, is:

RACK OF LAMB

[2 RIBS PER PERSON]

1 crown roast (2 ribs per person)	flour
	aluminum foil
salt and pepper	pimiento-stuffed olives
2 cloves garlic, sliced	or radishes

Have your butcher remove the backbone that runs
along the thick ends of the chops and tie the rack
together to form a circle. Rub salt and pepper all
over the meat, insert slivers of garlic, and then
dredge with flour. Cover the rib bone ends with
foil. Put the lamb on a rack in a shallow pan and
roast it in oven preheated to 300 degrees for 30
minutes to the pound. Potatoes and cabbage are

great staples in Ireland, and over there they combine the two in a dish which is great to use as a stuffing for a crown roast of lamb, and which the Irish call:

COLCANNON

[SERVES THREE TO FOUR]

1 pound potatoes, boiled	4 tablespoons fat
2 cups cabbage, boiled	salt and pepper
1 onion, minced	

Mash the potatoes and chop up the cooked cabbage and then sauté the minced onion in hot fat. Mix everything together and stuff it into the crown roast 20 minutes before the meat is finished. Make a gravy with the pan drippings, pour it over the Colcannon, take foil off rib ends and put a pimiento-filled olive or radish on each rib end. If anybody in your family or one of your guests happens to know how to play the bagpipes, have him pipe you into the dining room as you bear the crown roast in triumphantly. And don't tell us only the Scotch play bagpipes; the Irish do, too. And the sounds are just as dreadful, too, as when the Scotch play them.

This poor slob, one of those unfortunates whose failure in life seems to have been foreordained, was once described by a friend of ours as having been "born two dollars short." He went to a psychologist and unburdened himself of his troubles. "Every job I get," he said, "I lose. I have no friends. My relatives despise and shun me. The only thing I am successful at is having children. I can't support even one child and a wife, and we have twelve already. Every year, regular as clockwork my wife has another baby. What should I do?"

The psychologist, a learned man who had studied under a famous Viennese quack, gave him a look of scorn and loathing, for he knew he wasn't going to be paid for this consultation. "Don't," said the psychologist, "do anything." You'll be a hit with your family if you do:

BAKED LAMB CHOPS

[SERVES TWO]

4 lamb chops
⅛ teaspoon pepper
1 teaspoon salt
¼ cup flour

2 tablespoons butter, fat
    or oil
½ can tomato soup
½ cup water
½ cup onions, chopped

Trim fat off the chops and rub in salt and pepper. Cover thoroughly with flour and put them in a buttered baking pan. Preheat your oven to 325 degrees. While oven is heating up, mix the soup and water in a saucepan, and bring it to a boil. Toss the chopped onions on top of the chops, pour the boiling soup-water mixture over all, cover the pan, and bake the chops for 1½ hours.

The young man came to the office of his father, a very rich man, to ask for an increase in his allowance. What, the father wanted to know, would he do with more money? The lad said he would go back to college and get his master's degree. "So," said the father, "then what?" So, said the son, he'd be able to get a better job. And, asked the father, suppose he did get a better job? Then he might be able to meet a nice girl.

"So after you meet a nice girl," asked the father, "what will happen?" The young fellow said then maybe he would get married. And what, asked papa, would happen as a result of the marriage? "Then I'd be happy!" cried out the son. The father shrugged, "So, all right, you're happy," he said, "then what?" Everybody will be happy if you cook:

BAKED STUFFED LAMB CHOPS

[SERVES FOUR]

chicken fat or oil
2 chicken livers
1 small onion, chopped
salt and pepper

1 teaspoon parsley
4 chops, 2-inches thick
½ cup dry red drinking
   wine

Hot up the fat, sauté the chicken livers gently, and then cut them up fine. Sauté the chopped onion and combine the chicken livers and onion with seasoning and parsley. Wipe chops with damp cloth, dry them and then cut off the bones, and trim some of the fat. Cut a slit horizontally into the thick part of the chop and stuff some of the chicken liver-onion mixture into the slit. Shape each chop into a round piece and tie it up with string. Now sear them in a hot skillet on both sides and put them into a pan with the wine. Cover the pan and bake the chops in oven preheated to 350 degrees until they are done—about 45 minutes. There will be some fine pan dripping which you can thicken with a little flour.

What should you have with this? Well, why not some dry red wine? Did you notice that in the listing of ingredients we said "½ cup dry red *drinking* wine"? What we mean is, if something can't be used for drinking, it shouldn't be used for cooking, see? A baked potato—which will take about the same time (45 minutes) in your 350 degree oven—is a fine accompaniment to this stuffed lamb chop. The skin of the potato, when it is baked crisp, is delicious and it is full of nourishment. After the potato is thoroughly scrubbed, rub it with a little oil or fat. After 45 minutes of baking, protect your hand with a pot holder and squeeze the potato; if it yields to slight pressure, it is done. Prick the skin of each potato with a fork several places to allow the steam to escape, and the potato will be mealier, which is the way it should be.

🙊 **T**wo young fellows on our block set out to raise mustaches, and everyone was most interested in their efforts, because these young fellows never seemed to have accomplished very much before. After a couple of weeks, one of them had a fairly good-sized mustache, but the other's was not at all discernible to the naked eye. We were told about a conversation they had one day.

"I can't understand," said the lad whose mustache didn't seem to be growing, "why I can't raise a mustache. My father has a wonderful mustache." The other fellow pondered this problem. "It may be," he said finally, "that you take after your mother more than you take after your father." His mother makes wonderful:

LAMB AND CABBAGE

[SERVES FIVE TO SIX]

3 onions	2 teaspoons salt
3 tomatoes, mashed	¼ teaspoon pepper
3 pounds cabbage	½ teaspoon oregano
2 pounds lamb, cubed (or ham or beef)	3 cups stock

Chop up the onions, tomatoes, and cabbage. Get hold of a casserole, put in a layer of meat. (We keep reading cooking directions that say, "put such-and-such on the bottom of a casserole . . . ." Did you ever hear of such nonsense?) Dust it with some salt and pepper, then add a layer of cabbage, sprinkle that with salt and pepper and oregano, and finally a layer of onions. Keep making layers like that until you've used up all the meat, cabbage and onions, and salt and pepper. Now spill the stock into the casserole and put the tomatoes on top of everything. Cover the casserole and cook it over medium heat until the meat is tender, which should take about 2 hours.

We used to live in a small town that had one rich man, a very rich one. And he was just as stingy as he was rich, we are sorry to say. On the day that his new house was finished and furnished, he invited everyone in town to come and look over his magnificent mansion. He led us through every room in the house, being very careful to tell us just how much everything cost, because he was just as boastful as he was rich and stingy.

When we came to the dining room, he pointed proudly to a great table and exclaimed, "At this table, sixty people could sit down and eat." And then his face became red with anger, and he shouted, "God forbid!"

Here's a recipe we got from a young Italian friend of ours, a girl named Gina Lollobrigida, which will serve four people, and if you want to feed sixty people all you have to do is multiply all the ingredients by fifteen to make:

GINA'S SHASHLIK

[SERVES FOUR]

1½ pounds lamb	salt and pepper to taste
red wine (dry)	1 green pepper
wine vinegar	4 small onions
1 bay leaf	3 tablespoons olive oil
½ teaspoon marjoram	1 cup rice
½ teaspoon oregano	

Cut the meat into bite-size pieces and marinate them in a mixture of dry red wine and vinegar for several hours, along with the bay leaf, marjoram, oregano, salt, and pepper. Remove the seeds from the green pepper and cut the flesh into strips the same size as the pieces of meat. Boil some water and for five minutes cook the onions in it; drain them, and cut them in half. Okay, so you marinated the meat and you cooked the onions and cut them in half. Now get hold of four skewers, grease them lightly with olive oil, and thread them with alternate pieces of meat, green pepper, and onion-halves. Brush olive oil over everything and broil for 15 to 18 minutes, turning the skewers often. Lamb is best when it is pinkish in center. Serve this on a bed of plain, boiled rice, and Gina says have plenty of red wine handy.

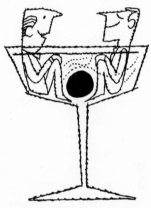

it was the first time the young fellow had come to his girl's house, and while he waited for her to finish dressing, the girl's father fawningly entertained him with jolly stories and funny sayings, for the old man wanted to make a good impression on the lad, who was a good marriage prospect for the girl. To tell the truth, the young fellow was rather annoyed, because the girl's old man was more than a bit of a bore, but he put up with him because he liked the girl.

"Would you have any objection," the father said at one point, "to a nice, icy-cold, dry, dry martini?" The young fellow considered this offer. "Well," he said, dryly and a bit icily, too, "I've never had one before." The girl's old man was astounded. "What?" he cried out. "You have never had a nice, icy-cold, dry, dry martini?" The young fellow shook his head haughtily. "No," he said, "I've never had an objection to one." No one will object if you give them:

BEERY BARBECUED LAMB SHANKS

[SERVES FOUR]

2 cloves garlic, sliced	½ cup (or more) beer
4 lamb shanks	2 bay leaves
3 tablespoons fat	4 peppercorns
flour	¼ cup lemon juice
salt and pepper	2 teaspoons lemon peel,
½ teaspoon paprika	grated

If you don't care too much for beer, don't be frightened away from this dish; the beery taste, if you don't like it, won't be discernible, but cooking in it adds a new dimension to the flavor of the lamb, and we think it will surprise and please you if you've never tried beer cookery.

Put slivers of garlic into the meat, melt the fat, and hot it up good. Sift the flour with the seasoning and roll the shanks in it. Brown the shanks all over. When the meat is thoroughly browned, add all the other ingredients, cover, and simmer over low heat for 2 hours. If it needs more liquid, add beer. We learned this recipe from a prominent Midwestern beer drinker named Frank Kohler, and we tried it and it proved to be as good as he told us it would be.

He told us about a prim little old Midwestern widow lady who was persuaded, by the husband of a friend, to have a glass of beer, something she insisted she had never had in her life. She took a timorous sip and she looked astounded. "My goodness!" she exclaimed. "It tastes just like the medicine my husband had been drinking every night of the 40 years we were married!"

When Charles Lamb was employed by the East India Company, the writer's superior chided him one day for his habitual tardiness in coming to the office. "I have noticed," said the stuffy little man, "that you are always at least one hour late in arriving each morning." Charles Lamb nodded agreement. "Yes," he said, "but you see, I make up for that by leaving one hour early each evening." Try that on your boss sometime, and also try:

IRISH LAMB STEW

[SERVES SIX TO EIGHT]

3 pounds boneless lamb	1 quart hot water
⅓ cup of flour	6 large onions
2 teaspoons salt	6 large potatoes
⅛ teaspoon pepper	3 carrots
3 tablespoons fat	3 celery ribs

Cut the lamb into bite-size pieces, removing any fat. Mix the flour and seasoning, dredge the meat in flour. In a Dutch oven, melt the fat and brown the meat all over, pouring off any excess fat. Pour in enough hot water to cover meat, cover oven, and simmer for 1½ hours, or until meat is fairly tender. Slice the onions, peel and quarter the potatoes. Slice the carrots into 1-inch pieces, slice the celery stalks, leaves and all, and add everything to the meat. Cover the Dutch oven again and simmer slowly for another 30 minutes, adding hot water—if needed—and stirring everything around once in awhile. Taste the cooking liquid and correct seasoning, if necessary. If you have to thicken it, take out ½ cup of cooking liquid, add a little flour, stir it in cup until smooth and add it to the rest of the stuff. If it needs thinning, or more liquid, add a little dry red wine, we suggest. Alcohol evaporates in the cooking process, you know, but the wine heightens the flavors of the meat and vegetables and adds a new dimension to it all.

For many centuries, Englishmen have been celebrating a peculiar holiday in the first week in May which they call, for some reason which has been obscured by time, "Furry Day." Everybody knocks off work on that day, and the men wear sprigs of hawthorn in their hair and go prancing around the countryside and through the streets singing a ditty called "Song of the Grey Goose Quill," raising merry hell all the way.

They ride people on a pole, induce boys to leave school, and demand tribute of money from all they met. Not the gentlefolk though. What the gentlefolk do, is go calling, going into the homes of their friends through the windows, if they feel like it, and they, too, dance in the streets all night long. From this sort of behavior there grew up, we imagine, the myth about "British reserve." And everyone will want you to re-serve this, if you ever cook:

LANCASHIRE HOTPOT

[SERVES THREE TO FOUR]

1½ pounds lamb, boneless	1½ pounds potatoes, also sliced thin
1 pound onions, sliced thin	2 teaspoons salt
	½ teaspoon pepper
	1 cup water

Cut the meat into bite-size pieces. Get a casserole that will hold at least 1½ quarts. Put in first a layer of meat, then a layer of onions, then a layer of potatoes. Sprinkle some salt and pepper on the potatoes. Now repeat layers until you have used everything. The top layer *must* be potatoes, sprinkled with salt and pepper. (You'll probably need more than ½ teaspoon of pepper.) Now add the water. The lid of the casserole should be real tight-fitting. Preheat your oven to 350 degrees and bake for at least 2 hours. The longer you cook the hotpot, the better it is, depending on how tight your casserole cover fits. If it is really tight, it can be cooked for as much as 6-8 hours. If your casserole cover doesn't fit snugly, here's what you do: Fold a piece of aluminum foil double and fit it over the casserole, then put on the cover. Okay? However long you cook the hotpot, remove the cover—and foil, if you've used it—30 minutes before serving, increase the heat of your oven to 400 degrees and cook until the top layer of potatoes is well and truly browned. With this hotpot we like a coldpot of beer or ale.

a Swedish meatball named Hedlund told us about a farmer from Norway who was being naturalized. The judge asked the man if he liked the kind of government we have here in the United States, and the man said he could make a couple of suggestions for improvements. "Oh, is that so?" said the judge. "Tell me just one thing you'd like to see changed." The farmer from Norway scratched his head and said, "Well for one thing, you could have more rain." Here's how the Norwegians:

ROAST FRESH HAM

[SERVES SIX TO EIGHT]

1½ tablespoons salt	1½ cups water, boiling
1½ teaspoons pepper	2 tablespoons butter
1 teaspoon nutmeg	2 tablespoons flour
1 5- to 6-pound fresh ham	½ teaspoon dry mustard

Rub the salt, pepper and nutmeg into the ham, and then make some gashes in the fat. With a knife, what else? Put the ham in a pan, and roast for 30 minutes in an oven preheated to 450 degrees. Now add the boiling water to the pan, reduce the temperature to 350 degrees, and roast 25 minutes more for each pound. Pour off the gravy and skim off the fat on surface. If the gravy is too thick, add a little water. Melt the butter in a saucepan, stir in the flour and mustard until mixture is smooth, add to the gravy, and heat to boiling point. Then you reduce the heat and cook for another 7 minutes.

A friend of ours who was becoming deaf was told by his doctor that if he laid off the booze, his hearing might improve. Our friend found this advice exceedingly difficult to follow, for he is an exceptionally social human being. But he did manage to stay on the wagon for one whole month. Two months after his relapse found him back at the doctor's office, deaf as a *matjes* herring. His doctor was bitter in his denunciation and he wound up by writing on his prescription pad, "I told you what would happen, didn't I?"

"Yes," our friend said wearily, "and I did follow your advice for one whole month. But I swear to you, Doctor, not one thing I heard while I was on the wagon was worth one shot of booze." There is Scotch liqueur in this recipe, but even our friend's doctor wouldn't call this boozing; for a dedicated boozer, it's not really enough.

FLAMING HAM STEAKS

[SERVES FOUR TO FIVE]

4 ½-pound ham steaks
1 package frozen
    baby peas, or 1
    10-ounce can
4 slices canned
    pineapple

8 maraschino cherries
1 8-ounce can sweet
    potatoes
5 marshmallows
6 ounces Scotch
    liqueur

Brown meat on both sides in skillet greased with fat trimmed from ham steaks. Remove from skillet and set aside between two warm plates. Cook peas. Cut ham steaks in half and arrange slices around edge of your best serving platter. Place half slice of pineapple on each piece of meat, put cherry in pineapple semi-circle, pour peas into center of platter and cover them with drained, heated sweet potatoes. Place lightly toasted marshmallow on top of potatoes. Now comes the delicate operation with the Scotch liqueur that separates the gourmet cook from the short-order, hamburger-joint fry cook.

In order to *flambé*, or flame, anything containing alcohol, the alcohol must first be warmed. Bring the decorative platter with the ham steaks and their garnishings to the table at the same time you fetch the warmed liqueur in a long-handled gravy boat or any lipped pitcher of crystal or china. The flaming action is quick, too quick to do any damage to your most delicate pieces. A slender taper candle or a long barbecue match is best to use in igniting the warmed liqueur. Pour the lighted liqueur over the contents of the serving platter. Keep in mind that the slower you pour, the more dramatic will be the effect. If you've taken a slug of the stuff in the kitchen first, your hand will be steadier, and the "oohs!" and "aahs!" of your family or guests won't make you jitter as you light and pour the liqueur. *Bon appétit!* (Frankly, we don't like marshmallows and maraschino cherries! Oh, well, some people do.)

The personnel manager was interviewing a girl who had applied for a job, and after testing her stenography and typing and after reading her letters of recommendation, he said, "This is very good, but perhaps you might be suited for another job, besides just taking dictation and typing. Do you have any other abilities?" The girl's face brightened. "Oh, yes," she said, "I made this dress myself, and I have won prizes in three newspaper contests." The personnel man smiled politely. "That's very nice," he said, "but what I mean is something you'd be good at during office hours."

"Oh," said the girl, "that's wonderful. Because I made this dress and won the contests during office hours." What you can cook quickly when you come home from your office is:

GLAZED HAM

[SERVES FIVE TO SIX]

1 3-pound precooked ham
1 clove, ground
1 9-ounce can crushed pineapple

½ cup brown sugar
¼ cup melted butter
1 teaspoon dry mustard

Cut the skin off the precooked ham, but leave some of the fat on. Now put everything else into an electric blender and run at high speed until thoroughly combined. Slash the fat, cover the ham with the glaze, and bake for 30 minutes in oven preheated to 350 degrees. Baste it once in awhile. It looks pretty, and tastes good, too, if you surround the ham with pineapple slices 10 minutes before the ham is finished.

If you happen to be passing by a town called New Glarus, Wisconsin, will you please find out and let us know if the Swiss-Americans who live there are still putting on Schiller's play about William Tell? They used to do that, first in German, and then, on Labor Day, in English. And they used to have a Yodel Club too, whose members used to yodel. Sounds like fun, doesn't it?

We know a prominent boor who picked up a piece of meat on his fork and asked his hostess, "Is this swine?" The lady, a sweet, gentle soul, sweetly and gently asked, "Which end of the fork are you referring to?" A good swine barbecue is:

PORK TENDERLOIN

[SERVES FOUR]

¼ cup honey	½ cup soy bean sauce
juice of one lemon	½ cup onion, chopped
½ cup sherry	1 tablespoon garlic
1 teaspoon dry	powder
mustard	2 pounds pork tenderloin

Stir together all ingredients until thoroughly combined, then marinate pork in mixture for several hours, turning pork every half hour or so. Drain the pork, reserving marinade, place it on spit, and cook it for about half-hour, 4 inches from source of heat, or until meat thermometer tells you that it has reached 180 degrees. (Put the thermometer into the thickest part of meat.) Keep basting the pork with the marinade.

When he was young and struggling for a toehold on the ladder of success, Dick Driver, the well-known sportsman (he drives sports cars, plays polo)—philanthropist (he supports three poor but honest chorus girls), once was awakened in the middle of the night by a burglar. Dick heard the window of his furnished room being opened stealthily, and then he saw a man quietly sneak inside from the fire escape. The burglar tiptoed over to the chair on which Dick's trousers were hanging and was going through the pockets when Dick couldn't restrain himself any longer.

"I burst out laughing," says Dick. "This flabbergasted the thief. He froze. I put on the bedside light and sat up. You never saw such a surprised-looking crook. 'Why are you laughing?' he asked. 'Why, you poor cretinous lout,' I replied, 'how do you think you're going to find any money in my pockets at night, when I can never find any there in the daytime?' " It won't cost you much if you make:

BREADED PORK CHOPS

[SERVES FOUR]

1½ pounds center pork chops	½ teaspoon pepper
	2 eggs, beaten
1 tablespoon salt	½ cup bread crumbs

With a damp cloth, wipe the chops, sprinkle all over with salt and pepper. Dip them in beaten eggs, then in bread crumbs, once again in eggs and a last time in bread crumbs. Put them in refrigerator between sheets of waxed paper for a couple of hours so the breading will stick. Best way of frying them is in a basket in deep fat. Fry them only until the crumbs are well browned, then drain the chops on paper toweling. Now grease a baking dish, put the pork chops in, and in an oven preheated to 350 degrees bake them for 40 to 50 minutes.

Dear Sir—

Anything you want you have to go after with great determination—we all know that, don't we? Like a girl we knew who finally got a job with a large business, where she had heard there were droves of well-paid, unmarried young men, some of whom were not very repulsive. She was turned down when she wrote her first letter applying for the job. "I am sorry," said the personnel manager in his letter, "but we are overstaffed and don't have enough work for everybody to do."

You know what made the man change his mind and hire her? Because she wrote back to him saying, "Don't worry about hiring me; no one will ever notice the little bit of work I will do." This will take very little work, but everybody will sit up and take notice:

BAKED PORK CHOPS

[SERVES TWO]

4 pork chops	2 tablespoons salad oil
1 tablespoon onion- soup mix	2 teaspoons salt dash of pepper
¼ cup water	2 cloves garlic,
juice of one lemon	crushed

Cut some fat from pork chops, melt it in skillet, then brown chops. Stir up all other ingredients, pour mixture over chops in skillet, cover it, and bake for about one hour in an oven preheated to 350 degrees.

around City Hall they tell this story about an old-time politician. Seems that this fellow ran a saloon before he was appointed a magistrate. One day a man was brought before him, charged with drunkenness, which is, you know, a violation against the station house. "Guilty or not guilty?" asked the former saloon keeper-magistrate. "Your Honor," the unfortunate fellow cried out piteously, "I have never touched a drop of liquor in my life!" "Well, then," remarked the absent-minded magistrate, "will you have a cigar instead?"

BARS AND LIQUOR STORES ARE CLOSED ON EVERY ELECTION DAY, SO PREPARE! Also try preparing:

BAKED PORK CHOPS IN SOUR CREAM

[SERVES TWO TO FOUR]

4 loin pork chops
flour
4 cloves garlic
½ cup sour cream
1 small bay leaf

1 tablespoon sugar
½ cup water
1 tablespoon vinegar
salt and pepper to taste

Trim fat off chops and save the fat. Dredge the chops with flour. (Note for brides: Dredging means putting some flour in a heavy brown paper bag, putting in the chops, and bouncing them around.) Now melt the fat from the chops and, after putting a clove of garlic in each one, brown them in a frying pan. Place chops in a baking dish. Mix all the other ingredients and pour over the chops. Cover and bake in oven preheated to 350 degrees for one hour, or until they're done.

*T*his young fellow—well, he wasn't such a young fellow, really, he was rapidly getting past the age when he should have been married already, and he wasn't really very sharp-witted either, it is sad to say—was being coached by his uncle about how to converse with a certain girl—well, she really wasn't a girl any longer, she was really a woman, who also should have been married by then. "There are three things that interest a woman," said the uncle, who had been married three times and therefore considered himself an expert on women, "and the first one is her family, the second one is food, and the third is a sense of humor."

When this fellow met the woman, he said, remembering his uncle's coaching, "Do you have any brothers or sisters?" The woman shook her head. "No," she said happily. "Do you like braised pigs' knuckles with sauerkraut?" the fellow asked her, remembering his uncle's second lesson. "No," she said, wiping a tear from her eye. "Well," said the fellow wittily, remembering the third injunction, "if you had brothers and sisters, do you think they would have liked braised pigs' knuckles with sauerkraut?" Here's how to make:

BRAISED PIGS' KNUCKLES WITH SAUERKRAUT

[SERVES FOUR]

4 fresh pigs' knuckles	3 cups sauerkraut
2 teaspoons salt	2 big potatoes, peeled
½ teaspoon pepper	and quartered
1 teaspoon celery seeds	

Wipe the pigs' knuckles with a damp cloth, put them in a big pot, add water to cover, and pour in the salt. Cover the pot and simmer until the meat is tender, which will take 2 hours or maybe a little more. Half an hour before the knuckles are finished, sprinkle with pepper and add the celery seeds, sauerkraut, and potatoes.

Variety Meats

several decades ago, it used to be fairly common to read in the newspapers that some chorus girl or actress was suing some foolish millionaire for breach of promise, which meant that the cad had promised to marry the wily chick and then had reneged on his promise. And the letters that those dopey millionaires wrote to those heartbroken girls! And which the newspapers used to print! Myomymy! And the money those girls used to collect! Myomymy!

Which reminds us of the two lawyers. FIRST LAWYER: "What was your last case?" SECOND LAWYER: "Breach of promise. My client, a girl, claimed her heart was broken and the jury gave her $50,-000. What was your last case?" FIRST LAWYER: "My client, a woman, was hit by a car and had her leg broken. The jury gave her $475. Which proves it is cheaper to break a girl's leg than her heart." Which reminds us of:

HAMBURGER WITH A HEART

[SERVES FIVE TO SIX]

1 veal heart	½ teaspoon salt
2 pounds chuck steak	¼ teaspoon pepper
2 small onions, finely chopped	2 teaspoons prepared mustard
½ teaspoon oregano	charcoal seasoning

Have the butcher remove veins and arteries from top of heart and have him grind the heart and the chuck together, twice. Spread the mixture flat; sprinkle chopped onion, oregano, salt, and pepper all over; spread it with the mustard; knead it together well to distribute the seasoning throughout; shape into hamburger-sized hamburgers and sprinkle on top of each some charcoal seasoning. Broil for four minutes on each side in a preheated broiler, three inches from source of heat. This is a recipe we got from a colleague, a 6-foot-4-inch fellow named Jerry Mulford, who has a terrible time not weighing more than several hundred pounds, because he is so good with a knife and fork.

The manager of the nightclub was trying to convince a friend that today's showgirls are much better educated and much more aware of the world around them than the giddy creatures of past decades, who were interested only in diamonds and the millionaires who could afford to bestow them on the girls of their choice.

"Why, these girls today," he said, motioning to the lovely girls who were rehearsing a new routine, "not only read newspapers and books, but they go to college and take drama and all sorts of other lessons. I'll prove it to you." And he called one of the tall young beauties. "Ask her anything," he said to his friend. The friend said, "Well, what do you think of Red China, dear?"

Dear pondered the question, then shrugged her pretty shoulders. "It's a little gaudy," she said, "but I guess it's okay if it doesn't clash with the table-cloth." On red, green, blue, or even white china, what looks and tastes great is:

SHARP TONGUE

[SERVES SIX TO EIGHT]

1 4- to 5-pound beef tongue, fresh, smoked or cooked
1 onion, minced
1 clove garlic, minced
2 tablespoons olive oil
4 anchovy fillets, drained and chopped
1 tablespoon capers, chopped

2 teaspoons parsley, chopped
½ teaspoon pepper
¼ teaspoon dry mustard
1 cup beef bouillon (if you use a smoked tongue)
1 cup dry white wine

If you can get only a fresh tongue, that makes more work. What you do in that case is put the fresh tongue in salted water to cover, put a bay leaf in a cheesecloth bag with half a dozen peppercorns, and add that to the water with a sliced onion, a pinch of basil, or thyme, 2 stalks of celery, 2 carrots, and bring it to a boil, then simmer for 2 to 3 hours, depending on size, until it's tender. Then you strain the broth, hold on to it, and throw all the vegetables and the cheesecloth bag away.

But if you buy a smoked tongue what you do is: Boil it for 2 to 3 hours, depending on size, and then make the sauce. You sauté the onion and garlic until they are both soft—in the hot olive oil— then add to the saucepan the chopped anchovies and capers, the parsley, pepper, dry mustard, and 1 cup of the broth from the boiled tongue—or 1 cup of beef bouillon if you use a smoked tongue. Lastly, add the wine, stir it all around for a couple of minutes, let it get good and hot, then slice the tongue, and pour the sauce over all.

We have a fat friend who is the greatest man on the East Coast, south of Boston, with a knife and fork. What we mean is, he likes very much to eat. And one of his continuous gripes is that portions of food in restaurants, especially the expensive ones, are getting smaller and smaller all the time. He has all kinds of ways to get portions that are to his liking, and we were with him in a restaurant when he was inspired to try a new one.

The waiter had wheeled over to our table a cart, and the captain in charge of our table, with a flourish, served our friend the dish he had ordered.

Our friend winced when he saw the dainty portion he'd been given, but to the captain he said, "That's grand! That's just what I wanted! Now that you've shown me a sample, bring me a whole portion!" So the captain came back with a double portion of:

TRIPE À LA MODE DE CAËN

[SERVES SIX TO EIGHT]

2 pounds honeycomb tripe
1 pound bacon
1 calf's foot
1 quart beef stock (or bouillon)
4 large onions, whole
2 stalks celery
1 green pepper, chopped

2 cloves garlic, chopped
1 tablespoon parsley
1 pinch each of thyme, mace, and cayenne
6 peppercorns and 1 bay leaf in cheesecloth bag
1 cup brandy
6 scallions, chopped fine

Clean the tripe well and cut it into strips about 2 to 3 inches long and 2 inches wide, put them into water to cover, bring to a boil, and let boil for 5 minutes. Drain the tripe. Chop the bacon, cut meat off bone of calf's foot. Put everything—except the brandy and chopped scallions—into a large casserole with a cover that fits very tight. Preheat your oven to 275 degrees and bake for at least 6 hours. About 30 minutes before serving, take dish from oven, discard cheesecloth bag, add scallions and brandy, stir, and put it back into oven for last half-hour, uncovered. If the casserole cover isn't really tight, it may be too dry; in that case, before you add the brandy, put into casserole some more beef stock or bouillon. All our fat friends love this.

doesn't it make you mad as anything, all those awful stories comedians tell on the television about how terrible, or stupid, or something, their wives are? Like this one: There was this sad man who came into a restaurant and said to the waitress, "Please bring me some lukewarm, greasy chicken soup, a piece of liver fried until it's like shoe leather, a cup of coffee with lipstick on it, and then sit down with me and nag, nag, nag."

The waitress stared at him. "What are you," she asked, "some kind of nut or something?" The man shook his head sadly. "No," he said, "I'm far from home and I'm homesick." Isn't that awful? Your husband will never tell stories like that if you cook:

BRAISED LIVER

[SERVES THREE TO FOUR]

1 pound beef liver	2 cups bouillon
2 tablespoons butter or fat	2 tablespoons vinegar
2 medium onions, minced	1½ tablespoons flour
	½ teaspoon salt
1 teaspoon parsley, chopped	dash of pepper

Wipe liver with a damp cloth and dry it. Sauté onions and parsley until onions are soft but not brown. Pour in bouillon, vinegar, flour, salt, and pepper, and stir like crazy. Now put in the liver, cover it and simmer over low heat for 10 minutes, and then turn the liver and simmer for another 10 minutes. That makes 20 minutes altogether. When you serve, pour the gravy over the liver.

The young fellow had been wooing the prettiest girl in town for a long time, and no one was more surprised than he when she accepted his proposal of marriage. "I will do my best to make you happy, darling," he said. "I will work hard and you will have a good life." The girl smiled. "Yes," she said, "I know." He told her that she was the most beautiful girl in the world. She did not disagree with him. "I know," he said humbly, "that I'm not much to look at." She agreed with him. "But that doesn't matter, sweetheart," she whispered sweetly, "you'll be working day and night, anyway." Here are a couple of ways to do:

SWEETBREADS

But first let us tell you something about sweetbreads, and how you should prepare them no matter how you cook them. First, you soak them in very cold water for 30 minutes to 1 hour. Then, you boil enough water to cover the sweetbreads, add 1 teaspoon of vinegar or lemon juice and 1 teaspoon of salt, plunge the sweetbreads into the boiling water, and simmer them for 15 minutes. After 15 minutes, plunge them into very cold water to make them firm enough to handle, and then remove any skin and tubes from them, being careful not to break them. You know what sweetbreads are, don't you? They're glands near the neck and heart of a calf and they make great eating. Here's how to cook:

SAUTÉED SWEETBREADS

[SERVES THREE TO FOUR]

2 pairs sweetbreads	1 stick of butter
3 tablespoons flour	2 teaspoons parsley,
salt and pepper	chopped
1 egg, beaten	lemon wedges
bread crumbs	

After preparing the sweetbreads, dip them first in seasoned flour, then in beaten egg, finally in bread crumbs. Hot up the butter and let it get slightly brown. Fry the sweetbreads until they are brown on both sides, about 3 minutes per side. Remove them to serving platter, pour over them the browned butter, sprinkle with chopped parsley, and serve to 3 or 4 people with wedges of lemon.

And here's how to cook:

BROILED SWEETBREADS

[SERVES THREE TO FOUR]

2 pairs sweetbreads	melted butter
salt and pepper to taste	1 tablespoon brandy
bacon	

Cut the sweetbreads into fairly large pieces after preparing them for cooking. Sprinkle them with a little salt and pepper, roll each piece in a strip of bacon, and fasten with toothpicks. Broil them, turning frequently, and baste them with the bacon drippings and, if necessary, with melted butter. Add a tablespoon of brandy to the gravy, and pour it over the sweetbreads. Remove toothpicks.

Everyone was congratulating John Lachaud because he had won a great fortune playing the numbers game. He was so happy that he even bought drinks for everyone, something no one had ever seen him do before. A friend asked him what number he had picked. "136," said John proudly. And how, he was asked, did he come to select that number to bet on? He smiled smugly.

"One night," he declared pompously, "I had a dream. In my dream I saw the number 21. In color. The next night I saw the same number again, also in color. Then for four nights more I had the same dream, the number 21 in color. Then the dream did not come back. But I had dreamed that number six times, right? So I used my brains, and I multiplied 21 by 6, and I bet on 136."

There was a stunned silence, and then his friend shouted, "Oh, you big dope! 21 multiplied by 6 is 126, not 136!" John smiled. "Okay," he said, "you be the mathematician, but I used *my* brains and won a fortune!" If you have calf's brains, what you should do is have:

SAUTÉED CALF'S BRAINS

[SERVES FOUR]

1 pound calf's brains	1½ tablespoons lemon
flour (maybe ¼ cup)	juice or vinegar
salt and pepper	2 tablespoons sherry
1 stick of butter, or	1 tablespoon parsley,
oil, or fat	chopped

Before you begin, prepare the calf's brains the same way as sweetbreads: soak them first in icy-cold, salted water. Then plunge into boiling water to which salt and lemon juice or vinegar have been added; simmer for 15 minutes. Cool and put them into refrigerator for a couple of hours, or plunge them into icy-cold water so they'll not come apart when you handle them.

Now, remove the membranes and slice brains into thick pieces. Season the flour and roll the brains in it, getting the pieces well coated. Now hot up the butter, getting it slightly brown, and fry the brains on all sides over low heat. Put the brains on a platter, add the lemon juice—or vinegar—to the pan, along with the sherry. Increase the heat and stir the sauce until it boils. Pour it over the brains and sprinkle with parsley.

Calf's brains, after they are prepared for cooking, can also be dipped in a beaten egg, then in seasoned flour, and fried in hot butter, fat, or olive oil in which minced garlic has first been sautéed. They are wonderful, too, in omelets. And a few chopped capers go well in any calf's brains dishes.

A young mother we know tells us that the other night she found her handsome young husband standing next to their infant son's crib. "He had such a wonderful, strange, adoring expression as he looked at our little child," she said, "that tears came to my eyes. I whispered to him as I put my head on his shoulder, 'Darling, what are you thinking?' " Her husband started, she said, and then shook his head in bewilderment. "I was just trying to figure out," he said, "how the devil can they build a wonderful crib like that for only $8.95?" Everyone will wonder how you did it if you serve:

BREADED BRAINS

[SERVES SIX TO EIGHT]

2 pounds calf's brains
2 cups water
1 tablespoon vinegar
1 cup bread crumbs
1 tablespoon parsley, chopped
1 tablespoon Parmesan cheese, grated

1 small onion, chopped fine
1 teaspoon garlic powder
1 teaspoon salt
½ teaspoon pepper
2 beaten eggs
¼ cup olive oil

Wash the brains, then put in a pan with the water and vinegar. Boil for 10 minutes. Drain, and then drop the brains into a pan with cold water and let stand for 30 minutes. Drain and remove the membranes. Cut brains into 3-inch pieces. Now mix together the bread crumbs, parsley, cheese, onion, garlic powder, and salt and pepper. Dip the brains first into beaten eggs, then into the mixture, back into eggs, and then once more into mixture, getting them thoroughly coated. Get the oil good and hot in a frying pan. Fry the brains until they are a golden brown all over.

wo old friends met after a long separation, and they began that tiresome, boring business of reminiscing, you know—"Whatever happened to Sam Schmulowitz?" and "Whatever became of Joe Schimshireis?" and "Do you ever see Max Mitnick?" and all the rest of that dreary kind of guff.

Well, it developed that one of their friends, Jerry Anthrobuby, had become very rich, and another one, Max Maxstein, had become very poor. How did Jerry get rich, one of them asked. "By wise speculation and shrewd investments," he was told. And Max, how did he lose all his money? "By gambling," he was told, "on the stock market." You won't be gambling if you cook:

WINEY BEEF KIDNEYS ON TOAST

[SERVES FOUR]

4 beef kidneys	1 green pepper, chopped
salt and pepper	½ cup beef broth (or
flour	hot water and
3 tablespoons oil or	bouillon cube)
fat, or butter	⅛ teaspoon oregano
1 medium onion,	½ cup red wine
chopped	4 slices toast

Wash the kidneys thoroughly under cold water, remove membranes, and cut kidneys into 1-inch slices. Mix salt and pepper with the flour, and dredge the kidney slices with the seasoned flour.

Hot up the oil, fat, butter, or whatever, and sauté the onions and green pepper until they are soft. Add the kidneys and stir-fry them for about 5 minutes. Add the broth and the oregano, cover the pan, and simmer over low heat for about 20 minutes. Taste one of the kidney slices: if it's tender, add the wine, stir, and cook for about 2 minutes longer. Pour over toast for four people. Serve with this a salad of red radishes, cucumber slices, and scallions or onion rings, on a bed of lettuce with lemon juice and olive oil on the side, so each person can choose how much of each to use. And let each person judge how much salt and freshly ground pepper he wants. We think it's kind of presumptuous for someone to tell us how much salt and pepper to put on a salad, don't you? We know how much we like; who knows, but you, how much you like. We know a couple of people who say that salt is poison, and they won't have any in their house. We ate there once.

Y ou may have noticed that we are a repository of many little-known facts—most of them utterly useless—and here we have for you a lulu. In New Hampshire, the fourth Monday in April is a legal holiday, did you know that? It is a fast day up there. After intensive research—by a very nice man at the New York Public Library—we learned that the fourth Monday in April each year used to be a fast day in all the New England states, a custom which began in colonial days, when they began observing Thanksgiving Day, to give thanks for a bountiful harvest. So they thought, back in those days, that it was proper and fitting to have a day at the beginning of the planting season to pray for a good crop, and they fasted on that day. Every state in New England dropped that custom quite awhile ago, but not New Hampshire, where on the fourth Monday in April no one will eat:

KISHKE

[SERVES THREE TO SIX]

1 beef casing, 12 inches long	1 teaspoon parsley, chopped
1 cup flour	½ teaspoon salt
3 tablespoons bread crumbs or cracker meal	⅛ teaspoon pepper
1 onion, grated	½ cup melted shortening or fat
	½ teaspoon paprika

You get the beef casing in a butcher shop, and when you get it home wash it in cold running water, scrape the fat off inside and out, then wash it again in warm water, and dry it thoroughly. Now sew up one end of the tube. Roll it up as you would a stocking, combine all the ingredients thoroughly, and stuff the *kishke* with it, but don't stuff it too tight. (As you stuff, you unroll the *kishke*, naturally.) When you've got the casing filled, sew up open end, and drop it into boiling water for 1 or 2 minutes, which will shrink the casing. You can rub it with melted fat and roast it all by itself on a bed of sliced onions, but it is better to put it right in the roasting pan when you roast a chicken, duck, turkey, goose, or even beef, for all of which it makes a splendid accompaniment. When it is done, slice it in 2-inch lengths.

This reminds us of a story—we don't know why it should remind us—that Buddy Hackett once told us. Seems his wife told the comedian that she wanted their children to get religious training, and Buddy asked, "Why?" Mrs. Hackett said she wanted the children to know that they were Jewish, that's why. "Oh, they know they're Jewish," said Buddy. "They got heartburn."

Poultry

you know that Englishmen—and English-women, too—love to go on walking tours, and they walk all over their own country and any accessible foreign one. The nicest people do that, even university dons. But here you see a fellow on the road, and immediately you think, "He's a bum." Isn't that terrible?

A friend of ours who went to school in England decided last summer to walk through the Tennessee hills. Late one afternoon, feeling tired, he hitched a ride from a passing motorist. Suddenly, the driver pulled out a gun and ordered our friend to take a bottle of moonshine booze out of the glove compartment. Then he made our friend take a drink, which he did, shuddering and choking on the horrible stuff. The man handed our friend the gun then and said, "Okay, now make me take a drink." You won't have to pull a gun on your family to make them eat:

BAKED CHICKEN

[SERVES FOUR TO FIVE]

1½ cups corn flakes, crumbled
2 teaspoons salt
½ teaspoon pepper
1 3- to 4-pound fryer, disjointed

2 eggs, beaten
⅓ cup chicken fat or butter
2 onions, sliced
1 clove garlic, chopped

Combine the crumbled corn flakes with seasoning. Dip chicken parts first in the eggs, then roll them in corn flakes, getting them well coated. Get your fat good and hot, brown the chicken parts on both sides. Now sauté the onions and garlic until they are soft. Put the chicken parts into a baking dish, toss in the cooked onions and garlic, and in oven preheated to 350 degrees bake for 45 minutes. We didn't list it in the ingredients but you know what's nice? If you pour half a cup of a dry white wine into the baking dish with the chicken, that's what's nice.

Ⓞne evening a friend of ours named Nellie Myers was beguiling her husband, grumpy and damp from dealing all day with all manner of importunate but mainly unimportant folk in his office in the City Hall district, with stories of her childhood in Kansas while she was preparing dinner for which he was ravening. "This young lad, a distant relation aged four, from Landgrove, Vermont, also named Myers by an odd quirk, once swallowed a shotgun shell his daddy, an extremely heedless fellow, had left lying around," she said gaily but breathlessly, as she prepared to bake chicken parts in fragrant herbs.

"Well, sir," gaily continued Nellie Myers (remember her from up there at the top?), "of course they called the doctor, who said the boy would have to be fattened up for a few days before he was operated on. 'But until the operation,' said the sage medico, 'keep the tyke in bed quietly and, above all, don't point him at anyone!'" Nellie chortled, and her dear husband grinned strongly and manfully as she placed in the oven:

HERB-BAKED CHICKEN

[SERVES THREE TO FOUR]

½ cup butter, margarine, or chicken fat

2 teaspoons mixed dried herbs (thyme, marjoram, basil, rosemary)

1 clove garlic (some people say optional, but we say if no garlic, the hell with it)

salt and pepper

1 3-pound broiler chicken, disjointed (means cut up, see?)

1 small onion, chopped fine

1 teaspoon parsley, chopped

Melt butter in large saucepan, add herbs, garlic, salt, and pepper, and roll chicken parts around in the stuff so they are coated thoroughly. Put chicken parts in large, flat casserole, skin side up, sprinkle with chopped onion and parsley, and bake for 15 minutes in oven preheated to 400 degrees. After 15 minutes lower heat to 300 degrees and bake 45 minutes to one hour. Stop when chicken is golden brown and tender unless you like chicken when it is incinerated. If you've got any old white wine lying around you got no use for, maybe you'd like to pour it into the casserole. Who'd know—or care—except you, anyway?

*D*ick Driver was a poor but not very honest boy. It happened that one summer Dick was invited to stay in the country with a farmer friend of his father. One morning, after he had done his chores, Dick washed up in the kitchen. On the table was a chicken cooked by the farmer's wife for their midday dinner. A growing boy, Dick always was hungry. He fought temptation but lost. He snatched up a chicken leg and gnawed it to the bone.

At dinner, when the farmer served the chicken, he saw that a leg was missing. "Who," he asked, "ate the leg off this chicken?" Dick smiled angelically. "This chicken," he said, "must have been run over by an auto and had its leg amputated. It happened to a friend of mine once."

Next day, Dick Driver and the farmer walked through the barnyard. Dick saw a chicken standing on one leg. "Look! Look," he shouted, "there's another one-legged chicken!" The farmer threw a pebble at the chicken, which skittered away. On two legs. The farmer sneered at Dick Driver. "You know," said Dick, who detested sneerers, "if only you'd had a pebble yesterday to throw at the chicken we had for dinner, we might have had two legs, instead of just one."

This is the recipe the farmer's wife, who had been a sophisticated model in the big city before she married him, had followed to cook the chicken in wine:

CHICKEN WINO

[SERVES SIX TO EIGHT]

6 tablespoons olive oil
2 teaspoons salt
1 teaspoon pepper
1 tablespoon flour
2 3-pound chickens,
    cut up
2 medium onions,
    chopped
1 cup dry white wine
    (not sweet, see?)

1 tablespoon tomato
    paste
1 bouillon cube,
    dissolved in 1 cup
    hot water
¼ cup wine vinegar
2 cloves garlic
1 teaspoon capers
2 tablespoons parsley,
    chopped

Heat olive oil in skillet, rub salt, pepper, and flour into chicken parts with great dispatch. Sauté onions until soft, add chicken, and brown all over. Pour wine into skillet (take sip from bottle if you have to; leave cup of wine for cooking!) and cook at high heat for 5 minutes. Mix tomato paste and bouillon and pour mixture into skillet, stirring with vigor and steadiness. Lower heat to medium, cover skillet, and cook until chicken is tender, about 45 minutes. (You can bring wine bottle to living room and entertain guests while chicken is cooking.)

When chicken is done, transfer contents of skillet to hot serving dish. Boil vinegar for one minute (just 1 minute, you hear?) in skillet in which chicken was cooking, add garlic, capers, and parsley, and cook for one minute more. Scrape up goodies left in skillet after chicken was cooked, pour contents over chicken, and serve.

in Puerto Rico the birthday of José de Diego is celebrated on April 16th, for in the 1890's he was a hero of the movement to free the island from domination of the Spaniards. De Diego was a poet and a lawyer. He was educated at the University of Barcelona and at Havana University and became President of the House of Delegates. In Puerto Rico they have a marvelous chicken and rice dish which is dearly beloved and which is called:

ASOPAO

[SERVES THREE TO FIVE]

1 2½- to 3-pound chicken
1 tablespoon salt
1 teaspoon oregano
1 clove garlic, pressed
  or mashed
2 tablespoons fat
2 ounces boiled ham,
  chopped
1 medium onion,
  chopped
1 green pepper, chopped

1 cup canned whole
  tomatoes, peeled
6 cups water, boiling
1 tablespoon capers,
  chopped
¼ cup green, pimiento-
  stuffed olives
2 cups rice
1 cup peas, cooked
pimiento strips

The list of ingredients is long, but don't be intimidated because this isn't a complicated recipe at all. Cut the chicken into serving pieces. (Of course you can use chicken parts, which is much easier.) Rub each piece of chicken with salt, oregano, and garlic. In a large saucepan, brown the parts in fat—you may need more than 2 tablespoons—and then add the chopped ham, onion, chopped green pepper, and the tomatoes with liquid. Cover the pan and simmer for 30 minutes. After half an hour, remove the chicken parts from pan, and separate the meat from the bones. Put chicken meat back in the pan, throw away the bones. Now add the water, capers, and olives and cook for about 5 minutes, after which you taste the sauce, correct the seasoning, if necessary, and add the rice. Cover the saucepan and over low fire simmer until the rice has absorbed most of the liquid. The rice should be tender and moist. Empty everything into a large serving platter and garnish it with cooked peas and pimiento strips. Grated Parmesan cheese should be at the table. A popular cold drink in Puerto Rico is called:

SANGRÍA

[EIGHT TO TEN LONG ONES]

1 cup lime juice	2 cups dry red wine
2 cups sugar	3 cups water

Heat the lime juice, stir in the sugar, and dissolve it. Add the other ingredients, let it cool, and then refrigerate it for hours.

a middle-aged, prosperous-looking man walked into an art gallery, and the owner smiled happily to see such a well-heeled prospective client. "Is there anything I can do for you?" he asked, smiling a revolting, fraudulent smile of graciousness. "Yes," said the man, "there is. You know that painting you have in your window, that abstract painting with all those vari-colored dots all over it?"

The art dealer's smile became even more repulsively charming. "Certainly," he said, "shall I take it out of the window for you?" The man nodded and said, "Yes, please do just that. And don't ever put it back in the window. It makes me ill whenever I pass by here and see it." People who come to your house will be made happy when they see that you have for them:

CHICKEN STROGANOFF

[SERVES SIX TO SEVEN]

1 cup oil	½ pound fresh mushrooms
salt and pepper	1 onion, or 4 to 5 green
½ cup flour	onions, chopped
1 5-pound roaster-	2 cloves garlic, crushed
fryer, cut up	½ cup sour cream
3 tablespoons chicken	½ cup heavy cream
fat or butter	1 tablespoon lemon juice
giblets	more salt and pepper

Isn't that a ridiculous name? Chicken Stroganoff, indeed! But you know what it's generally called, don't you? Smothered chicken, that's what it's generally called, and that's even dopier. Let's just call it "chicken-in-sour-cream," shall we? Okay, let's go. Wash the giblets well, trim off fat, cut them up and simmer in ½ cup of water for 30 minutes. Get the oil hot, season the flour, rub the flour into the chicken parts, and brown them in the oil. Now grease a roasting pan heavily, put in the chicken parts, pour the cut-up giblets and their broth—be sure there is no gristle in the giblets—over the chicken and in oven preheated to 350 degrees bake until the chicken is tender. Now make the sauce.

Get the chicken fat or butter—we prefer chicken fat—hot and cook the mushrooms, onions, and garlic until the onions are soft. Now add the two creams, the lemon juice, salt and pepper to this pan and cook, stirring all the while until it is quite hot. But DON'T let it boil. When the chicken parts are done, put them on your best serving platter, pour the sauce all over it. What's good with this is a roll, toasted, with which to sop up the lovely sauce, and don't let anybody tell you different.

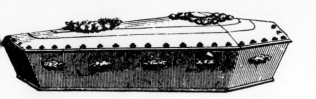

He was a fine man, the friend told the widow of the deceased, and he was sure to be mourned by his many, many friends. "Ah, yes," the widow said with a sigh, "his brothers in his two lodges, his brothers in his union, his poker-night buddies, and his pals down at the political club will all miss him, I'm sure. But I did never get to know him very well." Maybe if this nice widow lady had ever tried something special for him at the stove, she might have had a chance to get acquainted with her husband. Like this, for instance:

CHICKEN OREGANATO

[SERVES FIVE TO SIX]

2 tablespoons lemon juice	⅛ pound butter
1 tablespoon olive oil	1 cup canned whole
1 teaspoon salt	tomatoes
1 4½-pound roasting	½ teaspoon pepper
chicken	1 teaspoon oregano

Mix the lemon juice, olive oil, and salt well and rub it into the chicken. Rub, rub, rub inside as well as outside. What do you rub it with? Your hands, what else? Preheat your oven to 375 degrees, put the chicken in a roasting pan, and put it into the oven for one hour. In a saucepan, melt the butter, squash the tomatoes and dump them into the pan, and add the pepper and oregano. Cook this stuff for about 10 minutes, and every once in awhile agitate it. Now take the chicken out of the oven, pour the contents of the saucepan over it, and put it back into the oven at a reduced heat, 350 degrees, for another hour. Look at the pretty bird once in awhile and baste it.

We heard about a novel way a fellow used to get in touch with his wife while she was downtown on a shopping expedition. He had to leave town that afternoon to make a short business trip to another city, and he knew that his wife would like to go along with him because this place has very good stores, also. What he did was call up each and every store where he and his wife had charge accounts, and told the credit departments of all the stores that he wanted to cancel their charge accounts.

Within the hour his wife was on the phone, sobbing pitifully. "What happened?" she sobbed. "Did you lose your job?" She thought it was a mean—though clever—scheme. But she was mollified when he bought her a lavish lunch where they ate:

DEVILED CHICKEN LEGS

[SERVES SIX TO EIGHT]

⅓ cup oil or butter
8 chicken legs
bread crumbs
¼ cup vinegar
1 clove garlic, mashed
1 teaspoon dry mustard

1 bay leaf
salt and pepper
1 teaspoon Worcestershire sauce
½ cup catsup

Hot up the oil or butter and fry the chicken legs until they are well browned all over. Roll them in bread crumbs and then fry them again until the crumbs are browned, too. Take the chicken out of pan and keep it warm. Add everything else, except the Worcestershire sauce and the catsup, and simmer until the sauce is somewhat reduced. Stir it all occasionally. When the stuff is reduced to about half, take out the bay leaf, throw it away, and add the Worcestershire sauce and catsup. Stir it all around until it is well and truly blended and pour it all over the chicken legs. Eight chicken legs should serve 6 to 8 people, right? If you like real hot stuff, you can add some crumbled red pepper flakes into the sauce before you cook to reduce the quantity, but you've got to be careful, this is really devilish.

A very nice lady named Sheila Grunwald wrote to tell us about a man who went to a psychiatrist and said, "Doctor, I know I'm a fool, but if you would tell me what to do about it, it might help me."

The psychiatrist said that if somebody acknowledges that he is a fool, then he is not a fool. "Then if I am not a fool," said the man, "why does everyone call me a fool?"

The psychiatrist looked at him scornfully. "Listen," said the doc, "if you pay attention to what other people tell you, then, boy, you sure are a fool."

Very funny story, Mrs. Grunwald, and you won't be a fool if you make:

BAKED CHICKEN WITH CURRY SAUCE AND COCONUT

[SERVES THREE TO FIVE]

¼ cup all-purpose flour   1 tablespoon butter
1 teaspoon salt
¼ teaspoon pepper
2- to 3-pound frying
     chicken, cut in
     serving pieces

Combine and mix well flour, salt and pepper. Coat chicken with flour mixture, put chicken pieces in a single layer, skin-side up, in a shallow roasting pan. Now dot each piece of chicken with butter, and bake in oven preheated to 475 degrees, for 15 to 20 minutes or until browned.

When the chicken is browned, remove it from oven and pour the curry sauce we're going to tell you about in just a minute all over the chicken.

CURRY SAUCE

½ cup onion, minced
1 tablespoon curry powder
1 tablespoon canned applesauce
½ pound bacon, cooked, chopped fine
1 tablespoon tomato paste
1 teaspoon granulated sugar

¼ cup lemon juice
1 tablespoon all-purpose flour
1 cup canned consommé
1 tablespoon cream
1 clove garlic, crushed
1 tablespoon coconut flakes

Put all the ingredients together (except coconut) in a saucepan and mix them up well until you have a paste. Cook it over medium heat, stirring frequently, for 10 to 15 minutes. Now you have the chicken parts out of the oven, haven't you? Okay, NOW pour the sauce over the chicken, sprinkle the flaked coconut over the sauce, and put it back in the oven for another 20 minutes, or until the chicken is tender.

Wife of a friend of ours seemed to be unusually quiet one evening, which delighted our friend. Up to a point. After dinner when he had finished reading the newspaper, he felt he really should disturb the peace because it was obvious that his wife was unhappy about something.

"What is the matter, dear?" he inquired with a sneer. "Is there something troubling you?" "Yes," she whimpered, "I'm worried about our next-door neighbor. She hasn't been to our apartment for three days, and I'm afraid I must have said something to make her angry or offend her." Her husband turned on the TV. "Well," he snarled, "you must be sure to find out precisely what it was, so we can try it on her again." You'll do it over and over if once you try:

CHICKEN CACCIATORE

[SERVES THREE TO FIVE]

1 4-pound roasting
    chicken
½ cup flour
salt and pepper
¼ cup olive oil
    (maybe more)
1 clove garlic, minced

1 green pepper
4 small onions
1 cup canned tomatoes
1 cup canned mush-
    rooms
2 slices pimiento,
    chopped

Disjoint the chicken—of course you can use chicken parts—then sift the flour with salt and pepper and coat the chicken parts with it. Heat the oil and brown chicken and garlic all over in it, adding oil as needed. Slice the pepper—we don't have to tell you to take out the seeds, do we?—slice the onions, and mash the tomatoes. Pour everything over the chicken, cover the pan and simmer it for 1½ hours.

Now add the mushrooms, simmer for another 30 minutes, garnish with pimientos, and serve. If you like, you can add half a cup of red wine, dry, to this when you add the mushrooms. Have Italian or French bread to sop up the juiciness.

We heard about a politician who, when he was campaigning during the last election, rang the doorbell of one of his constituents, who then tried to slam the door right in his face. But our man is a wily one, and he stopped the door with his foot and continued his spiel while the citizen became angrier and angrier. "And for all these reasons," the politician wound up, "we think you should vote for our candidate."

The angry man glared at the politician. "I would just as soon vote for the devil," he shouted, "as vote for your candidate!" The politician smiled charmingly. "Yes," he said sneeringly, "but in that case, will you vote for our man if your friend, the devil, isn't on the ticket?" If you like hot stuff here's how to make what the Italians call:

BROTHER DEVIL'S CHICKEN
(pollo fra Diavolo)

[SERVES TWO TO THREE]

1 3-pound broiling chicken	1 tablespoon red pepper flakes
olive oil	1 clove garlic
salt to taste	½ cup dry white wine

Cut chicken into serving pieces. (A 3-pound broiler will make two hearty eaters happy, may satisfy three light eaters.) Rub olive oil all over the chicken pieces, sprinkle with salt, and then with the red pepper flakes, which should be crumbled fine. Red pepper flakes are HOT, HOT HOT, so use discretion. If you want the chicken just a little bit devilish, cut down on the red pepper flakes. Preheat your broiler, first pouring a little olive oil on the broiling pan, and broil the chicken three inches from source of heat for about 15 minutes on each side. Watch it carefully, and baste it with more oil at least once on each side. It should be browned, but not charred. When the chicken is done, put the pieces on a plate, put the plate into the broiling compartment —with the heat turned off, of course—so the chicken will stay hot while you make the sauce, which takes just a minute. Mash up the garlic clove—a garlic press is what you need—and mix it up in the wonderful juices from the chicken in the broiling pan. Pour in the wine, and on top of your stove bring it to a boil. Now pour it over the chicken and serve it. It is devilishly good!

friend of ours back from Spain was full of stories about how she made a special effort to get off the well-beaten tourist track and found what she thought was wonderful, wild, unspoiled country and people in Jerez, the home of Spanish sherry. "I thought," she said, "that the people there were altogether untouched by modernity. Until the day I left, that's what I thought. I returned the burro I'd rented, and only then did I think to ask the peasant who owned it what the name of the creature was. He smiled a sweet snaggle-toothed smile and said, 'Elizabeth Taylor.'" Here's how a lady from Jerez, named Mrs. David Sandeman, makes an easy, uncomplicated, but delicious:

CHICKEN PAELLA

[SERVES EIGHT TO TEN]

2 large onions (or 4 small ones)
2 cloves garlic, minced
¼ cup olive oil
2 roasting chickens, cut-up (about 4 pounds each)
2 tablespoons salt

1 teaspoon pepper
¼ bottle cocktail sherry (yes, we said BOTTLE)
hot water
2 cups rice
1 can cooked peas
pimiento strips

Brown onions and garlic in hot oil in large skillet with a cover. Add chicken pieces and brown on all sides for about 10 minutes. Add salt and pepper, pour in the sherry and enough water to cover the chicken pieces. Cook for another 10 minutes, then add rice, and cook over low heat 30 minutes or until rice is done and chicken is tender. Garnish serving dish with peas and pimiento. You notice how lavish Mrs. Sandeman is with the sherry? Well, why not? Her husband is a sherry-pusher.

We have a new stenographer in our office, a very capable girl, but she doesn't seem to be able to come in on time in the morning, or after lunch, or after the coffee break. One morning, after she'd been late four days in a row, her supervisor confronted her. "You should have been here at 9 A.M.," he said. The girl opened her eyes wide in astonishment. "Why?" she asked. "What happened?"

And then the supervisor became angry, and said he would have to suspend her for one day. "When would you like to take that day?" The girl considered this problem. "May I," she asked sweetly, "use that day up by coming in one hour late every day for eight days?" It won't matter if anyone arrives late if you have:

FRICASSEED CHICKEN

[SERVES FIVE TO SIX]

1 4- to 5-pound stewing chicken	4 tablespoons chicken fat
1 large onion, chopped	4 tablespoons flour
1 tablespoon salt	3 cups chicken broth
1 small bay leaf, crumbled	¼ teaspoon pepper
2 cloves garlic, chopped fine	¼ cup white wine (optional)

Cut the chicken up in small pieces, put them in a pot with water to cover, and boil. Add the onion, salt, bay leaf, and garlic, reduce heat, and simmer for about 2½ hours. After that, take the chicken pieces out and strain the broth in the pot. In a separate saucepan, mix the chicken fat and flour and add 3 cups of the broth that you have strained, stirring wildly. Cook it until it gets thickened. Add the pepper and more salt—if you need it—and pour in the wine (save this last step until everyone is ready to eat). Put the chicken pieces into saucepan, stir it all around, and cook for about 5 minutes.

In a cemetery out in Queens, a silly fellow who was putting some flowers on a grave saw a Chinese gentleman put a bowl of rice at the bottom of a gravestone. This, he thought, was very quaint. "Say," he said to the Chinese gentleman, "when do you expect your friend to come and eat that rice?"

The Chinese gentleman smiled urbanely. "Thank you for asking," he said. "I think my friend will come up to eat his rice about the same time that your friend will come up to smell his flowers." Here's how the Chinese do:

CHICKEN WITH ASPARAGUS

[SERVES FOUR TO SIX]

4 chicken breasts
1 pound asparagus
2 tablespoons black beans
2 cloves garlic
2 teaspoons cornstarch
2 teaspoons water
¼ teaspoon sugar

½ teaspoon monosodium glutamate
dash of pepper
2 tablespoons vegetable oil
½ teaspoon salt
½ cup chicken stock
1 tablespoon sherry

Black beans can be bought in Chinese groceries, and by mail order from the Oriental Food Shop, 1302 Amsterdam Ave., New York 27, N.Y., and Eastern Trading Co., 2801 Broadway, New York 25, N.Y. Bone and cut chicken into thin slices, and slice the asparagus extremely thin, diagonally. If the asparagus is young, leave the tips whole—otherwise, cut them in half. Rinse, then mince the black beans. Mince garlic. Now stir cornstarch in water and mix this up with sugar, monosodium glutamate, and pepper. Heat 1 tablespoon oil and add ½ teaspoon salt, the black beans, and the garlic. In half a minute, the beans will give off a pungent, wonderful odor. This is when you add the asparagus. Stir for half a minute and add stock. Cover pan and cook over low heat for 2 minutes. Now remove the asparagus and add the remaining oil. Put chicken in pan and stir it around for a minute or so and pour in the sherry. (You like sherry? Then use more than 1 tablespoon of it.) Flatten the chicken down in pan, and cook until color is nice and dark on bottom. Turn slices over and treat it that way again, and add asparagus. Now put in the cornstarch mixture and agitate the stuff in the pan until the gravy gets thick.

Sundown marks the beginning of the Eighth Day of Tabernacles, the climax of the Jewish holy season, which serves as a reminder of the days of wandering in Biblical days, when the Hebrews were a tribal, farming people. And then comes *Simhat Torah*, the day of Rejoicing of the Law, when thanks are given and joy is expressed for the gift of the Torah.

One hot summer day an old man was overcome by the heat in front of a candy store in the Bronx. Of course, a crowd gathered. An officious passerby pushed the people back and yelled, "Water! Water! Someone get some water!" The stricken man raised himself up on his elbow. "No, no," he said peevishly, "seltzer!" Here's a way to:

ROAST CAPON

[SERVES SIX]

2 cups mashed potatoes	2 teaspoons salt
2 tablespoons chicken fat, melted	¾ teaspoon pepper
½ teaspoon ginger	1 5-pound capon
½ cup onion, chopped and browned	½ cup water, boiling

Stir together the potatoes, fat, ginger, onions, and half the salt and pepper, stuff the bird with it and sew it up. Rub the remaining seasonings all over the outside. Preheat your oven to 425 degrees and roast the stuffed bird for 45 minutes at this heat, turning it several times to brown it evenly. Now add the boiling water to the pan, reduce the heat to 350, and, basting it once in awhile, roast it until it is tender, which should take another hour and a half or so.

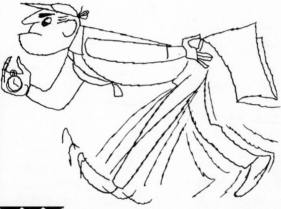

We used to work for a newspaper where the managing editor was quite a card. One night, he was angrily pacing up and down the city room, muttering. Did we say muttering? What he was doing was growling. And he looked very unhappy. The city editor, who was quite a card himself, stopped the managing editor and asked, "What's the matter, old friend? Why are you pacing up and down, muttering, or growling, or whatever it is you are doing to yourself?"

The managing editor glared at him. "Why shouldn't I pace, or mutter, or growl?" he snarled. "Do you know that nothing terrible has happened all day long? What are we going to put on page one if nothing terrible has happened in the city all day long? If somebody doesn't do something terrible pretty soon, we'll have nothing for page one."

The city editor smiled a dreadfully insincere smile. "Don't worry," he said. "Someone will do something terrible soon. You got to have faith in human nature." Your faith in your cooking style will be renewed if you get a:

CHICKEN PICKLED

[SERVES THREE TO FOUR]

1 2½- to 3-pound chicken

3 cloves garlic, minced

1 green pepper, sliced thin

1 pound onions, sliced thin

½ cup vinegar

1 cup olive oil

2 teaspoons salt

½ teaspoon pepper

Cut the chicken up and put it into a pot with everything else. Cover the pot and cook it over medium heat for about 30 minutes. Did somebody ask, "Do you really mean to say use 3 cloves of garlic?" Yes, we said use 3 cloves of garlic. Listen, if you don't like garlic, don't quarrel with us. Just make something else, because garlic lovers, of whom we are one, have their rights, just the same as anyone else. What you should do with the garlic is chop it up fine before you throw it in that pot. And did someone ask: "Did you really mean to say use 1 whole pound of onions?" Yes, we did. And what you should do with the onions is cut them up thin. And also cut the green pepper up thin, while you are at it. THEN, throw everything in the pot. Okay. You've got everything in the pot now? And it has cooked over medium heat for 30 minutes. So now what you do is take the cover off the pot and cook that well-pickled chicken for another 30 minutes. Will your kitchen smell delicious! And how aromatic you will be too, when you eat this dish which is a favorite in the Caribbean.

*T*his teacher, a pretty young girl not much older than some of her pupils, was trying to explain to her class the difference between the words "concrete" and "abstract." The word "concrete," she explained, means something that you can see and feel; while "abstract" means something that you can't see, like an idea.

"Now," she said, "can anyone give us a sentence using both these words?" A sturdy young lout in the first row held up his hand. "My pants," he said as he rose to his full height of 6 feet, 3 inches, "are concrete, teacher, but yours are abstract." Here's something a teacher of cooking we know named Frank Kohler gave us:

BEERY BAKED CHICKEN

[SERVES SIX]

6 chicken breasts
1 can cream of mushroom soup
⅓ cup beer
⅛ teaspoon thyme, chopped fine
2 tablespoons onion, minced
2 tablespoons parsley, minced
1 clove garlic, pressed
½ teaspoon dried tarragon
2 teaspoons salt
1 teaspoon pepper

Place each chicken breast in center of a large square of double-strength aluminum foil. Salt and pepper them, and fold up sides of foil toward the center to form a dish. Heat the mushroom soup and beer in a saucepan, stir until smooth, then pour in all other ingredients. Pour the liquid over each chicken breast and fold and seal each package tightly so the liquid cannot run out. In an oven preheated to 400 degrees bake for 20 minutes; then turn the packages over and bake for another 20 minutes, making 40 minutes baking time in all. This is delicious even if you are not too crazy about beer, because in cooking, the beery taste and smell disappear, but it adds a lot to the flavor of the chicken or whatever you cook with it.

he two dress manufacturers decided to spend a different kind of vacation, so they went on a safari in Africa. Somehow, they both became separated from the rest of their hunting party. They were wandering around the jungle bewilderedly, when one of them heard a noise behind him which he was sure was made by an animal. "Hey, Sam," he shouted, "I'm afraid to look. What is that behind me? A lion? A tiger? A leopard?" His friend shouted back, "Don't be a fool. How should I know? I'm not a furrier!" In Liberia they like this:

CHICKEN AND RICE

[SERVES SIX TO EIGHT]

2 teaspoons salt
2 3-pound chickens,
    cut up in serving
    pieces
¼ pound butter
3 tablespoons salad oil
4 medium onions,
    chopped

3 green peppers,
    chopped
2 cans tomato paste
2 cups water
1 teaspoon pepper
2 cups rice

Sprinkle half the salt on chicken parts, melt the butter in frying pan, get it very hot but don't let it smoke, and brown the chicken pieces all over. Cover the pan, lower the heat, and cook until tender (about 40 minutes), turning occasionally.

In a separate saucepan, heat the oil, add the onions and green peppers, and sauté until they are lightly browned. Now add tomato paste, the water, pepper, and the rest of the salt. Pour the rice into the tomato-onion-green pepper mixture, cover the pan, and cook until the rice is tender. If liquid becomes absorbed before rice is as you like it, add a little water. When the rice is done, pour all contents of that pan into chicken, stir it all around gaily, and serve.

On August 20th is celebrated the feast of St. Stephen of Hungary, the patron saint of that country, its first king, and the man who converted it to Christianity in the year 985. They don't celebrate it in Hungary these days, but Hungarians everywhere around the world remember the great procession in Budapest and the week-long feasting which always followed. One day they ate goulash, the next:

PAPRIKA CHICKEN

[SERVES THREE TO FOUR]

1 tablespoon salt
1 2½- to 3-pound chicken, disjointed
3 tablespoons butter
1 cup onion, chopped
2 cups chicken stock, or consommé

2 tablespoons paprika
1 bay leaf, crumbled
1 teaspoon flour
1 cup sour cream

Rub salt into cut-up chicken pieces, melt the butter in pot, and toss in onions and brown them. Then add stock, paprika, and bay leaf, and bring to a boil. Now add the chicken, lower the heat, cover the pot, and simmer for 1½ hours, or until chicken is tender. Take chicken parts out. Mix flour into sour cream and pour it slowly into pot, stir, and then put chicken back in pot and cook for another 5 minutes. Plain boiled rice is good with the sauce. Let us have no bad Hungarian jokes about "First, you steal a chicken . . ."

The not-so-dopey chorus girl was sitting in the lap of her boy friend, a homely, elderly, but very rich investment banker from Wall Street. She was looking into a mirror and repairing her make-up. She spied his ugly face in the mirror and was inspired to ask, "Do you think that God made you?"

The foolish old man said, "Yes." Then the girl asked, "And did He make me too?" When she got another "yes," the little darling looked smugly at her own pretty face, smiled happily, and murmured contentedly, "Well, I suppose practice makes perfect, hey?" Very tasty, pretty to look at, and not difficult to make, is:

CURRIED CHICKEN

[SERVES FOUR TO SIX]

2 tablespoons butter
1 bay leaf, crumbled
    fine
3 teaspoons curry
    powder
¼ teaspoon dry mustard
several grains cayenne
    pepper
3 teaspoons salt

⅔ teaspoon brown sugar
2 medium onions,
    chopped fine
1 3½- to 4-pound
    chicken, cut in
    serving parts
1 tablespoon flour
1 cup water, boiling

In a deep pan, melt the butter and toss in everything EXCEPT the chicken, flour and boiling water. Hold on to the chicken and flour, hear? Over a low flame cook and stir until the onions are soft. NOW, put in the chicken parts, raise the heat, and fry it for about 20 minutes, turning once. Sprinkle the flour over all, cook on high heat for another 15 minutes, and pour in the boiling water. Cover the pan tightly and lower heat, so the stuff will simmer until the chicken is real tender.

When spring comes, the sun passes through Aries. And you know what else happens? The swallows return to Capistrano! That's what happens! And if they don't, the California Chamber of Commerce is terribly embarrassed, because a lot of tourists go to Capistrano on this day just to see the swallows returning. In Iran—which used to be Persia—the beginning of spring is also the New Year, according to the Zoroastrian calendar.

Many years ago, when spring came to New York, we were a young reporter and our city editor sent us to the corner of Broadway and Spring Street to cover the arrival of the new season. Exactly at 8:34 a.m., when the sun passed through Aries, a pretty young girl came along, and we asked her if she felt joy and gladness in her heart because spring was here, and you know what she said?

"Happast eight in the morning you're trying to pick up girls awready?" she said. "You want I should call a cop or something?" Anyway, in Iran, on the first day of spring they eat, among many other delicious dishes, what they call:

POLOU

[SERVES EIGHT]

2 cups rice, cooked	2 ounces cumin
½ cup olive oil	½ cup currants
2 3-pound chickens	1 teaspoon saffron
2 cups water, boiling	

Cook the rice according to directions. In a pot large enough to hold the chickens, hot up the oil and then sauté the chickens in the oil, turning them until they are well browned all over. Now add the water, cover the pot tightly, and simmer over low heat until the chickens are tender—about 2 hours. Now pour the broth from the pot into a large pan, put half of the cooked rice in the pan, put the chickens on top of the rice, sprinkle them with the cumin seeds and currants, and pour the rest of the rice on the chickens. In oven preheated to 350 degrees, roast dish for 20 minutes.

Put the chickens on a warmed serving platter, mix the saffron with some of the hot broth, and mix it into the rice, which should surround the chicken on the platter. Pickles are very good with this.

The ancient Persian kings and noblemen were fantastic eaters and drinkers, and the kings used to have cooking contests, with the winners getting thousands of pieces of gold! Darius the Great, who became King of the Persians in the year 521 B.C., wrote his own epitaph: "I was able to drink a great deal of wine, and to bear it well." Not like some of the people we know.

We were a dinner guest at the home of people who are very nice people, intelligent, charming, and attractive, but whose good qualities are negated by the fact that they are pitiless bores about the beauty, talent, and wit of their children. After dinner that night, they had their son, a nasty, impertinent little creature, play the piano (the rotten little kid didn't even have to be urged to play, that goes to show you how un-American this rotten little kid is).

Disregarding entirely the terrible performance the kid gave—he's a rotten piano player—the father remarked proudly, when the lad finished the piece he was playing and we guests had applauded hyprocritically, "That's an extremely difficult piece to play, you know."

There was a moment of silence, which was broken by one of his other guests, a wonderful rude person whom we happen to admire, who said,

"Difficult is not good enough; I wish it had been *impossible."* It is difficult, but not impossible, to make:

DRUNKEN CHICKEN LEGS

[SERVES FOUR]

8 chicken legs with
    second joints
4 tablespoons butter
    or margarine
2 tablespoons onion,
    chopped
2 cloves garlic, chopped
2 tablespoons parsley,
    chopped

chicken livers and
    giblets from one
    fowl, chopped
salt and pepper to taste
2 cups white wine
6 tablespoons brandy

Lay off the wine and the brandy, please, until after you've got this dish finished, because you are going to need a hand as steady as a brain surgeon's for this dish, kiddies. First, you cut out the bones from the legs and second joints, leaving them all in one piece, with the incision on just one side. Now sauté in 2 tablespoons of the butter all of the other ingredients, except the wine and the brandy, starting first with the onions, which should be soft but not brown, then the garlic, parsley, chicken livers, and giblets, which have been cut up into small bits. Season the mixture to taste, let it cool so you can handle it. Now stuff the mixture into the chicken legs and sew them up. Put the chicken pieces into a large bowl, pour the wine over them, and let them marinate for 6 to 8 hours.

Heat the remaining butter in your largest skillet or frying pan and brown the chicken pieces lightly. You didn't throw away the wine in which they've been marinating, did you? Of course you didn't. Now put the chicken pieces into a baking pan, pour over them the butter in which they were sautéed, and over all this, pour the wine. Cover the pan tight and bake for 45 minutes in an oven preheated to 375 degrees.

Cut the threads on the chicken pieces and throw them away (not the chicken, it's the threads you throw away). Put the chicken pieces on your biggest and best serving platter, which you have warmed, of course, and put a ring of mashed potatoes around them. Heat the brandy, ignite it, and pour it over the chicken. You can let the lovely flame burn itself out, it won't spoil your dish.

HE: "If you're sitting on an elephant, how do you get down?"

SHE: "With a ladder?"

HE: "Nope."

SHE: "Jump?"

HE: "Nope."

SHE: "Then how do you get down from an elephant?"

HE: "You don't get down from an elephant. You get down from a duck."

What we want to get from a duck, however, is good eating, and here's how to cook:

BRAISED DUCKLING

[SERVES FOUR TO SIX]

½ cup flour
2 teaspoons salt
½ teaspoon pepper
1 3- to 4-pound
    duckling
¼ cup butter
¼ cup celery leaves

1 tablespoon tomato
    paste
rind of one orange,
    grated
1 cup orange juice
¼ cup dry white wine
⅛ teaspoon marjoram
½ teaspoon paprika

Season the flour with salt and pepper, cut the duckling up in quarters and dredge in the seasoned flour. Melt the butter and fry the duckling pieces until they are a beautiful golden brown color, all over. Now pour everything else into the pan right over the duckling pieces, sprinkle it all with the paprika, cover the pan, and simmer it over slow heat. If you need more liquid during cooking, which should take about 45 minutes, add a little wine or orange juice or both.

It was their twenty-fifth wedding anniversary, and the farmer's wife said, "You know, Shmendrick, we should do something special because it is our wedding anniversary." The farmer pondered this novel suggestion. "Well," he said, "what would you suggest that we do?" The farmer's wife smiled shyly. "How about," she said, "how about killing those two ducks?"

The farmer glared at his wife. "Kill those ducks?" he screamed politely. "How can you blame those poor creatures for a disaster that happened twenty-five years before they were born?" You make your ducks this way, ducks, and it will be no disaster:

DUCK WITH RICE

[SERVES SIX TO EIGHT]

¼ pound butter or fat
2 4-pound ducks, disjointed
6 cups stock
4 tablespoons tomato paste
2 teaspoons salt
1 teaspoon pepper
1 teaspoon paprika
1½ cups rice

1 cup green peas, cooked
¼ cup Gruyère cheese, grated
½ cup mushrooms, sliced and sautéed
½ pound cooked ham, cut in strips
2 pimientos, cut in strips

Melt half the butter in a large frying pan, brown the duck parts on all sides. Add 1½ cups of the stock, half the tomato paste, the salt, pepper, and paprika. Now cover the pan, lower the heat, and cook until the ducks are tender, about 1 to 1½ hours. Meanwhile, take another saucepan, melt the rest of the butter in it, and brown the rice, shaking pan from time to time. Pour the rest of the stock into the pan with rice, add tomato paste, and cover the pan. Cook over low heat for 20 minutes, at which time you add the peas and cheese. Cook for another five minutes. Add the mushrooms, the ham, and the pimientos, stir it all up, and add seasoning, if necessary. Before you pour the pan juices over the duck, sop up the surface fat with a paper towel. Fit for a silver anniversary, wouldn't you say?

All in one week in December comes Day of the December Moon, then Human Rights Day, and next the first day of Hannukah! And you know the following week? It's Bill of Rights Day, which marks the ratification in 1791 of the first ten amendments to the Constitution of the United States.

You know where we would be without those first ten amendments to the Constitution? Nowhere, nowhere at all, because on these amendments rest all of our most sacred rights. On this day everyone should have the right to:

ROAST DUCKLING WITH ORANGES

[SERVES SIX TO SEVEN]

1 6- to 7-pound
   duckling
2 teaspoons salt
¼ teaspoon pepper
1 cup water
2 teaspoons sugar

3 teaspoons cider vinegar
1 teaspoon flour
½ cup orange juice
rind of 1 orange
2 oranges, sliced

Rub the duckling inside and out with salt and pepper. Prick skin of duck all over with a fork, preheat your oven to 475 degrees, and roast at that high heat for 10 minutes. Pour off the fat, roast until fat accumulates in pan again—about 10 minutes more—and pour the fat off again. By now, a great deal of the duckling's excess fat is gone, so reduce the heat to 350 degrees, pour a cup of water into the pan, and keep roasting at that heat for about 2 hours. When the duck is finished, take it out of the pan, put it on a platter and put it back into the oven—with the heat turned off and the door open—to keep hot.

Now you make the orange sauce. Skim the fat off pan juice and then put the sugar into a small saucepan over low heat, caramelize it, and add the cider vinegar. Take some of the pan juice, stir the flour in, and then add it to the juice in the pan. Now stir into the gravy the vinegar-sugar and the orange juice, and keep stirring it until it gets thickened. Sprinkle the gravy with the grated orange rind and pour everything over the delicious duckling. Arrange the orange slices around the duck and everybody but the duck will be happy. And you don't have to drink champagne with duckling à l'orange, no matter what anybody says. You want to drink beer with it, drink beer. We have a Bill of Rights, don't we?

One of our more doltish acquaintances, a poor but dishonest fellow whom we may as well call Ignatz, since that is his name, was sentenced not long ago to the vilest sort of durance because he thought he could outwit not only the Feds but also a Long Island duck farmer, whose kind is among our wiliest citizens. Seems Ignatz came into possession of a large quantity of counterfeit $20 bills (he says he got it from a passing stranger), so he borrowed his girl's car, drove out to see the Island, and tried to figure a way of passing the phonies.

Deep in thought, he ran into a flock of fat young ducklings and brought several to an untimely end. Hearing the ruckus, the farmer rushed out. Ignatz dazedly gave him two of the phony $20s, the farmer gave him the slaughtered ducklings, and Ignatz drove off.

But not before the wily farmer noted down the license number. The Feds found Ignatz broiling the ducks on the estate of his girl's father, who promptly broke the engagement. This is how Iggy was broiling the ducklings, a way we recommend most highly, though we frown on how he got them:

CHARCOAL-BROILED DUCKLING

[SERVES FOUR TO FIVE]

1 4- to 4½-pound
    duckling
1 1-pound can jellied
    cranberry sauce

1 6-ounce can frozen
    orange juice,
    undiluted
1 7-ounce can whole-
    berry cranberry sauce

Thaw duckling if frozen; remove neck and giblets and the wings at second joint. (We always pass the first joint by; the second one is always much nicer and generally more fun, too.) Use small, sharp knife to quarter duckling by cutting through length of breastbone, then along length of back next to backbone, and across each half between thigh and breast. Trim off visible fat. (Let's have no wisecracks about whose visible fat should be trimmed.)

Put jellied cranberry sauce in large skillet together with undiluted orange juice and place over low heat—at edge of charcoal grill. Stir until smooth. Put duckling quarters in sauce, skin side down, simmer gently 15 minutes. Remove duckling quarters from skillet and put each one on piece of heavy duty foil (about 9 by 15 inches). Wrap loosely and place on grill over large bed of coals which have burned down to gray ash. Turn every 10 minutes, being careful not to allow drippings to cause flare-ups. For crisp, delicious skin, remove foil and put duckling on grill for 10 minutes over very low coals.

While duckling cooks, put sauce in a jar—remember the sauce?—and allow it to cool. Skim fat from top. Return skimmed sauce to pan, add whole-cranberry sauce, and heat. Pour over duckling quarters when serving. If you don't like tart sauce, add ¼ cup sugar to whole-berry sauce.

"**a**nd don't forget what I told you about waiting on table," the woman said to the new maid. "You serve each dish from the left, and you remove the plates from the right. It's very important." The maid smiled condescendingly. "Yes, sure," she said, "but what's the idea? You superstitious?"

It has probably been pointed out to you that the Old Farmer's Almanac advises the world to stay at home on Friday the 13th. But we say, "Go out," because it is in the home that most accidents occur. Did it ever occur to you, you lucky thing, to cook:

DUCK SALMI

[SERVES FOUR]

1 4-pound duck, with liver, heart, and gizzard, all cut up	⅛ teaspoon pepper
	1 teaspoon sage
3 cloves	1 bay leaf, crumbled
1 onion	1 cup dry white wine
½ cup olive oil	1 cup sherry
¼ teaspoon salt	4 slices bread, toasted

Skin the duck, or maybe you can get your butcher to do this for you. If your duck is frozen, thaw it and then cut the skin along the center of breast from the neck to the vent, then along the back.

Pull the skin away from the flesh, cutting close to the flesh with a sharp knife as you pull the skin back. Of course, it's easier to disjoint the duck first —you have to do it anyway with this dish—and then skin each piece separately, so why don't you just forget what we told you about skinning a whole duck? Okay? So now you wash and dry each hunk of duck. Do the same with the giblets, removing any fat and cut them up in small pieces. Remember those 3 cloves we told you about? Stick them into the onion. Now get hold of a large casserole and put in the olive oil; then add the cut-up giblets, the seasoning, the sage, and the crumbled bay leaf. After that add the duck pieces and, finally, pour over it all the dry white wine and the sherry. Now cover the casserole with a double sheet of foil or brown paper, fixing it so no edges stick out, and put on the casserole cover. Cook it over moderate heat for 1 hour and 20 minutes, or 20 minutes to the pound. When it's done, put the duck hunks on pieces of toast, strain the gravy, and pour it over all. Aren't you the lucky ones!

For all we know, they may still be telling, in poultry-raising circles, the old story about the city man who bought a farm for a hobby and decided to breed turkeys, unaware that these birds are delicate creatures and are prey to many ailments.

He wrote to the Department of Agriculture, the story goes, and said, "Every morning when I come into the barnyard, two or three of my turkeys are lying on their backs on the ground, their feet up in the air, and they are stiff as a board. Can you tell me what is wrong with them?" Some time passed, and then came a letter from the Department of Agriculture. "Dear Sir," it read, "your turkeys are dead." It doesn't, you know, have to be Thanksgiving in order to:

ROAST TURKEY
WITH RICE-CHICKEN-LIVER STUFFING

[SERVES EIGHT TO TEN]

fat or butter
2 cups rice
giblets
½ pound chicken livers
3 large onions sliced
½ pound mushrooms, sliced

3 cloves garlic, sliced
2 tablespoons parsley, chopped
1 teaspoon thyme
salt and pepper
1 8- to 10-pound turkey

To make the stuffing, melt a little fat in a large pan and pour in the rice. Over medium heat, stir-fry the rice, browning it all. Now cook the rice according to directions. Wash and remove fat from giblets and cook them for at least 30 minutes. Wash and separate chicken livers and remove any fat or membranes. Slice—not too fine—the onions, mushrooms, and garlic, and sauté them all in hot fat. Now fry the chicken livers gently on all sides. By this time, the rice should be finished, so put it into a large bowl. Cut up the chicken livers, the giblets—removing gristle—and mix everything, including parsley, thyme, and salt and pepper to taste, into the rice. This should make approximately 8 to 10 cups of stuffing.

Wash and then dry the turkey carefully inside and out and rub some salt and pepper inside and out, also. There should be approximately 1 cup of stuffing for every pound of bird, but don't try to cram the stuffing down, or it may burst open during roasting. Put the stuffing in loosely; if there's any left over, put it in oven-proof dish covered with foil and bake it while the turkey roasts. Sew the turkey up, smear it heavily with melted fat, and put it, breast side up, on a shallow roasting pan with a rack.

Soak in fat a length of cheesecloth large enough to cover top and sides of turkey, cover the bird with it, and cook for 3 to 3½ hours in oven preheated to 350 degrees. (Allow 25 minutes to the pound for a turkey under 15 pounds, less time to the pound for bigger birds.) If the cloth becomes dry during first 2 hours, soak it with more melted fat. Turkeys have very little fat, and there's nothing more depressing than a dry turkey, but this process will make it nice and juicy. During last half hour of roasting, remove cheesecloth so the skin can become crisp.

The turkey is done when you can move the drumstick up and down easily and when the meat on the thickest part of the drumstick is soft when you press it. Don't carve it immediately on taking it out of the oven; let it rest for about 15 minutes. Somehow, it gets even juicier that way. Make a gravy with the pan drippings and give thanks.

This city fellow had made a pile, and so he moved to the country to be a gentleman farmer. This made his wife and his daughter pretty snobbish, sad to say, and one day the wife of a neighbor, a real farmer, asked the daughter about various aspects of the farm.

"And how are your turkeys?" the farmer's wife asked. "Are they breeding?" The daughter of the city fellow looked down her nose to the farmer's lady. "Of course," she said haughtily, "they could if they wanted to, but they don't have to, you know."

FRIED TURKEY

[THREE-QUARTERS TO ONE POUND PER SERVING]

Disjoint a turkey and cut into serving portions. Dredge with seasoned flour, brown in ½ inch of hot fat, on all sides. Cover pan tight, reduce heat and steam until the meatiest pieces are tender. For crisp skin, remove cover after the meatiest pieces are thoroughly cooked and fry pieces until they're as you like them.

an in this restaurant asked the waiter to bring him a nice turkey sandwich. "I'm sorry, sir," said the servitor, "but we are all out of turkey." The customer pondered the menu and then said, "Okay, then I'll have a chicken sandwich." The waiter sneered. "Don't be foolish," he said obsequiously. "If we had chicken, wouldn't I give you a turkey sandwich?" In his restaurant, John Bruno, the eminent horseman-restauranteur, serves with a special sauce:

TURKEY AND HAM

[SERVES ONE]

1 teaspoon English mustard	1 teaspoon lemon juice
¼ teaspoon salt	3 ounces heavy cream
¼ teaspoon pepper	2 thin slices baked ham
1 ounce Escoffier Sauce Diable	1 slice dry toast
	2 thin slices roast turkey

Mix together mustard, salt, pepper, Sauce Diable, and lemon juice. Bring it to a boil, add the cream, stir it all madly, lower the heat, and let it simmer for about 15 minutes. Put the ham on the toast, place the turkey slices over the ham, and pour the sauce all over it heedlessly. *Molto bene!*

Geese are probably the most misunderstood and, therefore, the most sadly neglected birds in America. Take, as a case in point, one of the more famous gentlemen cookery writers who once wrote: "Goose is a delicious, though not at all an economical bird. Geese are exceedingly fat . . . and the comparatively small amount of meat makes them rather expensive." Well. This is an open-and-shut case of libel on a noble bird. Pound for pound, a goose provides as much meat as any other bird, if not more—meat which is far and away more delicious than that carried about by any other barnyard creature. There are three in our family, and a 10-pound goose provides us with two hearty meals and several wonderful snacks.

It is true that a goose is fat, but since goose fat is far better than any other for many kinds of cooking, we regard the fatness of a goose as an added boon, rather than a handicap. (That cookery writer, by the way, is no sylph himself.) The trick is to roast the goose so it is beautifully juicy, but not fatty, and to save the fat rendered in cooking for later use. (We make enough geese each winter to give us a supply of goose fat for the whole year. You know, we have a friend named John Reidy who becomes angry every time we tell him we've "made" a goose. "Listen," he tells us grouchily, "God makes a goose—you cook it.")

ROAST GOOSE

[SERVES SIX TO EIGHT]

1 10-pound (approximately) goose	goose fat
	orange juice
10 cups stuffing	port wine

What we do with a goose of about 10 pounds is first remove all the visible fat. Then we wash and dry it, inside and out, and rub some salt on and in the goose. The giblets are washed and cleaned (see recipe for ROAST TURKEY, page 205) and the liver is set aside to be sautéed gently and eaten as an appetizer; it is much too good to use as part of the stuffing.

For the stuffing, we stick to the one we have in this book for roast turkey — really a highly over-rated bird and inferior by far to the brave goose. (Why, a turkey is such a macilent bird that you have to drench it in fat to make it edible.) This is a stuffing compounded of fried rice, chicken livers, mushrooms, onions, etc., and it will be found, as we have said under ROAST TURKEY. Indeed, everyone in our family likes this stuffing so much that we use it to stuff chickens, ducks, and almost anything else that will take a stuffing, including ourselves, because sometimes we just make the stuffing, all by itself, and make a meal of just that. (No one has ever described us as sylph-like, either.)

Anyway, after the goose is stuffed and trussed, we preheat the oven to 425 degrees. AND WE DO NOT PRICK THE SKIN. In a fairly deep pan (the dear bird sheds so much fat that you *need* a deep pan) we set the goose on its side. AND WE DO NOT PUT ANY HOT WATER IN THE PAN. (Everything in capital letters is contrary to the instructions given by most cookery writers, but *ish kabibble;* when it comes to cooking, we are fearless.) What we do put into the pan is a couple of spoonfuls of hot fat we got from rendering some of the goose's generosity with the stuff, so the creature won't get stuck to the pan.

Every 15 minutes, we look at the goose and drain off the fat, which we save, of course. At this temperature—425 degrees—a 10-pound goose should be done in approximately 2½ hours, not counting the time it is out of the oven for the double purposes of draining off the fat and turning the bird from one side to the other, which we do at the end of the first hour. For the last half-hour lay the the bird gently on its back, so the breast skin will get good and brown and deliciously crackly. Indeed, the skin of the goose will probably be the most sought-after part of the dear thing. We said a goose should be roasted 15 minutes to the pound at 425 degrees, didn't we? Well, you know, ovens are tricky devils, and no two behave in exactly the same way, we don't care what the manufacturers tell you. So if your goose seems to be browning too quickly, reduce the temperature to 400 or maybe even to 375 degrees. Anyway, in the last hour, the goose should be basted, lest it become too dry. Make a basting sauce of equal parts of goose fat, orange juice, and a good port wine and douse the bird generously with this mixture. When the bird is done, do not pour this into the clear, pure rendered fat. Put this basting sauce into a separate heat-proof container, for it, too, can be used as a fat in cookery, where an orangey-winey flavor is desirable, as on a duck, and especially on a raunchy old turkey.

A

nd who has not eaten *gansene griebernüsse* may not, as far as we're concerned, say that he has truly feasted.

GANSENE GRIEBERNÜSSE

hunks of fat from the goose	excess skin from neck of goose, cut into 2-inch squares
1 large onion, chopped	salt and pepper

Render the fat over medium heat, and throw away all the small pieces which won't melt down. Pour all but 3 tablespoons into a heat-proof container, let it cool, and refrigerate it. In the 3 tablespoons of fat, fry the chopped-up onion until it is well and truly browned, remove onion from pan, and set it aside. Pour off fat in pan, leaving only a thin film in it. Put in the cut-up neck skin of the goose. (It's easier to cut the skin with scissors than with a knife.) Over low heat, fry the skin, turning the pieces from time to time, occasionally pouring off excess fat, until skin becomes a dark golden-brown. It should be quite crisp, but don't be impatient, because it takes quite a while. Sprinkle with salt and pepper and stir it around. Now what you do is put the onions back into the pan and combine with the fried neck skin—and you know what you did? You made *gansene griebernüsse!* That's what you did! So put some on an unsalted cracker—and eat it! It's just as good, almost, when it's cold, so you can put it in the frig.

You know, sometimes we wish we'd never before eaten *gansene griebernüsse,* just so we could eat it for the first time! What a treat!

a man we know named Joe McCarthy, to whom we are indebted for many past favors, says he saw a notice in a newspaper out his way on Long Island that has all the husbands out there livid with rage, and all the wives filled with triumph, if not smugness. A man put a notice in the paper which said, approximately:

"I will be responsible for all obligations of my wife, Pauline V. During twenty years of marriage, she has given me great happiness, comfort, counsel, and six fine children. As we begin our twenty-first year, I am proud to assume any and all of her obligations."

Well, if your husband hasn't paid for an advertisement like that, maybe it's because you never made for him this delicious dish, which would melt a heart of stone:

SAUTÉED CHICKEN LIVERS

[SERVES FOUR TO SIX]

12 chicken livers
3 tablespoons onion, chopped
2 tablespoons butter
½ cup chicken stock

½ teaspoon Worcestershire sauce
salt and pepper to taste
dash of paprika

Cut chicken livers apart, wash thoroughly, and remove fat. Sauté onion until it is soft, add chicken livers, and sauté tenderly until they are brown. Add stock slowly, then Worcestershire, salt and pepper, and paprika. Don't overcook—chicken livers are delicate little things and must be nurtured carefully. Same goes for husbands, too.

On New Year's Eve we generally go to a nightclub where we take into our system much more of food and drink than it really requires, and we make prominent fools of ourselves; or else we do the same thing at the home of someone who immediately becomes a former friend. In other countries, however, they have really charming, quaint customs.

In Denmark, for instance, people save their broken crockery all year, and on New Year's Eve they throw it against the front door of someone they like and admire, and the people who have the most broken crockery slammed at them are considered the most popular people in town and they invite everybody in to eat:

BAKED GEHAKTE LEBER
(Baked Chopped Liver)

[SERVES SIX TO EIGHT]

2 pounds chicken, calf, or beef liver
1 small onion, minced
1¼ cups bread crumbs

3 eggs, beaten
2 tablespoons water (milk is better)
2 anchovy fillets, chopped

Grind or chop the liver fine after you've washed it and removed any membranes. Mix together all the ingredients. Preheat your oven to 350 degrees, grease a pan and pour everything into it; bake this for 1½ hours. Let it cool, refrigerate it, and when your friends come smashing crockery against your doorway at midnight, slice the baked liver thin and serve the slices on pumpernickel or rye bread.

Sebastian was riding in the dining car of a railroad train. When the train pulled into a station, a tall, powerful, angry-looking man strode into the dining car and marched down the aisle yelling in a loud voice, "LanFranco! LanFranco! LanFranco!"

Sebastian, who had just finished his meal, stood up and happened to be facing the angry man as he came back down the aisle between the tables, still yelling, "LanFranco!"

A polite, helpful little fellow, Sebastian, who wanted to be of assistance, said, "Sir . . ." And that's as far as he got when the angry man punched him in the nose, twice, and then ran down the aisle, out of the train, and away. Sebastian, who had just finished a delicious dinner of chicken livers and corn meal, called *polenta* in Italy, his father's native country, had been knocked to the floor of the dining car, his nose streaming blood. But his mingled expression of hurt and surprise was so comical that everyone in the car couldn't help but laugh at him. So Sebastian, being a nice fellow, laughed too.

A fellow passenger helped him to his feet and said, "But why are you laughing? That terrible man gave you your lumps." "Yes," replied Sebastian, "but the joke is on him; he gave the wrong man his lumps. My name is not LanFranco, it is Sebastian."

CHICKEN LIVERS AND CORNMEAL
(Polenta) [SERVES FOUR TO SIX]

1½ quarts of water	10 chicken livers, cut up
1 teaspoon salt	dash of pepper
3 cups cornmeal	1 bouillon cube (dissolved
¼ pound butter	in cup of water)
3 slices bacon, cooked	
and diced	

Bring water to boil, add salt. Pour in corn meal slowly, *stirring constantly,* or else the meal will be lumpy. Cook corn meal 30 minutes, stirring occasionally. While corn meal cooks, melt butter in saucepan, add bacon, chicken livers, and pepper. Sauté over low heat for 5 minutes. Add bouillon and cook for another 10 minutes. Taste and correct seasoning, if necessary. Drain corn meal in colander and pour into large serving dish. Place the chicken livers-bacon sauce over corn meal and serve. If you stir corn meal, unlike Sebastian, you won't get lumps.

Vegetables, Salads, Dressings, Potatoes and Even Some Fruits

This book salesman was touring through the New England states trying to peddle books on scientific farming and the poor slob wasn't getting anywhere at all. When he returned to his home office, he sadly told his boss about a typical New England farmer's reaction to books on scientific farming.

"They would look through one book after another, listen to my pitch," he said, "and then they would say, 'Nope.' Every book I showed them, no matter how hard my sell was, all they'd say was, 'Nope.' I told one fellow that if he would buy these books it would help him to farm twice as good as he was farming now. And you know what he said? He said, 'Young feller, I ain't farming half as good right now as I already know!' " Here are a bunch of vegetables raised by farmers who may or may not be scientific:

ROAST CORN

Strip down husks from ear of corn, but DO NOT tear husks off. Remove silk, melt 1 tablespoon butter for each ear of corn, and spread butter over ear (of corn, silly). Add salt and pepper to taste. Replace husks the way you found them, tie up ends with twine, and cook for half-hour two inches from firebed, turning the ears from time to time. Or, place the corn right on the coals if it is a medium fire, for 20 minutes, turning the ears several times. (Of course, you can use aluminum foil, and throw away the corn husks, if you want to take the easy way out.)

FRIED CUCUMBERS

[SERVES SIX TO EIGHT]

2 tablespoons butter
2 tablespoons onion,
    chopped
¼ cup water
4 large cucumbers, peeled
    and sliced
½ cup sour cream

1 egg yolk, beaten
2 tablespoons sugar
3 tablespoons vinegar
1½ teaspoons salt
⅛ teaspoon pepper
⅛ teaspoon paprika

Fry chopped onion until brown. Add water and sliced cucumbers. Cook until cucumbers are brown and water is absorbed. Mix sour cream, beaten egg yolk, sugar, vinegar, salt, pepper, and paprika. Pour over cucumbers in pan, cook at low heat until liquid boils.

EGGPLANT AND TOMATOES

[SERVES FOUR TO SIX]

1 eggplant
½ teaspoon salt

1 1-pound can tomatoes
    (mash them up good)
¼ teaspoon pepper

Peel eggplant and cut it into ½-inch cubes. In a pot cover it with water, bring it to a boil, add salt, cover pot, and simmer on low heat for about 20 minutes, or until the eggplant is tender. Taste it, that's how you'll know. When it is tender, drain it, and mix it with tomatoes and pepper. Pour it all into a buttered casserole, cover it, and bake for 20 minutes in oven preheated to 350 degrees. Delicious!

ESCALLOPED TOMATOES
(We can't figure out when a tomato is scalloped and when it is e-scalloped, can you?)

[SERVES SIX TO EIGHT]

2 cups bread crumbs
2½ cups whole, peeled
    tomatoes

2 tablespoons butter
salt, pepper, garlic powder
    (we told you we like
    garlic, didn't we?)

Get hold of a baking dish and grease it. Now sprinkle half those bread crumbs up there on the bottom of the greased dish. (On the INSIDE of the bottom, not the outside, you hear?) Throw the tomatoes right on top of those crumbs. Use as much seasoning as you like and don't let anybody tell you different. Just leave this stuff alone while you melt the butter and sauté the rest of those bread crumbs we told you about. Sprinkle this stuff on top of the tomatoes, and put the whole thing into an oven preheated to 350 degrees, for 30 minutes. Promise him anything but give him tomatoes.

BAKED TOMATOES

[SERVES FOUR TO EIGHT]

4 tomatoes
1 cup seasoned bread
    stuffing

2 tablespoons butter or
    margarine

Cut the tomatoes in half, circumferentially. (Listen, we're not going to have to tell you to wash the tomatoes first, are we? Not our readers, no siree. We might just as well tell you, "First, wash your hands." You'd find that insulting, wouldn't you?) Put the tomato halves into a baking pan and distribute bread stuffing on top of each half. Now put a little hunk of butter on top of each, and put the pan in 325-degree oven for 20 minutes.

WILTED LETTUCE

[SERVES FOUR TO FIVE]

1 head of lettuce	1 clove garlic, chopped
4 slices bacon, minced	¼ cup wine vinegar
1 onion, chopped	coarse pepper to taste

Break up the lettuce. Mince bacon and fry it until crisp, pouring off most of the fat and saving it for later use. Add the chopped onion and chopped garlic and fry until they are soft. Now add the vinegar, pour fat back into the pan, and when the liquid comes to a boil, pour everything over the lettuce, stir it all around, and serve immediately. This is wilted lettuce. You don't need salt for this, because the bacon has enough saltiness; let each person at table add pepper according to taste. Pepper mills add class, don't you think?

All over the Near and Middle East they like as an accompaniment to meat dishes, something like:

LEEKY OLIVES

[SERVES SIX TO EIGHT]

1 pound leeks, chopped	3½ tablespoons tomato paste
1 cup green olives (pitless)	2 teaspoons salt
1 tablespoon olive or salad oil	¼ teaspoon pepper
2 tablespoons flour	1½ tablespoons lemon juice
1½ cups water	

Chop up the leeks, put them in a saucepan. Now chop the olives. Now mix together all the remaining ingredients and add the chopped olives. Pour everything into the saucepan on top of the chopped leeks, stir it all around wildly. Bring it to a boil, reduce the heat and simmer, covered, for 20 minutes, stirring the mixture occasionally. Serve it hot with hamburgers or any other kind of meat. Will you be aromatic!

SPANISH CAULIFLOWER

[SERVES FOUR TO SIX]

1 cauliflower	1 medium onion, chopped
2 cups water	1 clove garlic, minced
3 teaspoons salt	2 tablespoons vinegar
4 tablespoons olive oil	¼ teaspoon pepper

Separate the cauliflower flowerets, place in saucepan with the water and 2 teaspoons of the salt, and boil for 10 minutes. Drain. In a separate saucepan, heat the oil and sauté the onion and garlic, stirring all the while, until onion is slightly browned. Now add the cauliflower, vinegar, pepper, and the rest of the salt and cook over low, low heat for 10 minutes.

The elderly business man opened the door to the apartment in which the beautiful but smart young showgirl lived—you see, he had his own key, because he was paying the rent—and then he sat, or, rather, slumped, on the mink-covered sofa.

"What's the matter, honey?" asked the beautiful young girl. "Oh woe is me," said the business man, "for I have lost all my money and I am bankrupt." The little dear smiled affectionately. "Oh, that doesn't matter, because I will always love you,"

she said, "even if I never, never see you again."
You will love this:

ASPARAGUS TART

½ cup Parmesan cheese, grated
4 slices bacon, cooked and crumbled
2 tablespoons butter or margarine
¼ cup parsley, chopped
1½ cups asparagus, cooked and sliced

1½ teaspoons salt
dash of pepper
1 tablespoon cider vinegar
2 eggs, slightly beaten
1 cup light cream
2 tablespoons onion, grated
1 9-inch pie shell, unbaked and chilled

Sprinkle cheese and bacon into pie shell. (Of course, you've cooked and drained the bacon, haven't you?) Preheat your oven to 350 degrees. In a medium skillet, melt the butter or margarine and add the parsley and the asparagus, which should be sliced in diagonal pieces. Cook for 5 minutes, remove from heat, add all the remaining ingredients which you have mixed together, and pour it all into the pie shell. Bake it until the filling is firm and the crust is golden.

The fresh asparagus season runs from February to June, but asparagus can be bought all year 'round in jars, tins, or in frozen packs. You should allow 2 pounds for 4 servings. Fresh asparagus should be cooked not more than 15 minutes. With the other kinds, just follow directions on jar, can, or package. Asparagus is great with almost everything —fish, meat of any kind, and fowl of any kind.

CREAMED ONION PIE

[SERVES FOUR]

2 cups fluffy mashed potatoes
2 tablespoons butter, melted
1½ tablespoons flour
1 cup milk

½ teaspoon salt
⅛ teaspoon pepper
1 cup small white onions, cooked
dash of paprika

Put thin layer of mashed potatoes in 9-inch pie

plate. Melt butter, stir in flour, add milk gradually, add seasoning and you'll have what is called by some "cream sauce." Then pour sauce on top of potatoes which are on bottom of pie plate, place the small cooked onions artistically into the sauce, top with rest of mashed potatoes, and on top of it all, delicately sprinkle the paprika. Bake for 25 minutes in oven preheated to 375 degrees. We like onions, and you?

ONION-STRING BEAN SALAD

[SERVES FOUR TO SIX]

1 package frozen string beans	1 tablespoon parsley, minced
2 cucumbers, sliced	1 teaspoon garlic salt
1 large or 2 small onions, chopped	4 lettuce leaves

Cook the string beans, drain and then chill them. Mix everything together and pile it on the lettuce leaves. Some people like French dressing with this. Okay, you like French dressing, who's going to .stop you.

A friend of ours who had gone to the Garrison Health Club to lose weight tells us that some men go there to gain, and that the sight of the weight-gainers plying their knives and forks on choice viands often saddens the fatties. On his way to his own seat in the dining room, our fat friend told us that he passed by one of the skinnies, who had before him an enormous charcoal-grilled steak that must have weighed a pound and a half. "You're not going to eat that all alone?" he asked the skinny, who grinned smugly. "Oh, no," said skinny with a repulsive chuckle, "not alone. With the steak I'm going to have:

HASH-BROWNED POTATOES WITH ONIONS

[SERVES SIX TO EIGHT]

½ cup butter or fat or margarine

2 medium onions, sliced

8 large raw potatoes, peeled and cubed

1 cup water

Sauté the onions until they are soft but not brown. Then toss in the potatoes and brown them. Pour the water into pan, cover it tightly, and simmer for 15 minutes over low heat. Now uncover the pan and continue cooking and stirring potatoes and onions until all the liquid is absorbed.

We know a lady (actually, she's not a lady at all; and she's not very nice, really) who is proud of the fact that she is a tyrant to her husband, a meek little slob who, all of his friends have long suspected, never did have all of his buttons. Or his marbles, either. Anyway, we were visting them one day when she decided to prove to us how thoroughly she had mastered this poor little man.

"Herman," she said, "get under the table." (Did we forget to say that we were having dinner at their house?) Herman meekly got under the table. We are sorry to say that we giggled. Not from amusement, believe us, pray do, but from embarrassment. "Come out from under the table," commanded this awful woman. And to the amazement of all of us, and even probably to himself, Herman rebelled.

"I WILL NOT," he roared. "I'LL SHOW YOU WHO IS THE BOSS IN THIS HOUSE!" And sure enough, there he stayed, under the table, while we all made believe he wasn't there and ate this delicious dish, for though this woman is a terrible wife to Herman, she does feed him well:

EGYPTIAN BEANS

[SERVES FOUR TO FIVE]

1½ cups dried white beans	½ cup olive oil
3 scallions, cut thin	¼ cup lemon juice
1 large cucumber, peeled and sliced thin	2 cloves garlic, minced
	2 teaspoons salt

Wash beans, cover with water, and soak overnight. Drain, cover with fresh water. Cook about 2 hours, until skins on beans are split. Drain and allow to cool. Put beans in a bowl, add everything else, stir it up, and chill for several hours. This makes a fine accompaniment to any meat dish. Poor Herman. Wonder if he ever got out from under that table.

A low fellow we know had the misfortune to sit next to a lady who is a prominent East Side bore, all the time talking about her distinguished ancestors. So he, being a prominent West Side boor, countered by telling her funny stories about his disreputable relatives, which didn't amuse her one bit.

"I always say," she said frostily, "that breeding is everything." The fellow laughed raucously. "There you go exaggerating again!" he cried. "It is *not* everything." He paused for a moment and added, "But I will admit that it can be fun." It is great fun to eat:

EGGPLANT PARMESAN

[SERVES FOUR]

2 cloves garlic, minced
½ cup olive oil
1 1-pound can peeled tomatoes
1 6-ounce can tomato paste
1 large or 2 small eggplants

salt and pepper to taste
2 cups bread crumbs
½ cup Parmesan cheese, grated
½ pound Mozzarella cheese

Brown the minced garlic in 2 tablespoons of the oil, then add the tomatoes and tomato paste, and simmer for 20 minutes. Meanwhile, peel the eggplant, slice into ½-inch pieces, and fry them in the rest of the oil until they are soft and browned all over. Sprinkle the eggplant with salt and pepper and remove from the pan. Now mix together the bread crumbs and Parmesan cheese. Put a layer of fried eggplant in a baking dish (you know how directions keep saying 'put . . . in bottom of baking dish'? Wonder why?), pour on some of the bread crumb-cheese mixture, then some of the tomato sauce, and keep making alternate layers until you've used everything up. Slice the Mozzarella cheese about ⅓ of an inch thick and cover the top layer with this. Bake it in a 350-degree oven until the Mozzarella melts. About 10 minutes. This is a nice lunch dish for four people.

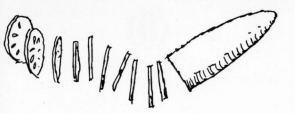

CUCUMBER SALAD

[SERVES FIVE TO SIX]

4 cucumbers
2 cloves garlic (okay,
    optional, but we
    keep telling you
    garlic is lovely)
2 tablespoons lemon juice

1 teaspoon salt
2 cups sour cream
1 teaspoon dill, chopped
2 tablespoons olive oil
1 tablespoon parsley,
    chopped

Peel the cucumbers and cut them in very thin slices. (We happen to like cucumber peel, but it sure takes all kinds, doesn't it?) Squeeze the garlic in a press and put the lovely stuff into the lemon juice. You did this in a cup, didn't you? Well, put the sliced cukes into a bowl and sprinkle them with the salt we told you about. Now take another bowl and put into it the sour cream, the dill, and the garlicked lemon juice. Stir it around until the stuff is smooth. Now, spill it all over the cukes, and stir THEM around. At this juncture, you dump the olive oil all over everything, stir, and sprinkle the chopped parsley over all. Put it in the refrigerator. Eat it later.

ANOTHER ONE

[SERVES FIVE TO SIX]

4 cucumbers, peeled,
    sliced thin
2½ teaspoons salt
3 scallions

½ cup cider vinegar
3 tablespoons cold water
½ teaspoon sugar
¼ teaspoon pepper

Sprinkle the cucumber slices with salt and let them stand for ½ hour. Slice the scallions, using some of the tops, mix everything up thoroughly, and refrigerate it for hours before serving.

ONION-TOMATO SALAD

[SERVES FIVE TO SIX]

2 onions
5 tomatoes
1 tablespoon salt

1 teaspoon oregano
¼ cup olive oil
pepper

Slice the onions thin, cube the tomatoes. Mix everything together, refrigerate it, and serve on crisp leaves of lettuce.

NUTTY POTATO SALAD

[SERVES EIGHT TO TEN]

6 potatoes, peeled, boiled
    and cubed
1 tablespoon onion,
    grated
1 stalk celery, chopped
1 tablespoon salt

3 tablespoons olive oil
1 cup chopped Brazil nuts
1 hard-boiled egg,
    sliced
lettuce

Mix up everything except the sliced egg and the lettuce. Now put the mixture on a bed of lettuce and garnish it with sliced egg. You can add black or green pitted olives or slices of pickle to the garnish. Who's going to stop you?

TROPICAL SALAD

[SERVES EIGHT TO TEN]

½ head of cabbage
1 cucumber, pared
1 green pepper
6 onions
6 radishes
1 large avocado, peeled

½ cup olive oil
¼ cup vinegar
¼ teaspoon lime juice
½ teaspoon salt
⅛ teaspoon pepper
1 tablespoon sugar

Shred the cabbage and slice all the vegetables very thin. (Listen, we don't have to tell you to peel an onion and throw the skin away, do we?) Now mix all the vegetables together. Mix all the other ingredients separately, then dump all the liquid stuff into the vegetables and agitate them severely.

POTATO SALAD

[SERVES FOUR TO SIX]

2½ pounds potatoes
1 egg yolk
2 tablespoons vinegar
½ cup olive oil

1 large onion, chopped
2 teaspoons salt
¼ teaspoon pepper

Put the potatoes in boiling water for about 20 minutes, or until they are cooked thoroughly but not mushy. Drain, peel, and cube them. Beat up the egg yolk with the vinegar and add the olive oil, beating steadily. Now pour this mixture over the cubed potatoes, and add the chopped onion, salt, and pepper. Toss it around wildly in a saucepan over a low heat. Some like it cold; we like it hot, summer or winter.

Ash Wednesday is the beginning of Lent, but before that penitential period comes the Carnival season, which is observed in many different ways in different parts of the world. "*Carnevale,*" of course, means, "Goodbye, meat," and this is a period of feasting and drinking. Lots of each.

The Monday before Lent in England is called "Collop Monday," and in the old days housewives used to serve up all the dried and salted meats, or collops, in the house. In Denmark, the same day is called *Fastelaven,* and children wake up early in the morning, take twigs, go into the bedroom of their parents, and beat them, shouting, "*Fastenlavensboller!*" which means, "Lenten buns." And the punishment of the parents stops only when the children are given the buns.

In Rio de Janeiro, people get loaded and squirt ether at each other. In Syria, the Thursday before Lent is known as "Drunkard's Thursday," because that's when they drink the most and when they roast a sheep and stuff grape leaves with all kinds of stuff that's good to eat. Here's how to stuff:

STUFFED GRAPEVINE LEAVES

[SERVES FIVE TO SEVEN]

¼ cup rice, half-cooked
1 tablespoon onion, chopped
1 tablespoon seedless raisins
1 tablespoon pine nuts, or blanched, slivered almonds

2 tablespoons olive oil
15 grapevine leaves (or lettuce, if you can't get vine leaves)
1 cup water, boiling

While the rice is being half-cooked, fry the onions, raisins, and pine nuts in hot oil, until the onion is slightly browned. Boil the vine leaves for 5 minutes and drain them. Drain the rice when it is half-cooked and mix into it the fried onion, raisins, and nuts. Spread the vine leaves out on a board or large plate, put a teaspoon of the rice mixture on each leaf. Now get a large pot ready and line it with a large piece of aluminum foil, so edges stick out over the top. (You'll see why, later; just be patient.)

Now fold over each leaf and put them all into the pot, folded sides down. Add one cup of boiling water, and put a heavy plate right into the pot, over the folded-up vine leaves—so they won't move around—cover the pot and let it simmer over low heat for 30 to 40 minutes, or until all the water is gone. Now lift out the foil, vine leaves, plate, and all. Drain the leaves, cool, and then refrigerate them for a couple of hours. Serve 2 or 3 to each person, with a lemon slice. After you get the hang of this, try varying the stuffing with chick peas, maybe pistachio nuts, or mushrooms. Whatever you like. And, if you can't get grapevine leaves—many markets around town have them—use lettuce leaves. Almost as good.

BAKED STRING BEANS

[SERVES FIVE TO SIX]

2 boxes frozen string
    beans

1 can cream soup (what-
    ever you prefer)

Cook the string beans, drain them, put them in a casserole, add the can of soup, and stir. Cover the casserole and bake it for 30 minutes in oven pre-heated to 350 degrees.

SPINACH DUMPLINGS

[SERVES THREE TO FOUR]

1 package frozen spinach,
    cooked and chopped
salt and pepper to taste
dash of nutmeg

2 tablespoons Parmesan
    cheese
1 egg, beaten
¼ cup flour

Mix the spinach with salt, pepper, cheese, and nutmeg. Add the egg and then the flour to the spinach. Now shape mixture into balls and drop them into a stew for 15 minutes, before the stew is done.

CHEESY ASPARAGUS

[SERVES THREE TO FOUR]

1 1-pound can asparagus
2 tablespoons butter

salt and pepper to taste
Parmesan cheese, grated

Put the asparagus on a baking sheet, put dots of butter on the spears, sprinkle them with salt and pepper, and pour grated cheese over all with a lavish hand. Put the asparagus-loaded baking sheet in the broiler 4 inches from the heat and broil until the cheese is melted. About 4 minutes.

One of the mental patients stood by and watched the farmer unload his truckload of zucchini, tomatoes, and mushrooms. He sidled closer to the farmer. "You know," he said with a revoltingly ingratiating smile, "I used to be a farmer myself." The farmer, slightly nervous, said, "Zat so?"

"Yes," said the patient. "Say, did you ever try being nuts?" The farmer shuddered. "No," he said. "Well," said the patient, "you ought to try it sometime. Sure beats farming." Did you ever have:

STUFFED TOMATO?

[SERVES EIGHT]

8 tomatoes
8 ounces (2 cups)
    blue cheese,
    crumbled
4 cups rice, cooked

4 scallions (including
    tops), chopped
6 tablespoons oil
2 tablespoons lemon juice
¼ teaspoon black pepper

Slice off tomato tops, scoop out the pulp, and mash it up. Drain the mashed pulp, mix it up with all of the other ingredients, and stuff all into the tomato shells. Put the stuffed tomatoes in a shallow pan and in an oven preheated to 350 degrees, bake them for 15 minutes. (If you like, serve this cold. Just omit the baking.) Here's a:

MUSHROOM SOUFFLÉ

[SERVES FOUR TO SIX]

1 cup (4 ounces)
    blue cheese,
    crumbled

16-24 large mushrooms
4 eggs, separated
1 tablespoon lemon juice

Mash the cheese, chop up the stems of the mushrooms very fine, and then mix them together. Beat the egg yolks until yellow and fold into the cheese-mushroom mixture. Now beat the whites until stiff. Beat the lemon juice slowly into the whites and fold all this into the cheese mixture. Fill the mushroom caps with the mixture and bake them at 400 degrees in a shallow, greased pan for 10 minutes, or until the filling is puffed up, and browned.

Some other time use blue cheese in a:

STUFFED SQUASH

[SERVES THREE TO FOUR]

1 large zucchini or yellow summer squash (or two small squashes; and don't tell us that the plural of squash is squash)

¼ cup butter
½ cup onion, chopped
4 cups soft bread cubes
1 cup blue cheese, crumbled
½ teaspoon oregano

Cut the top off the zucchini or squash and scoop out the flesh. Leave a shell about ¼ inch thick. Now chop up the flesh and cook it in the butter until soft. Add to mixture the bread, onion, cheese, and oregano. Stuff all into the shell. Put a little water in a baking pan, arrange the stuffed vegetables on it, and bake for about 30 minutes, or until the vegetables are tender and the stuffing brown, in an oven preheated to 350 degrees.

In the year 1381 on November 12th, the Count of Cleves gathered a group of his friends and founded "The Brotherhood of Fools." The purpose of the organization was to improve the morals of the people of that time. The Count decided to call the organization "Brotherhood of Fools" because he knew that only fools would try to dissuade those people from boozing, gambling, and conspicuous lewdness. Sad, isn't it?

We know a couple of fools who went out for a walk. One of them had an umbrella. Suddenly, it began to rain. "Quick," said the second fool, "open your umbrella." "Won't do any good," the first replied. "Why not?" "Because," the umbrella-bearer replied, "it's full of holes." The second fool wanted to know why he had brought along the useless umbrella. "Well," said the first, "you see, I didn't think it would rain." You will be far from foolish if you make:

FISHY POTATOES

[SERVES SIX]

6 baking potatoes
1 cup milk
4 tablespoons butter
½ teaspoon salt
¼ teaspoon pepper

2 cups canned salmon,
    tuna, or other fish,
    drained and flaked
paprika

Half-bake the potatoes. (You know how good baked-potato skins are, don't you? And how nutritious? So we don't have to tell you to scrub them first, do we?) Okay. You get them half-baked? Let them cool, so you can handle them, slit the largest end, and scoop out the insides. Mix with the milk until smooth. Mix in the butter, salt, and pepper and then mix in with this the fish which you have flaked. Stuff this mixture back into the potato skins, sprinkle the top with paprika, and bake until done.

GARBANZOS (chick peas)

[SERVES FOUR]

½ cup olive oil
1 onion, chopped
2 cloves garlic, chopped

1 1-pound can garbanzos
1½ quarts water
salt and pepper to taste

In a good-sized pot heat the oil and sauté the onion and garlic until they are soft. Add everything else and cook over low heat—just until *garbanzos* are hot. Drain and serve hot. A nice change from potatoes, rice, etc.

The city man who was spending the summer in the country got pretty friendly with one of the farmers in the area, who took him around the place, showing him the barn, the fields, and the equipment he used. It was a miserable place. The barn looked as though it would collapse any minute, the fields were full of rocks and tree stumps, and the farm equipment was all outmoded and rusty and seemed utterly useless.

The city man couldn't restrain himself. "My goodness," he cried, "this is terrible! I just can't see how you get along here! How can you possibly make a go of it on a place like this?" The farmer yawned. "Aw, now, things ain't as bad as you think. Why, I don't own this miserable farm!" Things will be very good, indeed, if you try some of these vegetable and salad dressing recipes

Did we tell you the pathetic story of an expatriate Frenchman we know named J. Lachaud, now living in New York, whose eyes fill with tears whenever he or anyone else mentions "Paris"? "I had to leave Paris," he once whined, "because French is such a beautiful language.

"You see, every time I heard a train departure announced, I would be so thrilled I wanted to enlist in the Foreign Legion." Everyone will want to stay home, if you give them:

BAKED MUSHROOM CASSEROLE

[SERVES THREE]

1 large onion, chopped (don't get discouraged if you don't have a large one in the house, just use a couple of small ones)
¼ cup butter
2 eggs
½ cup light cream
4 4-ounce cans mushrooms, sliced

¾ cup mushroom liquid
½ teaspoon salt
¼ teaspoon coarse-ground black pepper
1 cup saltine cracker crumbs (this will take about 25 finely crumbled ones)
4 ounces pasteurized process cheese spread, cubed

Sauté the onion in the butter and then mix in a large bowl all of the other ingredients.

Now stir into this mixture the sautéed onion. Get hold of a 1½-quart oven-proof dish, grease it well, and pour everything into it, pell mell, willy nilly. Now cover the dish and bake the casserole in the oven, which has been preheated to 350 degrees, for 30 minutes. After 30 minutes, take the cover off the dish and put the casserole back into the oven and continue baking for 30 minutes.

This bride called her mother long-distance to complain about the cookbook she had been given as a wedding present by one of her disappointed suitors. "He must have given it to me out of spite," she wailed long distance, "because the instructions in it are all wrong." When her mother asked what had happened, the silly girl said, "I was trying to make a sauce, and the book says to bring it to a boil, and then beat it for 15 minutes." So what happened? the mother wanted to know.

"Well," the dopey bride whined, "I beat it for 15 minutes, like the book says, but when I came back, it was all burned up." A young St. Louis woman we know named Beulah Schacht, who travels all over the country eating well and having fun, gave us this recipe for what she calls, for some odd reason:

WOOD POTATOES

[SERVES FOUR TO SIX]

6 large potatoes	1 medium onion, chopped
8 slices processed cheese	fine
salt and pepper to taste	1 tablespoon flour
2 tablespoons butter or	milk
margarine	paprika

Peel and slice potatoes and boil until tender but not mushy. Drain the potatoes. Grease a casserole, put in half the potatoes, and cover them with 4 cheese slices. Add salt and pepper. Now put the other half of potatoes on top of cheese and add remaining cheese slices. Melt one tablespoon butter or margarine and sauté the chopped onion. Add to onion flour and enough milk to make a thin cream sauce, stirring constantly as the stuff cooks, until it is smooth. Pour the cream sauce into casserole, sprinkle with paprika, cover, and bake for about 1 hour, or until it is browned on top in oven preheated to 350 degrees.

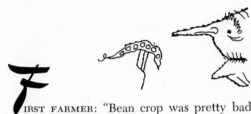

FIRST FARMER: "Bean crop was pretty bad this year."

SECOND FARMER: "Yup. But not so bad as back in '36. Why, I remember back then, the bean crop was so incredibly bad my old grandpa, at just one dinner, ate nineteen acres of string beans."

Your family will eat real good if you give them our:

AUNT MIL'S HUNGARIAN STRING BEANS

[SERVES FOUR TO SIX]

1 medium onion, quartered and sliced thin
1½ cups water
1 pound string beans, cut in 1-inch lengths
juice of ½ lemon
2 medium tomatoes, peeled and sliced thin

½ green pepper, cut into small strips
1 teaspoon salt
1 scant tablespoon sugar
dash of garlic powder (you can go heavier on garlic powder if you like)
1 tablespoon corn oil

Simmer onion in the water for 15 minutes. Add all the other ingredients, cover pan, and cook slowly for 30 minutes, or until beans are tender. It was the French who were the first Europeans—the Chinese knew the secret long before that—to learn that vegetables taste much better and retain more of their goodness with shorter cooking time. So the French figured that if they cut a string bean in half, lengthwise, the cooking time could be reduced drastically. And they were right! This is a good accompaniment to meat or fish.

TOMATO DRESSING

[ABOUT ONE AND ONE-HALF CUPS]

2 slices white bread	1½ teaspoons salt
1 8-ounce can tomato sauce	¼ teaspoon pepper
	¼ cup cider vinegar
1 clove garlic, mashed	½ teaspoon paprika
⅓ cup salad oil	

Cut crusts off bread and throw them away. Crumble the bread and mix everything up wildly. If you have a blender, all you do is put everything into the container and run it at high speed for 45 seconds. Chill it and shake well before using.

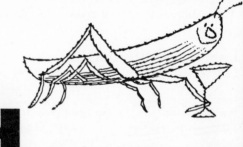

Harry Lee, the well known bartender and wit, was astonished one day recently when he saw a grasshopper hop into his restaurant and hop up onto the bar. "A grasshopper on Second Avenue!" Harry exclaimed quietly, so as not to startle his skittish clientele. "Will wonders never cease?" And to the grasshopper, he said, "Young fellow, do you know we sometimes serve a drink which is named after you?"

Now it was the grasshopper's turn to be startled. "You mean," he exclaimed shrilly (for that is how grasshoppers speak), "that you serve a drink named

Max?" We don't think there are any grasshoppers in Hawaii, but in the Islands this is how they make:

CHICKEN SALAD

[SERVES THREE TO FOUR]

2½ tablespoons lemon juice
⅛ teaspoon salt
2½ tablespoons salad oil
2½ cups chicken, cooked and cut up in ½-inch squares

1 14-ounce can pineapple pieces, drained
1 cup celery, cut in ½-inch pieces
5 tablespoons mayonnaise
lettuce
½ cup coconut, flaked

Stir up lemon juice, salt, and salad oil and then toss in the chicken, pineapple, and celery, and stir around well. Put in the refrigerator for a couple of hours, stirring occasionally. Just before serving, add mayonnaise, stir everything up like anything, spread it all out on some lettuce and sprinkle the coconut over all. If you put whipped cream on this, just don't invite us, that's all.

It was a very dull dinner party, and it was made more irksome for the young fellow because the girl next to him was nasty. So he picked up the dish of vegetables and dumped them on her head. "How dare you drop that broccoli all over me?" she shrieked. "Broccoli?" he said, horrified. "I thought it was spinach!" On the broccoli was:

SAUCE OLIVEDAISE

[ABOUT ONE AND ONE-HALF CUPS]

2 tablespoons butter
⅓ cup stuffed green olives
1 cup mayonnaise
2 to 4 tablespoons lemon juice, depending on how tart you like food

dash of Worcestershire sauce

Soften butter, but do not melt it. Slice the olives and mix all the ingredients together. This makes less than two cups of sauce. This is excellent sauce, hot or cold. If you want it hot, just before serving heat the sauce over low heat, stirring frequently. But it is just as good cold, and when it's served cold on hot vegetables, it is a wonderful taste sensation.

On asparagus or artichokes, this olivedaise sauce makes a festive dish worthy of being featured at any dinner. But it makes even such ordinary, commonplace vegetables as carrots, broccoli, cauliflower, or Brussels sprouts appealing even to the meat-and-potatoes set, which generally shuns vegetables. It's an easy sauce to stir up at the last minute, but you can make up a batch in advance and store it in the refrigerator.

ROQUEFORT CHEESE DRESSING

[ABOUT ONE CUP]

¼ pound Roquefort cheese
5 tablespoons cream
4 tablespoons lemon juice
dash of Worcestershire sauce
⅛ teaspoon salt
¼ teaspoon paprika

Rub the cheese through a sieve, mix it gradually first with the cream, then with the lemon juice. When you've got it completely agitated, add the salt, Worcestershire sauce, and the paprika.

Man in our office came back from his vacation—his name is Fred Dickinson, if you have to know—and somebody asked him if he'd had fun and what did he do. "Well," said Fred, who is a chronic whiner, "there wasn't much for me to do, but my wife and three daughters certainly had a busy time dressing for breakfast, lunch, and dinner." Here's a salad dressing which a friend of ours calls:

A KIND OF CAESAR SALAD DRESSING

[ONE AND ONE-HALF CUPS]

1 tablespoon prepared mustard
½ teaspoon salt
¼ teaspoon pepper
1 clove garlic, crushed
5 ounces cider vinegar
dash of Worcestershire sauce

1 cup olive oil or salad oil
1 raw egg
4 anchovy fillets, chopped
green vegetables for 6 people
1 tablespoon Parmesan cheese, grated
croutons (about 20)

Whip the first 6 ingredients together unmercifully, then slowly add the olive oil, beating, beating, beating, all the time. When it becomes slightly thickened, stir in the raw egg and then sprinkle it all with the chopped anchovies. Put your green vegetables in a large bowl, pour some of the mixture over it all, add the cheese and the croutons, and toss it with much abandon. Use as much of this dressing as you like, but if there's any left over, don't worry. Store it in the frig because it keeps real well. This can be a wonderful complete lunch.

At the Garrison Health Club on the Hudson River, where fat and thin men (but all pretty well-to-do, skinny or fat) go to have their problems in weight corrected, two new members met in the swimming pool. "Ho-ho-ho," ho-hoed the fat one, "from the looks of you, people would say there was a famine on here." The other man, who was skinny, sneered. "Yes," he snarled, "and from the looks of you, they'd say you had caused it."

Elsa Prunty, the dietician there who helps see to it that the fatties lose and the skinnies gain, says that exercise is just as important as diet in gaining or losing weight, and that even a low-calorie diet must be tasty or no one will stick with it for very long. Here is a salad dressing, equally popular with fat and thin, which she calls:

PARISIENNE DRESSING

[ABOUT TWO CUPS]

1 cup olive oil
½ cup tarragon vinegar
1 teaspoon salt
½ teaspoon celery salt
½ teaspoon sugar
¼ teaspoon dry mustard
¼ teaspoon paprika
¼ teaspoon pepper
1 tablespoon Worcestershire sauce
¼ cup catsup

¼ teaspoon onion juice
1 whole clove garlic
1 tablespoon Bermuda onion, chopped
2 tablespoons parsley, chopped
1 tablespoon pimiento, chopped
1 tablespoon green pepper, chopped

All these ingredients are placed in a jar that can be tightly capped and kept in refrigerator. It must be shaken well before each use. We recommend it highly for mixed green salads, and though it may seem chock full of calories, only a few dashes on a salad makes it very appetizing, even to men who are salad-shy. In another version, Elsa Prunty makes:

HAWAIIAN DRESSING

[ABOUT TWO CUPS]

1 cup olive oil
¼ teaspoon celery salt
½ teaspoon sugar
⅛ cup catsup
1 whole clove garlic
1 tablespoon parsley, chopped

1 tablespoon pimiento, chopped
1 tablespoon green pepper, chopped
¼ cup lemon juice
¼ cup pineapple juice
¼ cup orange juice
¼ cup apple juice

This dressing is good for fruit salads with lettuce and cottage cheese.

er young daughter wondered why Shelley Winters was rushing through dinner at her home, after she had done a matinee performance one Saturday recently. "I've got to go back to the theater," Shelley explained, "because I have another show to do tonight."

The child looked puzzled. "But you did one this afternoon," she said. "Yes," said Shelley, "but I've got to do it over again tonight." The child looked even more puzzled. "Why?" she asked. "Did you do something wrong?"

You won't be doing anything wrong if you give your family these dishes, built on fruits and melons in season:

RINGAROUND SALAD

[SERVES TWELVE]

1 envelope gelatin (plain)	6 3-ounce packages cream cheese
2 cups milk	4 ounces Roquefort or blue cheese
½ teaspoon salt	
½ teaspoon onion, grated	12 cantaloupe slices
¼ teaspoon Worcestershire sauce	12 pineapple slices
	assorted fresh fruit

Soak gelatin in ½ cup milk; dissolve in rest of milk, which you've brought to the boiling point. Add salt, onion, and Worcestershire sauce. Now chill it all until it is slightly thick. Blend softened cheeses and fold gelatin mixture into the cheeses. Agitate madly and put the stuff into 2- or 3-ounce soufflé cups. Refrigerate until firm. Place the cantaloupe slices on a tray with a pineapple slice on each one. Unmold the cheese salad and put in center of fruit slices. With this, a selection of available fruits goes great.

Cantaloupes, casabas, and cranshaws—all melons in season are cheap. So if you serve the delicious-looking and-tasting stuff above, you'll be as wise as this lady we heard about who was delighted to hear from her husband that their bank had returned the check with which she had paid for a new fur coat. "Oh, goodie," she cried, "now I can buy a new suite of furniture with the same check!" Here's a fruity dessert which is healthy, wise, and inexpensive:

HONEY MELON BOWL

[SERVES EIGHT TO TEN]

1 cup honey	½ cup lemon juice
⅔ cup water	1 teaspoon orange peel, grated
3 cardamom seeds	
⅔ cup orange juice	½ cup sherry
2 tablespoons chopped mint	large bowl of assorted melon balls

Mix honey and water (oil and water don't mix, but if you warm the water, it will mix with honey). Then peel the cardamom seeds and crush them without pity with a rolling pin or smash them with a blunt instrument. Put crushed seeds into honey, simmer for about 5 minutes, and pour over the chopped mint. Pour in the orange and lemon juice, the orange peel, and the wine. (If you've got to hit the sherry, leave that ½ cup alone—take a sip from the bottle.) Get a large bowl, make balls out of cantaloupe, watermelon, cranshaw, or whatever melons are in your market, and pour the strained syrup over all. Put it all into the refrigerator until it's all icy cold and frosty. Mint looks nice as a garnish. (Some day, if you really want to know, we'll tell you how to use mint in a julep. Real tasty, too.)

Eggs and Cheese Dishes

a social-climbing chiropodist named Richard (Dick the Driver) Welsh was in bed at home one night when his wife nudged him. "Dick," she whispered, "I hear a noise downstairs; I fear there are burglars in our home." Dick, who had his head under the covers, for he also had heard the noise, whispered back, "Yes, dear, I have heard the noise also, and I think you are right in assuming it is being made by burglarious folk!"

His wife nudged him again, harder. "So get up!" she whispered fiercely. "Aren't you going to go downstairs and do something about it?" Dick the Driver whimpered. "Oh, no," he cried softly, "I couldn't go downstairs, for I would die of embarrassment to face those robbers, for there isn't a thing in the house worth stealing!"

After the noises had stopped, Dick waited until he was certain the burglars had left, and then he went downstairs and cooked himself this delicious midnight feast—it would be good for dinner or lunch as well—to quieten his badly shattered nerves:

BEL PAESE CHEESE OMELET WITH RED SALMON CAVIAR

[SERVES TWO]

2 eggs, beaten
¼ cup milk
⅛ teaspoon pepper (we use no salt, for salmon caviar is quite salty, see?)
3 tablespoons butter
1 small onion, chopped

⅛ pound Bel Paese cheese (or any other kind of cheese, but Bel Paese is best)
1 tablespoon red salmon caviar
1 tablespoon parsley, chopped (celery flakes are fine, too)

Beat the eggs viciously with the milk, pepper, and parsley. Hot up 1 tablespoon of butter and fry the chopped onion until it is soft, but don't let butter get brown. Take onion out of pan and mix it up thoroughly into the egg mixture. Melt remaining butter in the pan, pour in egg mixture and cook it over low heat and covered until eggs are set on bottom. When eggs are set, cut pieces of cheese into pan, distributing them over entire surface. Now put the pan into broiler, about 3 inches from source of heat, and broil it until eggs are set on top, and cheese is melted. Remove the omelet to a warm plate. We don't like to fold this omelet because it looks so pretty, dotted with little dollops of red caviar and the green of the parsley or celery in the eggs. Filled with this delicious repast, you will have the courage to face not only burglars, but possibly also a cruel master. We told you to use 2 eggs, didn't we? Well, this is for 2 persons; if there are any more of you, well, you can multiply, can't you?

These two college girls were having Bloody Marys to get their eyes open for their first class in the morning, and one of them became annoyed by something the other girl said. (They were both edgy and short-tempered, you see, because they'd stayed up late the night before, cramming for an examination.) "Listen, Jenny," she said, "why do you go on calling your mother 'the mater?' In the first place, it's only in old, corny joke books and in old, dopey novels that college girls and boys called their mother 'mater' and their father 'pater.' And in the second place, you don't call your father 'the pater,' you call him 'my father.'"

Jenny grinned viciously. "With my mother," she said sweetly, "it makes sense to call her that;

she's gotten my five sisters married off, and now she's working on my case." For a late Saturday or Sunday breakfast how would you like to work on a:

CHICKEN LIVER-CREAM CHEESE OMELET

[SERVES THREE]

6 chicken livers
lots of butter
1 large onion, chopped
1 tablespoon parsley,
   chopped

6 eggs
salt and pepper
1 3-ounce package cream
   cheese

This is for 3 people, maybe just for 2. Wash and separate the chicken livers, and remove fatty membranes. Melt 1 tablespoon of butter, sauté the chopped onion until it is soft, and then for 1 minute sauté the parsley. Empty the pan into a bowl containing the 6 eggs, add salt and pepper to taste, and beat it. Now melt some more butter in the pan and sauté the chicken livers lightly, turning them once. Don't overcook them or the chicken livers will become hard, which would be a pity. When the livers are finished, put them aside to keep warm. Melt some more butter and pour in the egg-onion mixture. When the bottom of the omelet is set, cut little dollops off the cream cheese and dollop them all over the omelet. Now put the pan in the broiler, and watch it carefully. When the cream cheese is melted, but the eggs are just the slightest bit moist, take the pan out of the broiler. Put the chicken livers on the omelet, fold it over, turn it out on a serving platter, and garnish with parsley.

This is, of course, as good a dish for lunch or a late supper as it is for a late breakfast, which we think is the best time for it. No, a thousand times no! We will not call it "brunch." What a terrible word!

What wonderful variations there can be on this omelet! Lox, for instance, instead of the chicken livers! Red salmon caviar instead of the chicken livers or lox! Sautéed mushrooms with any of these! Smoked whitefish, instead of the chicken livers, lox, red salmon caviar! Stop us, somebody!

LOXY EGGS

[SERVES ONE]

1 tablespoon butter
3 tablespoons onion, chopped
1 large slice lox (smoked salmon, for goodness sake), diced

2 eggs
dash black pepper
½ teaspoon parsley, chopped

Sauté the onion until soft but not brown; now delicately sauté the diced lox, stirring and turning the lox until golden. Beat up the eggs and pour them into the pan with onion and lox, sprinkle with pepper, and keep stirring. When eggs are set to consistency you prefer, sprinkle parsley on it, put it on a plate, and eat it. This is for one person, so if you're going to make two portions, just multiply by two, see?

CURRIED EGGS

[SERVES TWO]

4 hard-boiled eggs
1 slice white bread
½ cup hot milk
½ cup Cheddar cheese, diced

1 tablespoon flour
¼ teaspoon paprika
½ teaspoon curry powder
½ teaspoon salt
1 tablespoon butter

Slice the eggs and put them in a buttered baking dish. In blender, put broken pieces of bread, cover blender container, and blend on high speed for 5 seconds. Turn bread out of blender container and put in all ingredients except butter and bread crumbs. Cover blender container and blend on high speed for 10 seconds. Pour the mixture over eggs, sprinkle bread crumbs over all, and dot with butter. In oven preheated to 400 degrees bake for about 15 minutes, or until bread crumbs are browned.

At a hotel in the country last summer we shared a table with an uncouth lout who complained about everything that was served him. One day he had chicken for dinner and, as he chomped away at it, he remarked, "This, I know, is an incubator chicken." A deep silence fell over everyone at the table, for we all knew he was going to say something rotten.

Finally, he said, "Isn't anyone going to ask me how I know this is an incubator chicken?" And he looked around at us expectantly. "No?" he said. "Well, then, I'll tell you anyway. It's because no chicken with a mother could be this tough." No one would say that if this is the way you make:

CURRIED CHICKEN OMELET

[SERVES THREE OR FOUR]

1 tablespoon butter	1 teaspoon onion, minced
1 tablespoon flour	1 teaspoon curry powder
½ cup hot milk or cream	1 teaspoon lemon juice
½ teaspoon salt	1 cup chicken (leftovers
⅛ teaspoon pepper	are fine)

Melt the butter in saucepan, stir in the flour, and add the hot milk slowly, beating it all the time. Add all the ingredients except the chicken and keep beating it until it is smooth and boiling. When it boils, add the chicken, stir it all up good, lower the heat, cover the pan, and make the:

OMELET

6 eggs	salt and pepper
3 tablespoons milk (or cream)	3 tablespoons butter
parsley flakes, or chopped fresh parsley	

Beat the eggs with milk and all other ingredients, except the butter. Over medium heat, melt the butter, pour the egg mixture into pan and let eggs get set. This process can be hastened by lifting the edges of the omelet with a spatula and letting the loose egg mixture run down underneath. Also, you can put the pan in the broiler, but you have to keep watching it so it doesn't burn. Or, you can put a pot cover over the omelet so the reflected heat helps set the eggs. When the omelet is set the way you like it, loose or firm, turn it out on a plate, pour over it the curried chicken, and serve it, folded or unfolded, according to your taste.

This story is told about almost every distinguished Chinese visitor to this country, but it is said that it actually did happen when Dr. Wellington Koo, the diplomat, attended a formal dinner at Princeton. Seems that next to Dr. Koo was seated a large football player who, groping for conversation, turned to the cultured gentleman and asked, "Likee soupee?" Dr. Koo smiled affably and nodded. During the next course, the football played turned once more to Dr. Koo and asked, "Likee fishee?" Dr. Koo smiled and nodded again.

When the dinner was ended, Dr. Koo was asked to say a few words, and he did, in his usual urbane and clever manner, and in perfect English, of course. He returned to his seat at the table and smiled at the red-faced football player. "Likee speechee?" asked Dr. Koo. Football players—and almost everyone else—just love:

EGG FOO YOUNG

[SERVES THREE]

oil for deep frying (Chinese use peanut oil)
1 cup roast pork, diced (leftovers are fine)
½ cup minced onions
2 scallions, chopped (green part, too)
1 tablespoon soy sauce
1 cup canned bean sprouts, drained (you can get this in Chinese groceries and some fancy groceries; if you can't, simply omit them from recipe)
3 eggs

The oil should be a little more than 2 inches high in your frying pan. Get it good and hot. And while the oil is hotting up, mix everything else together in a bowl, in the order in which they're listed here. When the oil is boiling, get hold of a deep ladle, dip up about ⅓ of the mixture, put the ladle into the boiling oil, and tip out the contents. This should make one omelet, so you should do this operation twice more. When the three omelets rise to the top of the oil, turn them over to brown on the other side. Now make the:

EGG FOO YOUNG SAUCE

1 teaspoon cornstarch
2 tablespoons cold water
1½ cups chicken stock or bouillon
1 teaspoon molasses
1 teaspoon soy sauce
½ teaspoon salt
⅛ teaspoon pepper

Mix the cornstarch with the cold water and combine in a pan with all the other ingredients. Bring it to a boil and stir it until it is slightly thickened, which will happen in less than 1 minute. Pour this sauce over the 3 *egg foo young* omelets. This should serve 3 people nicely, maybe with some rice, fried or plain. As Harry Lee, our Chinese philosopher friend, says, *"Est gezinte late."*

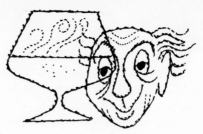

We met a man we hadn't seen for several years and he looked terrible. He was sallow, his face was deeply lined, he had heavy bags under his eyes, and he was about 30 pounds lighter than when we had last seen him. He looked so awful, in fact, that we couldn't help but ask why he looked so awful.

"I have insomnia," he explained. Well, we asked, don't you take anything for it? "Oh, sure," he replied, "every hour on the hour I take two ounces of brandy." And does that put you to sleep? we asked. The man shook his head. "No," he said, "but it makes me happy to be awake." Did you ever give your husband a:

BRANDIED OMELET?

[SERVES ONE]

2 eggs	2 tablespoons brandy
a dash of salt	1 tablespoon butter
pinch of pepper	1 tablespoon brown sugar

Beat the eggs up viciously with the salt, pepper, and one tablespoon brandy. Melt butter in frying pan, pour in egg-brandy mixture, and, over low heat, let it set. You will be able to hasten the process if you use a spatula to lift up the edges of the omelet and let the loose egg mixture run underneath. Keep doing this until the omelet is as firm as you like it, fold it over, slide it onto warm plate. Now mix the brown sugar with the remaining brandy —you can add more brandy if you like—pour it into the pan to heat for just ½ minute, and then pour it over the omelet. Now ignite the brandy and serve it flaming.

This Englishman had been sent by his employers, a large oil company, to the jungles of South America to explore for oil. He met there a man, bent on the same mission, with whom he became friendly. The fellow spoke pretty good English, the Englishman thought, but he couldn't decide whether the man was a Briton or merely a South American who had studied English. So he decided to inquire.

"Are you a foreigner here, too?" he asked. The fellow glared at him. "A foreigner!" the fellow exclaimed. "Hell, no! I'm from Brooklyn!" In Brooklyn, this is the way they make:

CHOPPED EGGS WITH TZIBBELE

[SERVES TWO TO THREE]

4 hard-boiled eggs	⅛ teaspoon pepper
¼ cup onion, finely chopped	⅛ teaspoon garlic powder
½ teaspoon salt	3 tablespoons chicken fat or butter

Chop up the eggs and mix them with the chopped *tzibbele* (onions). As you mix, add the seasonings and then work in the chicken fat or butter. Taste it and correct the seasoning, if necessary. You can use this as a spread. But you know how we like to do this? What we like to do is roll biscuit dough real thin, put some of this filling on top of one hunk of dough, put another piece of dough on top, and then bake it. How nice it makes the house smell!

Undoubtedly you are made aware by many thoughtful merchants whenever Mother's Day rolls around, and you are reminded that it would be nice if you would bring or send to her a slight token of your love, affection, remembrance, or, at least, esteem. But you may be surprised to learn that this custom is much older than you think, for many centuries ago they had a day in England around the middle of Lent called Mothering Sunday. Everyone went to see his mother on Mothering Sunday, and they carried gifts, and cakes, and all manner of goodies.

We heard a story from a Pennsylvania Dutch mother about a couple who were buying the farm next to hers. They came to the bank to close the deal after agreeing to pay $11,000 for the property. The woman was carrying a pail full of money, and after the papers had been signed, she emptied the pail on the banker's desk and they began counting the money. There was only $8,000 in the heap.

"Ach, Mama," said the husband, "you broughten der wrong pail!" For this day, the right dish for a Pennsylvania Dutch mother to give her gift-bearing children is:

CIDER OMELET

[SERVES THREE OR FOUR]

4 apples, stewed	½ teaspoon nutmeg
2 tablespoons butter	1 tablespoon cinnamon
½ cup sugar	4 eggs, beaten

Bring one pint of water to a boil, put the apples into the boiling water, and simmer until the apples are tender. Let them cool, then peel and core them. Put the apples through a sieve and combine with butter, sugar, nutmeg and cinnamon. When the mixture is quite cool, mix in the beaten eggs, combining thoroughly. Now butter a baking dish, pour the mixture into it, and in an oven preheated to 250 degrees bake it for about 20 to 25 minutes. Serve this hot, with a hot:

CIDER SAUCE

2 cups apple cider	¾ tablespoon flour
1 tablespoon butter	2 tablespoons sugar

Boil the cider until it is reduced to half the quantity. While this is going on, in a separate pan melt the butter over low heat and blend in the flour. Slowly add the reduced cider, stirring. Add the sugar and boil for 5 minutes or so. Pour this hot on the hot cider omelet.

A Pennsylvania Dutch poet named William J. Meter once wrote this Mother's Day poem: "I eat myself done and get all full,/And I feel like in Heaven then,/For *schnitz* and *knepp* the way Mom makes/Gives all that's good for us men." (*Schnitz* are apples, and *knepp* are buttons, and it is the name of a Pennsylvania Dutch dish with apples, ham, and a batter, a real hearty dish.)

Jack E. Leonard, the fat funny man, was seated at dinner one night next to a very serious-minded young lady who wanted to discuss with him all manner of weighty subjects, all of which Leonard turned into a joke. Finally, during dessert, the young woman turned to the rotund one and said, "I have noticed that even when you are not on stage you always try to get a laugh. Don't you ever want to do something else besides getting laughs?"

Jack E. pondered the question, and then said there was something he had always wanted to do, but hadn't yet been able to. "What is it?" the girl asked eagerly. "I have always wanted," he replied, "to throw an egg into an electric fan." Better to throw eggs in a pan and make a:

SPANISH OMELET

[SERVES THREE]

6 eggs	2 hot (Spanish or Italian) sausages, chopped fine
1 green pepper, chopped fine	3 tablespoons oil, butter, or margarine
1 large onion, chopped fine	¼ teaspoon salt
1 tomato, chopped fine	

Separate whites and yolks and beat them up separately. Mix together all the chopped vegetables and sausages. Heat oil in frying pan, combine whites and yolks of eggs and salt, and pour mixture into pan. When this is slightly set, pour vegetable-sausage mixture into pan. Put pan in oven preheated to 350 degrees until eggs are set and top of omelet is slightly browned.

Early in February each year, the people of Tampa, Florida—the Chamber of Commerce is mostly concerned in this—celebrate Gasparilla Day. Gasparilla—it sounds like a terrible soft drink, doesn't it?—was a bloodthirsty pirate who roamed the Spanish Main in the 19th century. He was most successful until one day in 1821, when he light-heartedly set out in pursuit of a vessel which, he discovered when it was just too late, was a U. S. Navy warship. So old Gasparilla jumped overboard rather than be captured, and he was last seen swimming out into the sunset towards Spain, which he probably never reached because he was near

Tampa when all this happened. In Tampa, and all over the Caribbean, they serve an egg dish fit for anybody with the hearty appetite of a pirate, called:

HUEVOS VINAGRETA

[SERVES THREE]

2 tomatoes	½ cup olive oil
2 onions	½ teaspoon salt
6 eggs	freshly ground black
3 tablespoons wine vinegar	pepper

Cut each tomato and onion into 3 slices. Put the tomato slices into a baking dish. Now remove enough center rings from the onion slices to form a nest for an egg, put the onion on top of the tomato slices, and break an egg into each onion nest. Mix together the vinegar, olive oil, and salt and pour the mixture over the eggs. Dust with freshly ground black pepper and bake, covered, for 30 minutes in an oven preheated to 325 degrees. This should suffice as an appetizer for 6 people or as a main course for 3.

A Viennese quack we know told us about one of his more peculiar couch-renters. "This fellow," he said, stroking his silly little Vandyke beard with what we suppose he thought was a meditative motion, "told me that he was in a terrible fix because he talked to himself." The good old doc laughed with mad abandon at the recollection. "I told him," he said, "that almost everyone talked to himself at one time or another. And do you know what the dolt said to me in answer?"

When we did not respond, the doc laughed more exuberantly than ever and continued. " 'I know,' the fellow told me, 'but you have no idea what a horrible bore I am.' " This unfortunate fellow kept talking, you see, about his mother's way of cooking:

CHICKEN-LIVER OMELET

[SERVES TWO]

1 small onion, chopped
(large, if you like
onions as much as
we do)
2 tablespoons butter
(listen, you can't
use too much butter
when you cook, you
know?)

4 chicken livers
4 eggs (this is for 2
people, unless you
are a glutton)
salt and pepper to taste
parsley, chopped

Sauté the onion in the butter, but don't let it get brown. While this is going on, wash and clean the chicken livers and separate them. Now dry them on a paper towel and put them in the pan with the onions. Keep turning the chicken livers; don't cook for more than 5 minutes over a low heat because chicken livers are darling, delicate little things and if you overcook them, don't invite us to your house, you hear? Don't beat the eggs, just excite them slightly with a fork with salt and pepper. Take the chicken livers and the onions out of the pan (put this stuff in a bowl or something and keep it warm) and pour the eggs into the pan. When the eggs are set, pour the livers *et cetera* on top and pop the pan into the broiler until the top of the eggs are as set as you like them. Don't fold the omelet, you hear? Sprinkle the parsley on top, and slide it on to a platter. Just as tasty as it is pretty.

One summer Jackie Gleason had all the flagstones on the walks outside his house torn up so he could put steam pipes underneath to melt any snow that might fall during the next winter. Reason for this, said the plump fellow, is because he and his houseman had a harrowing time one winter during one of the heavier snowfalls. "We were snowed in for two days," he told us, "and we weren't worried, because we had plenty of food and enough to drink to keep body and soul together. But by the third day, I felt I had to get my mail, which of course nothing, not heat, rain, sleet, or dark of night, not anything delays."

So Jackie and his man shoveled snow. They shoveled all morning. They shoveled all afternoon. They shoveled on late into the evening. Finally they reached the mailbox. "I opened the mailbox," said Jackie. "There was no mail." So now he has hot flagstones and he can sit in the house and watch the snow fall while he drinks orangeade and eats:

PIPERADE

[SERVES TWO]

1 small, sweet green pepper, sliced thin	2 tomatoes, chopped and peeled
3 tablespoons olive oil	1 tablespoon ham, chopped
salt and pepper to taste	
1 small onion, chopped	1 tablespoon butter
1 clove garlic, minced	4 eggs, beaten

Sauté green pepper in oil. Add salt, pepper, onion, garlic, tomatoes, and ham. Simmer slowly for about 25 minutes, or until vegetables are tender. Add butter, turn up heat, and add eggs. Stir rapidly until eggs are thickened, and now you've got an omelet to gladden anybody's heart, even a snow shoveler's. And isn't that a happy thought?

The cast of the TV show had been working all night, and during a short break, while the cameras were being moved, the elderly star fell asleep in his chair. "It's amazing," said one of the younger members of the cast, "how young he still looks." The others agreed with him. "And," said a young actress, "he is still one of the best actors in America." They agreed with her, too.

"And he is so kind, and helpful to everyone," another actor said. "He never shows any temperament," said still another. Everyone agreed, and then there was a long silence. The star opened his eyes. "Isn't anyone," he said, "going to say anything about how modest I am? Don't you think my modesty is worth noting?" What is worth noting is a:

BAKED CHICKEN OMELET

[SERVES THREE TO FOUR]

4 tablespoons olive oil	1-2 cups chicken, diced,
1 onion, sliced	(leftover or canned)
1 clove garlic, mashed	3 small potatoes, boiled
½ cup chicken consommé	and diced
salt and pepper to taste	4 eggs, separated
2 tomatoes, peeled and	
quartered	

Hot up the oil, brown the onion and garlic, and then add the consommé and seasoning. An easy way to peel tomatoes is to cover them with boiling water for a minute or two, then plunge them in cold water; the skin comes off easy that way. Okay, you've got the tomatoes peeled and quartered, so add them to the pan and cook everything for about 15 minutes, stirring occasionally. Now add the chicken and potatoes and cook for another 5 minutes. Put the contents of the pan in a greased casserole. Beat the egg yolks until they turn yellow.

Whip the egg whites until they are stiff, and fold them into the yolks. Now pour the eggs into the casserole and bake in an oven preheated to 400 degrees, until egg mixture is set. This should take about 8 to 10 minutes and it should serve 3 or 4 people.

We were walking with a friend one day and a panhandler came up to us and said, "Would you give me some money for a sandwich?" You know what our friend said? He said, "Well, I don't know; let's see the sandwich first." Wasn't that mean?

The bride and groom had returned from their honeymoon, and on their first morning in their own apartment the young bride was awakened by some noise coming from the direction of the kitchen, and then there was wafted to her delighted nose the delicious smell of fresh-brewed coffee. When her husband tiptoed into the bedroom, bearing a tray on which there was a glass of fruit juice, a large covered plate, a basket of toast thoughtfully covered with a napkin, a pot of steaming hot coffee, and the morning newspaper, the bride clapped her hands delightedly.

The bridegroom lifted the cover off the plate, showed her what was on it, and said, "You notice everything about this tray, darling." "Oh, yes, dearest," she cried out happily. "Well," said her husband, "that's the way I want you to bring it to me every morning." On the covered plate was a:

WESTERN OMELET

[SERVES ONE]

1 slice boiled ham	one small onion, chopped
2 tablespoons butter	2 tablespoons green
2 eggs (per serving),	pepper, chopped
beaten	dash of pepper

Fry ham in 1 teaspoon butter, then cut it up and mix it in with eggs, which you have beaten up lightly. Now sauté onion until soft and pour it into egg mixture, along with green pepper and pepper. Melt rest of butter in pan, pour in egg mixture, and cook slowly over low heat until it is set the way you like it. Use a spatula to fold it over and to slide it out of pan. You know what? In California, they don't know what you are talking about if you ask for a Western omelet. There, they call it a Denver omelet. But in Denver, they call it a chopped ham omelet with green pepper and onions. Once in Manila, we were told there is no such thing as a Manila envelope; they call it a brown paper envelope. And in Brazil they thought we were nuts when we asked about Brazil nuts. We never did find out what the hell they call Brazil nuts down there.

We were told about a poor fellow in the garment district who suffered terribly from insomnia. He spent thousands of dollars going to doctors, none of whom could help. One day his partner said, "Sam, did you ever try counting sheep? It's supposed to be infallible." Sam shrugged his shoulders sadly. "So," he said, "I'll try counting sheep."

At 4 a.m. his partner's phone rang. It was Sam. "Where," he asked his partner, "can we get linings for 24,000 men's suits?" The partner screamed with rage. "Are you out of your mind, at 4 a.m. you call me up with such a crazy question? Who needs 24,000 linings?" A deep, sad sigh came over the phone. "I counted sheep, like you said," said Sam.

"I got up to 24,000, and I still wasn't sleepy, so I fleeced the sheep. Then I had the wool woven and I started to make men's suits, and then came the problem: Where could I get 24,000 linings?" You will have no problems if you make:

FLORENTINE EGGS

[SERVES FOUR]

1 pound fresh or frozen spinach, chopped	4 eggs
3 tablespoons olive oil	4 or 5 tablespoons cheese, grated
salt and pepper to taste	

This is fine for a late Sunday breakfast—we loathe the word "brunch," don't you?—and it is as simple as it is novel. Thaw, if frozen, and drain the spinach. Hot up the oil in a double boiler. (You notice that when you read recipes they keep saying: ". . . in the top part of a double boiler"? Now who, in her or his right mind, would put an ingredient in the *bottom* part of a double boiler?) Well, all right, let's simmer down; let us be kind. Okay, you've got the spinach in the double boiler with the oil. Stir it all around and let it cook for about 8 minutes, covered. Add the salt and pepper, mixing it up well, and distribute the spinach among 4 ramekins. Put an egg in each ramekin. (We swear, once we saw a recipe which said, "break the egg and . . .") Oh, well. Now put one tablespoon of grated cheese on top of each egg and bake it in your oven, preheated to 325 degrees, until the egg white is firm. We didn't say what kind of grated cheese to use, because *any* grated cheese you like is good. And you can jazz this dish up by putting a slice of boiled ham between the spinach and egg, or a piece of lox (smoked salmon) or other smoked fish, or practically anything you like.

We all know, don't we, how frugal are French peasants? Well, here were these peasants leaving the home of some friends after an evening of anti-conviviality, and the guests were thanking their hosts for a splendid evening of fun. "Your *quiche Lorraine*," said M. Lachaud with his insufferable Gallic charm, "was exquisite. I could not resist, it was so delicious. I had two slices."

Mme. Josette Banzet, a descendant of the ancient nobility, smiled politely and prettily. "Thank you, Monsieur," she said, "you ate three, not two, but whoever said that I was an accountant?" This is how Mme. Banzet makes her:

QUICHE LORRAINE

[SERVES THREE TO FOUR]

1 9-inch pie crust, uncooked, with edges built high	1 tablespoon flour
	1½ cups milk
4 slices bacon, cooked	4 eggs
12 ounces cheese, grated (Cheddar, Swiss, American, what's in the house)	salt and pepper
	cayenne

You've got the pie shell prepared, haven't you? Okay. Now crumble and mix up the bacon (you got to cook the bacon first, didn't we tell you?), the cheese, and the flour and put them into the pie crust. Agitate the devil out of the milk, the eggs, the salt, and the pepper and pour them all over that stuff in the pie crust. When we mean cayenne pepper we'll tell you so. Just pay attention, please. NOW comes the cayenne pepper. Toss it over everything you've got there in that pie crust. In an oven which has been preheated to 400 degrees bake it for 15 minutes, then reduce the heat to 325 degrees and leave it there for another ½ hour. You can tell when your *quiche* (pronounced "keesh") is finished because it will show cracks, and all over the top there will be a delicious, golden-brown color. If you let the thing alone for 10 or 15 minutes before you cut it up like a pie, it will settle, sort of, and then if your guests can't count when you serve them slices of it, who could possibly blame them? You?

Two men, one of them carrying a shotgun on one shoulder and a heavy haversack on the other, met in the woods. "Any luck?" asked the unarmed man.

"Luck?" said the man with the gun. "I should say so! I've only been out two hours and I've got nine rabbits right here in the bag."

"Well, well," said the other, "and do you know who I am? This is my land, it's posted against hunting, and I'm the Justice of the Peace."

"Well, well," said the man with the gun, "do you know who I am? I am the biggest liar in Sullivan County, and I haven't got any rabbits." Here's how to make an old-fashioned:

WELSH RABBIT

[SERVES FOUR]

1½ tablespoons butter
3 cups cheese, grated
(Cheddar is best,
but you can use any
other kind you like)
1 teaspoon Worcestershire
sauce
½ teaspoon dry mustard
¼ teaspoon salt
⅛ teaspoon cayenne
2 egg yolks
½ cup beer
4 slices buttered toast,
decrusted
½ teaspoon paprika

Over hot, but not boiling, water, melt the butter and cheese, stirring constantly. When the cheese is melted, add the Worcestershire , mustard, salt, and cayenne, but don't stop stirring. Pour in the egg yolks one at a time, stirring all the time, and then slowly add the beer and keep stirring! Don't let the cheese bubble, and keep stirring until the mixture is quite smooth. It sounds like you might get stir crazy doing this, doesn't it? But Welsh rabbit has to be smooth, and you can't get it that way unless you stir, stir, stir. Well, when it's all nice and smooth and good and hot, ladle it over the toast, which should have the crusts removed. Or English muffins, if you like. Sprinkle some paprika on each serving.

In a cookbook we just got, there was a recipe which called for stirring, and the lady who wrote it said, ". . . stir clockwise," but she didn't say why. You suppose it's okay to stir counterclockwise below the Equator? Isn't that ridiculous? Stir clockwise, indeed. Some people, Nice Nellies, call this dish a Welsh rarebit, but that's pretty ridiculous, too. Welsh rabbit is what it was named when it was invented several centuries ago, and that's what it should be called, see?

Biscuits, Pizza
Brioche, Pastry, Scones
and Kreplach

We heard a terrible joke from a TV comedian the other day, one of those awful fellows who is always telling stories about how stupid his wife is. Don't you think there should be a law or something against comedians telling stories like that? He said that he had answered the telephone the night before and it was a next door neighbor. He shouted into the phone, "Of course, I'll be right over!" And he dashed into the kitchen, and then he was dashing for the front door when his wife stopped him and asked him where he was going. "Sam just called to ask if he could borrow a corkscrew, and I'm rushing over to bring it to him."

His wife looked puzzled. "Why can't you send our nine-year-old son over with the corkscrew?" she inquired politely. "This just proves that women are too dopey ever to be trusted to make important decisions," he says he told his loving wife, "because when a great opportunity arises, they will always mess it up." If you follow directions you won't mess up:

BACON BISCUITS

[MAKES TWENTY-FOUR]

4 cups flour	1 cup milk
3 teaspoons baking powder	½ cup cream
2 teaspoons salt	⅔ cup crisp bacon, crumbled
½ cup shortening	

Sift the flour, baking powder, and salt together. Blend in shortening, add the milk and cream, and work it until it has consistency of a heavy paste, but don't overwork the dough. Flour a board lightly, turn the dough out on the board, and flatten it with your hands. Sprinkle bacon crumbs evenly over all. Now sprinkle dough with flour—very little—and roll it out, gently, gently, with a rolling pin. You got a biscuit cutter? Good! Cut the dough with it, and put rounds on greased cooky sheets. In an oven preheated to 400 degress bake for 10 minutes.

It was a class in English history, and the teacher had asked the little girl, "Who followed Edward VI?" There was a long, long silence. "Don't you remember?" the teacher asked. "It was Mary, wasn't it?" The little girl agreed, happily.

"And now," said the teacher, "do you remember who followed Mary?" The little girl jumped up and down in her seat with excitement. "Oh," she cried happily, "I know that one! It was her little lamb!" If you have chicken soup, it follows that you should put into it:

MANDLEN (Soup nuts)

[SERVES SIX TO EIGHT]

1 cup matzo cake flour	3 eggs, beaten
1 tablespoon potato flour	shortening for deep frying
dash of salt	

Sift the matzo flour, potato flour, and salt together. Now beat the eggs and add enough flour mixture, mixing steadily, to make a stiff dough. Pat it out on a floured board until it is less than ½ inch thick. Cut it up into ½-inch squares, drop the *mandlen* into hot shortening, and fry them until they are nicely browned. Remove with a perforated spoon and put them into the soup just before you serve it. For variety, try:

EGG-MATZO FARFEL

[SERVES SIX TO EIGHT]

1 cup matzo farfel	1 tablespoon fat
2 eggs, beaten	

You can buy *matzo farfel* or you can make your own by crushing *matzos*. Beat up the eggs and heat the fat. Put the *farfel* into the pan and over low heat add the beaten eggs, stirring constantly, until the *farfel* is all separated. Let it stand until the *farfel* is dry. Add it to hot soup just before serving. And another wonderful chicken-soup accompaniment is:

CHICKEN-LIVER BALLS

[SERVES FOUR TO FIVE]

½ pound chicken livers
1 cup water
1 cup matzo farfel, or
matzo crumbs

1 egg, beaten
1 teaspoon onion, minced
1 teaspoon salt
⅛ teaspoon pepper

Wash livers, remove membranes, and then chop them fine. Heat the water, add the crumbs, and stir it into a paste. Let it cool; then add the beaten egg, the chopped livers, onion, and seasoning. Shape mixture into small balls. Let them cook in simmering soup for 15 minutes before serving.

I n England, on April 22nd, they have a double celebration. It is the Feast of St. George, patron saint of England, who is said to have spent most of his time traveling around England slaying dragons who were about to devour virgins. These days we don't believe that there were any such creatures (dragons) in England or anywhere else.

It is also the anniversary of the birth of William Shakespeare, and you know, of course, that there are people who are just as skeptical about Shakespeare's authorship of all those plays as they are about St. George's slaying of dragons. No matter; let us cast our doubts aside and join our British cousins in celebration by having:

CORNISH PASTIES

4 cups flour, sifted
¾ cup shortening
½ teaspoon salt
1 cup (approximately) water
2 cups raw beef, diced

2 cups potatoes, peeled and thinly sliced
1 medium onion, thinly sliced
1 teaspoon salt
¼ teaspoon pepper

First, make the dough by mixing the flour, shortening and ½ teaspoon salt and adding water until the dough is stiff enough to knead. Roll out the dough about ⅛ inch thick and cut 6-inch circles. Mix together the meat, potatoes, and onions, using a little water to moisten the mixture, and season with 1 teaspoon salt and ¼ teaspoon pepper. Fill each circle of dough with the mixture, fold the circle in half and press the edges together. In order to make this an authentic Cornish pastry, you have to make now what is called a "Cornish crimp." Flour your finger tips and fold a corner of the pasty over, just as though you were dog-earing the page of a book—which you should never, never do to a book—to mark your place. Crimp all around the pasty, puncture the top with a knife. Put pasties in a lightly greased baking dish and bake for 20 minutes in oven preheated to 400 degrees. After 20 minutes, reduce the heat to 325 degrees and bake for another hour. You know what the English like to have with this? Ale, that's what they like to have with this. A fellow named Ed Antrobus, a British agent in New York—his number is 000—tells us that Queen Elizabeth I used to drink a pint of ale at breakfast each morning. That's pretty jolly-making.

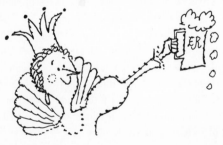

But a Bloody Mary for breakfast is even jollier, and so is an Elizabethan drink called:

SYLLABUB

[FOUR CUPS]

1 cup white wine
1 cup heavy cream
1½ cups milk
¼ cup brandy
1 teaspoon lemon juice

¼ cup sugar
¼ teaspoon rosemary
    leaves, crushed
¼ grated nutmeg

Put everything into bowl and beat it with a whisk for 5 minutes until it's foamy. Or put it all into an electric blender for 10 seconds. Chill it well. Mr. Antrobus tells us that in Elizabeth I's time, they used to milk a cow right into the bowl, but that isn't really necessary.

We think it is terrible, don't you, that all those television comedians, when they are not telling awful jokes about their wives, are telling appalling stories about their mothers-in-law? Even so, we can sympathize with the poor fellow we heard about who said, despairingly, to his wife's mother, "I don't suppose you'll ever come to visit us again, will you?"

His mother-in-law stared at him in amazement. "How can you say such a thing?" she asked. "Why, you have been wonderful to me. Why shouldn't I visit you again?" The man shook his head sadly.

"But how," he said, "can you visit us again, if you never leave?" If you serve this, no one will ever want to leave your house:

SPAGHETTI WITH WHITE CLAM SAUCE

[SERVES FOUR TO FIVE]

2 dozen cherrystone clams
1 cup water
4 tablespoons olive oil
1 small onion, chopped

2 cloves garlic, chopped fine
2 tablespoons parsley, chopped

Scrub the clams thoroughly, then steam them in the cup of water until the shells open. DON'T OVERCOOK! Save the liquid, remove clams from shells, and cut them up in small but not tiny pieces. Sauté the onion, garlic, and parsley in the olive oil until the onion is soft. Pour in the clam juice and the clams and keep over very low heat, covered, while you make the:

SPAGHETTI

4 quarts water
1 tablespoon salt

1 tablespoon olive oil
1 pound spaghetti

Bring the water to a boil, pour in salt, and olive oil, and then put in the spaghetti. Start timing when the water comes to a boil again. Stir the spaghetti around in the pot—the olive oil will prevent it from forming a lump, and so will occasional stirring. If you like it *al dente,* which in Italian means literally "for the teeth," or chewable, DON'T BOIL THE SPAGHETTI FOR MORE THAN EIGHT MINUTES. If you like it softer, cook for 10 to 12 minutes, but don't invite us. We like it *al dente.* Drain the spaghetti thoroughly, put it into a large serving dish, and douse it all with the clam sauce. *Mama mia!*

We have a friend who is a golf pro at one of those great big gaudy hotels in the country, and he tells some very sad stories about his experiences. Like the time that two young women, dressed in golfing clothes that were obviously brand new, came to see him at the clubhouse. "I smiled my most charming smile at the ladies," he told us, "and I said to one of them, 'Good morning! Would you like to have a golfing lesson?'

"And she threw her head back and laughed and laughed and laughed. 'Oh my,' she said, 'how silly! Don't you remember? I learned how to play golf yesterday—today my friend wants to learn.'" If you don't already know it, would you like to learn how to cook:

LASAGNE?

[SERVES FOUR TO SIX]

2 tablespoons fat or oil
2 large onions, chopped
1 clove garlic, pressed
    or mashed
¾ pound ground beef,
    ground fine
¾ pound ground veal,
    ground fine
¼ cup pignola nuts
1½ cups water
1 can tomato paste

½ teaspoon salt
½ teaspoon pepper
5 quarts water
3 tablespoons salt
1 tablespoon olive oil
1 pound lasagne
1 pound Mozzarella
    cheese, sliced thin
¾ pound ricotta cheese
lots of Parmesan cheese,
    grated

Heat the oil—you'll need a large, deep skillet for this—and sauté the onions and garlic until they are soft. Add the beef and veal—both ground fine, now—and brown the meat, stir-frying. Add the pignola nuts and stir to distribute them throughout. Now bring the 1½ cups of water to a boil in separate pan, stir the tomato paste into this until it dissolves, and add the salt and pepper. Combine both mixtures in large pan and stir. Cover the pan and reduce heat to minimum. Bring 5 quarts of water, with 3 tablespoons of salt and 1 tablespoon of olive oil, to a boil and put in the *lasagne*. Reduce the heat and boil the *lasagne* just long enough to make it tender but chewy—*al dente,* Italians call it, meaning "for the teeth," and that's the way it is best—which will take 15 to 18 minutes. The olive oil should prevent the *lasagne* from lumping up, but just to be sure, stir it once in awhile. Drain it thoroughly and let it cool so you can handle it. Then grease the bottom and sides of a large baking pan and put in first a layer of *lasagne*. Now put in some of the meat sauce, another layer of *lasagne,* a layer of Mozzarella, more *lasagne,* and a layer of ricotta. The top layer should be ricotta. Sprinkle it lavishly with grated Parmesan and in oven preheated to 375 degrees bake it for 20 to 25 minutes, when the Mozzarella cheese should be melted.

There are all sorts of variations to *lasagne*—using pork instead of veal, for instance, adding sautéed mushrooms or chopped red pepper to make it fiery —and if you like, you can invent some new ones.

The Old Farmer's Almanac, a wonderful source of useful information and very funny stories, tells us that in the first week of March, the maple sap starts to run in New England. When we were a small boy, we lived for several years in Sullivan County, and one of our neighbors was a farmer named Stratton who taught us how to get the sap out of a maple tree and boil it to make our own syrup. It was wonderful!

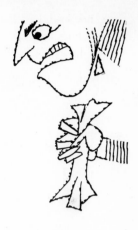

When we grew up we knew a reporter who called his editor a sap one day. "You're drunk," said the editor. "Yes," said the reporter, "but I'll be sober tomorrow, and you'll still be a sap." You know, of course, that maple syrup is wonderful with:

BUCKWHEAT CAKES

[MAKES TWELVE]

¾ cup flour
3½ teaspoons baking powder
¾ teaspoon salt
3 tablespoons sugar

¾ cup buckwheat flour
3 tablespoons butter
1 egg, beaten
1 cup milk
1 teaspoon molasses

Sift the flour with the baking powder, salt, and sugar and then add the buckwheat flour. Melt the butter and put that and everything else into the flour mixture, stirring it all around until you've got a smooth mixture. Put individual tablespoons of the batter on a hot, greased griddle and cook on both sides. Serve the cakes with plenty of butter and syrup. This will make about 12 buckwheat cakes, which is just about enough for one hungry boy, which we used to be. If you want to know how to tap a maple tree and how to make syrup we suggest you go to the library; we've forgotten how, so don't write to us. If you want to know what happened to that reporter who called his boss a sap, well, he fired us, that's what he did. What we learned how to make as a boy, and what we still like for breakfast, is:

SOUR CREAM BISCUITS

[MAKES TWELVE]

2 cups flour
½ teaspoon salt
½ teaspoon baking powder

4 tablespoons shortening
1 cup sour cream

Mix and sift together the dry ingredients. Then cut in the shortening and add the sour cream, combining it well. Flour a board and roll the dough, which should be soft, to a thickness of about ½ inch. Cut it up with a biscuit cutter, put the biscuits on a greased pan, and bake them in oven preheated to 400 degrees until they are well and truly browned. About 15 minutes. This should make about 1 dozen biscuits.

If you don't know what a bagel is, we feel sorry for you, but a loose definition might be a cruller-shaped bread form that fights back. Anyway, here is this bagel-baker who met a friend. The friend remarked that the bageler looked worried. "Of course I'm worried," said the bageler. "Why shouldn't I be? I keep losing money. Look, if I make the hole big, it takes an awful lot of dough to go around that hole." His friend laughed. "So," he said, "make the hole small." "Hah," the bagel-maker said, "you think you're so smart. If I make the hole small, it takes even more dough to fill up the bagel." Bagel-makers are a very proud people, and they guard the secrets of bagel making very carefully, but here is how to make a:

BRIOCHE

[MAKES TWENTY-FOUR]

1 cup milk	¼ cup water (warm)
½ cup butter	2 yeast cakes
1½ teaspoons salt	4 eggs, beaten
¼ cup sugar	4½ cups flour, sifted

Scald the milk, add butter, salt, and sugar, and stir it all until everything is dissolved. In the warm water, dissolve the yeast cakes and add to this mixture the beaten eggs. Then combine both mixtures and slowly pour in the flour, stirring wildly all the while. Now you've got dough, so beat it viciously for awhile until it fights back, put it in a warm place for 5 or 6 hours and it will rise. Punch it down. You got muffin tins? Okay, fill ⅓ of each cup with dough, brush with melted butter and let it all rise once more for about ½ hour. In oven preheated to 425 degrees bake them for 20 minutes, then take them out of the tins. This is what the French have for breakfast, and look at them, will you?

Passover is the eight-day celebration of the deliverance of the Hebrews from slavery in Egypt and though it is, in the main, a happy, festive time, there are rituals connected with the observance of this holiday which serve to remind Jews of the hardships and bitterness of the long, long Biblical trek to freedom. Throughout the eight days Jews may not, of course, eat leavened bread, but only matzos, which contain no leavening. Matzos are made under the supervision of rabbis to ensure that all the ritual regulations are observed. There is a folk tale concerning the revered rabbi of a small Eastern European town who was too sick, when the Passover was approaching, to undertake this task.

Several of his followers, worried, came to his bedside and pleaded with him to allow them to substitute for him. "Teach us," they asked, "all the things we must do." The sick man raised himself up in his bed. "What you must do, my sons," he said, "is to be sure that the women who bake the matzos are well paid for their work." Your efforts will be well repaid if you make:

BAKED MATZO-MARROW MUFFINS
(with chicken soup)

[SERVES TWELVE]

8 tablespoons marrow (from beef bones), or ⅓ cup chicken fat	½ cup water
	1 cup matzo meal
4 eggs	3 tablespoons onion, minced
1 teaspoon salt	
¼ teaspoon pepper	1 teaspoon parsley, chopped

Have your butcher split the beef bones, take out the uncooked marrow, and mash it, combining it with the eggs, salt, and pepper. Beat it all well, add half the water, and beat again. (If marrow bones are not available, use ⅓ cup melted chicken fat.) Now add matzo meal gradually, beating steadily. You should have a loose batter that can be poured easily. Add water as necessary while mixing the batter. Preheat your oven to 350 degrees. Sauté the minced onion until soft and add the parsley to the pan for a minute or two. Then add the onion-parsley mixture to the batter, stirring it in well to distribute it throughout. Grease a muffin pan and pour batter into each cup, filling it about ⅓. (A nice ploy here is to put in half this amount of batter, then put in 1 teaspoon of chopped liver, and then the rest of the batter.) Bake it for 15-20 minutes. It will puff up beautifully, so pop one right into each plate of chicken soup. This should make 12 big, baked matzo-marrow muffins, and one is enough for a plate of soup. They're good, too, as accompaniment to a meat course.

Elsewhere, we have a recipe for baked *gefilte* fish (see index) which we got years ago from a lady named Malvina Katz, and it is the best *gefilte* fish we ever caught. During *Pesach, gefilte* fish is practically obligatory, so if you don't like to *patchkeh* in the kitchen, or if you don't have time for it, there are, of course, store-boughten brands of *gefilte* fish which, like almost everything else, is *Kosher shel Pesach*. For those of you who don't dig, *Pesach* is Passover; *patchkeh* means to "fuss around," and *Kosher shel Pesach* means "for Passover use."

We have a friend who spent some time in Mississippi years ago, and he says he never once saw a girl there who was rounded out properly, and he always thought that it was because three times a day they ate:

HOMINY GRITS

[SERVES FOUR TO SIX]

1 cup hominy grits	2 teaspoons salt
3 cups water	

First you soak the grits for an hour in cold water. Then you drain them and cook in 3 cups of boiling water and salt. And what have you got? Three cups of boiled hominy grits. That's the way the poor people eat it. But the rich make tasty, nutritious patties out of it which are good when made like this:

1 cup hominy grits, cold and cooked	1 tablespoon flour
	milk
1 egg, beaten	salt and pepper
	1 tablespoon butter

Mix everything but butter, using just enough milk to make a stiff batter. Melt the butter, drop the batter in by the tablespoon, and fry the patties on both sides.

We went to a party one night not long ago where the host and hostess—very nice people except that they always want their guests to play games, which is such a drag (don't you think?)—made everybody get up, one at a time, and do imitations. Well, you never did hear such dreadful, idiotic performances. But then one man stood up and began singing and it was fantastic! This man is a lawyer, and we never even knew he could sing, though we've known him a long time. And yet, there he was singing an operatic aria in a beautiful, strong tenor voice that was tremendously thrilling.

When he finished singing, everybody stood up and shouted, "Bravo!" and cheered wildly and gathered around him. "I didn't know you could sing," we all exclaimed. And he replied, blushing modestly, "Oh, I can't really sing. I was just imitating Enrico Caruso." No one will think it is an imitation if you make this:

PIZZA

[SERVES TWO, MAYBE ONLY ONE]

2 tablespoons shortening	¼ cup water
1 cup self-rising flour	1 teaspoon olive oil

Blend the shortening into the flour until it looks like coarse meal. Add water and oil slowly and beat on it until it is nice and smooth. Roll it out—if you haven't got a rolling pin, and you'd be amazed how many people don't have one, use a beer can, or any other kind of can, for that matter—until it will cover a pan which is 8 by 10 inches. So put it in the pan and make:

TOPPING

½ pound Italian sausage
1 clove garlic, crushed
2 teaspoons oregano
1½ teaspoons basil
1 6-ounce can tomato
    paste

½ cup mushroom
    ends and pieces
6 ounces Mozzarella
    cheese
3 tablespoons Parmesan
    cheese, grated

Cut up the sausages into small, but not tiny, pieces and brown them well in a skillet, where else? Put a few drops of water in the pan and hot them up before you put the sausage pieces in. When they are browned, pour off fat and add the garlic, oregano, and basil. Mix it all up well. Now, remember the dough you put in the pan? Okay. Spread the tomato paste all over it and cover the paste with the sausage mixture. Drain the mushroom ends and pieces and put them on top of the sausage mixture. Then put over that the sliced Mozzarella cheese, sprinkle it all with the Parmesan cheese, and bake it in your oven which you have preheated to 450 degrees for 15 or 20 minutes, until the cheese is bubbling and the dough is baked. *Dus haste pizza! Mama mia!*

In Old England, October 6th was celebrated by maidens as St. Faith's Day. They would gather by threes, these English maidens, and bake a scone.

After they mixed the ingredients, they would place the cake on glowing ashes to bake, and each maiden would turn the cake three times. Then they would break the cake into three pieces, and each girl got one piece, which she would break into nine pieces. The crumbs were passed through a wedding ring borrowed from a woman who had been married exactly seven years, and then the maidens would go home.

ALL THIS TIME THEY WOULD KEEP ABSOLUTE SILENCE! Three maidens, all saying not one word? Incredible! Just before they got into bed that night, the maidens would eat their cake and recite:

> *"Oh good St. Faith, be kind this night*
> *And bring to me my heart's delight;*
> *Let me my future husband view*
> *And be my visions chaste and true."*

This is how you make:

SCONES

[MAKES ABOUT TEN]

1 egg	1 teaspoon baking
1 cup milk	powder
½ cup sifted flour	butter

Beat up the egg and milk. Sift the flour and baking powder into the milk and egg mixture and stir it smooth. Get a large frying pan and grease it lightly. By tablespoons, drop in the batter, which should be like thin cream, and fry over low heat, browning the scones lightly on both sides. Serve scones with lots of butter and maybe jelly or jam. We know a man named Cohen says he likes scones.

five

The committee from the lodge had come to the home of a well-to-do businessman to ask for a donation to buy matzos for some poor families, and the man sat down and wrote out a check. The chairman of the committee looked at the check and flushed with anger. "Brother," he said scornfully, "this you call a donation? Five dollars? Why, your son, he's not even working, he gave a check for $100." The rich man shrugged his shoulders. "Sure," he said, "he can afford it; he has a rich father; me— I'm an orphan." There is no end to the things you can do with _matzos_, and one unusual dish is:

BAKED MATZO SANDWICHES

[MAKES THREE]

3 matzos
2 eggs
salt and pepper
1 onion, chopped
chicken fat

sliced or chopped cooked
   chicken, meat,
   chicken livers, or
   fish

Break the _matzos_ in half and let them soak in water for 5 to 10 minutes until they are soft. Squeeze excess water out. Put the _matzos_—be careful not to crumble them—into a bowl. Beat the eggs with salt and pepper and pour the beaten eggs over the _matzos_. Let them soak, turning them at least once, so that each _matzo_ piece absorbs some egg. Sauté the chopped onion until it is soft. Now get hold of a large baking dish, grease it with the chicken fat, and put one layer of egg-soaked _matzos_ into it. Cover each _matzo_-half with chicken, meat, or whatever filling you are using. Sprinkle some of the sautéed onion on top and cover each one with another _matzo_-half. Brush some melted fat on each sandwich. Bake it in oven preheated to 325 degrees until the tops are browned, about 20 to 30 minutes.

Of course, you can make these sandwiches with any kind of filling you like. If you want a cheese filling, use butter instead of chicken fat. A fine dessert is:

MATZO PANCAKES

[SERVES TWO TO THREE]

3 matzos
milk
2 eggs, beaten
⅛ teaspoon salt

¼ cup butter
½ cup sweet wine
sugar

Break the matzos into a bowl, add milk, and let it soak for about 10 minutes. Squeeze milk out, add beaten, salted eggs to *matzos*, and stir thoroughly, so the *matzos* absorb all the egg. Melt half the butter in pan, drop the egg-soaked *matzos* in by the tablespoonful, brown on both sides. When they are all done, set them aside to keep warm. In a saucepan, add the rest of butter to the wine, bring to a boil, and then simmer until it is somewhat reduced. Pour the hot butter-wine sauce over the *matzo* pancakes and sprinkle with sugar.

A friend of ours who was having her hair done in a beauty parlor says that a lady came in, and, after arranging to have her hair washed and set, gave the beautician a dollar bill. "My goodness," said the homely beautician, a notorious gusher, "this is wonderful! You are such a nice lady! This is the first time anyone has ever given me a tip before I did any work on her!"

The woman sneered at the beautician. "That's not a tip," she snarled, "that's hush money." None of your family or friends will be able to keep quiet about it if you give them:

HUSH PUPPIES

[MAKES TWENTY-FOUR]

1½ cups cornmeal	1 small onion, chopped
3 tablespoons flour	2 tablespoons butter
1 teaspoon baking powder	2 eggs
1 teaspoon salt	1 pint milk
	deep hot fat for frying

Stir together and then sift the cornmeal, flour, baking powder, and salt. Melt the butter, beat the eggs up in it, add the milk, and then combine this mixture with the dry ingredients, agitating it all severely until smooth. Drop globs into deep hot fat from a large spoon and fry until the hush puppies are frizzled. Drain them before serving. With almost everything, our mother, who didn't care what we were as long as we were fat, used to give us:

CORN BREAD

[SERVES SIX TO EIGHT]

1 teaspoon salt	1¼ cups sifted flour
¾ teaspoon soda	1 cup cornmeal
2 tablespoons sugar	2 eggs, beaten
2 teaspoons baking powder	1¼ cups buttermilk
	3 tablespoons shortening

Add salt, soda, sugar, and baking powder to flour and sift. Now mix in the cornmeal. Stir up the eggs —beat them first—the buttermilk, and melted shortening, add them to that other stuff, and mix it all up strenuously. Get hold of a pan, grease it well, and bake the bread in an oven preheated to 425 degrees for about 40 minutes.

We know a man, really we do—his name is Selig A—who keeps going to the South Pole for his vacations, who says he met a fox-huntin' type of Englishman who told him this story about his first visit to the North Pole.

"First time I tried to drive a dog team, I yelled at them, 'Tally-ho! Tally-ho!' but the bloomin' dogs didn't stir at all. They just all turned around and laughed in my face." Our friend smiled superciliously, as is his custom. "You should have said 'Mush!'" he said. The Englishman shrugged. "Okay, they turned around and laughed in my mush." You ever make:

MUSH?

[SERVES FOUR TO SIX]

1 cup cornmeal	1½ teaspoons salt
1 cup water, cold	4 cups water, boiling

Mix up the cornmeal, cold water, and salt. Put the boiling water in the top of a double boiler, slowly pour in the meal mixture, and cook it over high heat for 10 minutes, stirring. Now cover it and steam it over boiling water for at least 1 hour, stirring it up from time to time. That may sound dreary, but it isn't really. Anyway, this is much more interesting:

CORNY TART

[SERVES FOUR TO SIX]

¼ pound butter
1½ cups corn kernels
1 teaspoon salt
¾ cup sugar

3 eggs
1¼ cups milk
1 teaspoon vanilla

Melt the butter and mix with corn, salt, and sugar. Beat eggs and milk together and combine with butter-corn mixture. Add vanilla. Pour into a greased baking dish and bake for 1 hour in oven preheated to 375 degrees.

MAMALIGA

[SERVES FOUR]

1 quart water
1 teaspoon salt
1 cup yellow cornmeal
¼ cup butter, melted

¼ cup cheese, grated
(Swiss or Parmesan
or Gruyere)

This is Rumanian, and Rumanians eat this often instead of bread. Boil the water and salt and slowly add the cornmeal, stirring steadily until it is thick. Cook for 20 minutes over moderate heat. Now butter a pan about 8-inches square, pour in the *mamaliga,* let it cool, then refrigerate it for a couple of hours. On a lightly floured board, turn it out carefully so it doesn't break up and cut it into ½-inch slices. Now butter a baking dish, put in a layer of *mamaliga* slices and douse it with the melted butter. Sprinkle it with half the cheese, put on a second layer of *mamaliga* slices, and use up rest of cheese. Now bake it for 25 minutes in oven preheated to 375 degrees. It should be nicely browned when done. Serve it hot.

Several of our neighbors' children were playing out in front of our house one day, and they played and hollered and oh, they had a wonderful time! Which means, of course, that they were awfully noisy. So, finally, in order to get a modicum of peace and quiet in the neighborhood, just for a little while, anyway, we called them into our kitchen and gave them all slices of bread and butter and glasses of milk.

One of the little boys, a very nice little boy named Paul, looked up at us, his bright little face all alight with happiness, and, as we handed him his slice of bread and butter, he said, smiling, "Thank you, thank you very, very much." We were startled, because none of the other children had said a word. "You are a very nice, polite little boy, Paul," we said. "You think so?" he asked. "Certainly," we said. Paul sneered at us.

"Well," he said, "if you really want to hear some politeness, you just smear some jam on this here piece of crummy bread and butter." If you really want to hear politeness, give everyone some:

MEAT-FILLED KREPLACH

[MAKES ABOUT TWELVE]

FILLING (do this first)

½ cup onions, minced
1 tablespoon fat (chicken fat, preferably)
½ pound ground beef
¾ teaspoon salt
¼ teaspoon pepper

First, brown onions in hotted-up fat; then, brown

the meat, stirring it together with the onions. Pour in salt and pepper and stir. Now make the:

KREPLACH

| 2 eggs | ½ teaspoon salt |
| 2 cups flour | water |

Put flour into a bowl or on a board and make a well in the center. Drop in the eggs and salt and work the eggs into the flour. Add sufficient water to make dough. Knead it until the dough is nice and smooth, then roll it out, stretching it as thin as you can get it. Cut the dough into 3-inch squares, put a tablespoon of meat filling into the center of each, fold the dough into a triangle, and press the edges together with a bit of water. Cook in soup or salted, boiling water until the *kreplach* rise to the top, which should take about 20 minutes. The Italians call *kreplach ravioli,* the Chinese call them *won ton,* and every other people in the world has its own name for *kreplach!*

Desserts

COOL RUM PIE

*T*his lady from Sayreville, New Jersey, wanted to know if we have a recipe for "a moist rum" dessert. "We had a baker," she wrote us, "who would make a delicious rum cake for special occasions." And then she added, sort of pathetically, we thought—it brought tears to our eyes— "I have looked for a recipe for so long, but cannot find one that makes a nice, moist, rum cake."

Lady, weep, seek no more. Here is a recipe for a dessert that is moist. It is the moistest. It isn't cake, it's a pie, but if this doesn't make your most special guests on your most special occasions moan with pleasure or, at least, scream with joy when they eat this, then we will come all the way out to Sayreville and eat it. You start out with a bottle of rum, but don't do anything with this bottle until we tell you. First, make the:

CRUST

½ box of zwieback   ½ cup nuts, chopped
½ stick butter, melted   (pecans or walnuts)

Break up the zwieback and mix with melted butter and nuts. (Keep rum bottle handy; if smashing up zwieback exhausts you, take a swig of rum and resume zwieback-breaking when strength returns.) Okay, now you got everything mixed together. Spread mixture on Pyrex pie plate and bake 15 minutes in moderate oven, 375 degrees. Here come the filling directions:

FILLING

1 envelope gelatin   1 pint heavy cream,
½ cup water   whipped
6 egg yolks   ½ cup rum
1 cup sugar

Dissolve gelatin in water in saucepan and bring to a boil. Beat up egg yolks and sugar with much vigor and pour into boiling gelatin, stirring strenuously all the while you are pouring. Did we tell you to whip the cream? Well, whip it until it is stiff. Please pay attention, and let us have no jokes which are in poor taste. Fold the whipped cream into the egg mixture.

You remember that ½ cup rum we mentioned a while back? Okay, pour the rum into the filling mixture and set it all aside to cool. Take small taste of filling. If it isn't moist enough, sprinkle rum over it until you are pleased. Spread filling over crust which has cooled by this time, and place it in refrigerator to chill. Now take a cold shower and wait until special guests come for special occasion. Serve pie real cool.

BISCUIT TORTONI

[SERVES EIGHT]

⅓ cup toasted almonds, blanched	3 egg yolks
	2 tablespoons sherry
2 tablespoons water	1 cup heavy cream
⅓ cup sugar	

You blanch almonds by covering them with boiling water. But first you shell them, if they have shells. Let them stand in the hot water for five minutes, drain them, pour cold water over them, and then take them one by one and slip off the skins. Easy as pie. (What does that mean, anyway, "easy as pie"? You know any easy pies?)

After the almonds have been blanched and toasted by browning them in pan, cut them in quarters and put them into your blender container. (Say, if you haven't GOT a blender, forget the whole thing, and maybe bake an easy pie instead of making *biscuit tortoni*.) Cover the container and let it run on high speed for about 5 seconds or until the nuts are ground up. Turn the nuts out into a saucer. Put the water and sugar into a small saucepan, bring to a boil, and let boil for 3 minutes. Now put the 3 egg yolks and the sherry into the blender container, cover it, and turn the motor on high. Take the cover off, letting the motor run, and pour in the hot water-sugar syrup slowly but steadily. After you've poured in all the syrup, turn motor off, remove contents of container to a bowl. Whip the cream mercilessly, fold the yolk-sherry-syrup mixture into the whipped cream. Now, on a refrigerator tray arrange 8 paper cups and pour the whole business into the cups, sprinkle the ground nuts on top, and freeze for 4 to 5 hours. Aren't you the clever one, making *biscuit tortoni* right there in your own little kitchen?

BANANA PIE

[SERVES SIX]

2 eggs, beaten	½ teaspoon salt
3 bananas (do we have to tell you to peel them?)	1 teaspoon baking powder
4 tablespoons butter	¼ cup coconut flakes
½ cup sugar	¼ cup brown sugar
1 cup flour	2 tablespoons lemon juice

Preheat your oven to 350 degrees. Beat the eggs. Split bananas lengthwise. Now cream the butter and add sugar slowly, beating, beating, beating until it's fluffy. Now add the eggs and beat all this up, too. Sift the flour, salt, and baking powder and add it to that other stuff and beat. Grease and then dust with flour a pan about 8- or 10-inches square. Pour mixture into the pan. Set the banana halves on top and sprinkle them with the coconut flakes, brown sugar, and lemon juice. It will take about 30 minutes to bake. Let it cool and serve with whipped cream or heavy sweet cream.

LEMON MERINGUE PIE

[SERVES SIX]

3 eggs, separated	¼ cup lemon juice
¾ cup sugar	rind of 1 lemon
¼ cup cornstarch	1 tablespoon butter
dash of salt	⅓ cup sugar
1 cup water	1 9-inch baked pie shell

Into your blender container put everything except the egg whites, ⅓ cup sugar, and, of course, that baked pie shell, because you are going to need it in a little while. Run the blender at high speed for 20 seconds, pour contents of container into a saucepan, and cook it over low heat, stirring all the time. When it is all thick and smooth, pour it into the baked pie shell. Now beat on the egg whites, gradually adding the sugar by the tablespoon until it is quite stiff and shiny. Spread this all over the filling in your pie shell. Preheat oven to 350 degrees, pop your pie into the oven, and bake for 15 minutes. *Formidable!*

LEMONY PECAN CAKE

[SERVES SIX TO EIGHT]

1 pound butter	½ teaspoon salt
2¼ cups sugar	¼ pound candied
6 eggs	pineapple
3 ounces lemon extract	½ pound candied cherries
4 cups flour	4 cups (1 pound) pecans
1½ teaspoons baking powder	

Cream the butter and sugar and beat up the eggs. Combine eggs and butter-sugar mixture and agitate it all severely. Blend in the lemon extract. Now sift together the flour, baking powder, and salt, and add all this to the butter-egg mixture. Stir it all up and add the nuts and fruits. In an oven preheated to 300 degrees bake it in loaf pans for 1½ to 2 hours.

ERMINE COLLARS

[MAKES FOUR]

1 egg white	4 sponge-cake shells
¼ cup granulated sugar	¼ cup glazed chocolate
¼ teaspoon lemon juice	chips
12 canned apricot halves	1 teaspoon cornstarch
½ cup apricot syrup	1 tablespoon water, cold

Beat egg white until it is foamy, add sugar, 2 tablespoons at a time, and keep beating. Add lemon juice, beating until stiff, shiny peaks form. Heat the apricots and the apricot syrup; drain and hold on to the syrup. Put three apricot halves on each sponge-cake shell and spread the sides of each shell with the meringue. Press the chocolate chips into the meringue and bake in 400-degree oven until the meringue is browned, which will take about 5 minutes. While this is baking, mix the cornstarch with the cold water, add it to the syrup you've been holding on to, heat it, and stir until it is thickened. Pour it over the ermine collars—you think this looks like ermine?—just before serving. Maybe it doesn't look like ermine, but it tastes great.

NUT CRUMB PIE CRUST

1½ cups zwieback, crumbled	sugar to taste
½ cup butter, melted	½ cup nuts, finely chopped

Mix crumbs, butter, sugar, and nuts and spread on the bottom and sides of a pie pan. Now you got a crust. Fill it with whatever you like and bake it. Now you got a pie.

JAMMED COFFEE CAKE

3 cups biscuit mix	1 cup jam (we like strawberry)
3 tablespoons sugar	⅓ cup coconut flakes
2 eggs	
1 cup milk	

Mix together all ingredients except the jam and coconut. Beat it up pitilessly. Get a pan and grease it up well. Spread the batter on the pan and pour the jam over it, spreading it so it is distributed evenly. Now sprinkle over it the flaked coconut. Bake for 30 minutes in oven preheated to 400 degrees.

RUMMY RICE PUDDING

[SERVES EIGHT TO TEN]

1½ cups rice
2 eggs, beaten
1 cup sugar
2 cups seedless raisins
1 teaspoon cinnamon

2 tablespoons butter,
   melted
rum or brandy (you
   decide how much)
powdered sugar

Cook the rice and mix it with eggs, sugar, raisins,
cinnamon, and butter. Get a casserole, butter it
up, and put the rice mixture in. In an oven preheated to 300 degrees bake it for 45 minutes. Turn
it out, pour in rum or brandy, pour on powdered
sugar, and serve sliced with light sweet cream.
Great.

This is not a Hungarian dessert, but a pesty
fellow we know from Buda loves:

WINEY FARINA

[SERVES FOUR TO SIX]

½ cup dry red wine
1 cup sugar
¼ cup butter
3 cups farina, cooked

½ cup honey
½ cup nuts, chopped
   (not salted ones,
   PLEASE)

For 15 minutes boil the wine and the sugar and
you'll have a thick syrup. So now dump in the
butter and the farina and stir it all up like mad until
it's nice and thick. Pour the stuff into bowls,
saucers, anything you like, and serve hot with the
honey and chopped nuts on top of each serving.
(A dry red wine goes nice with this, you know?)

FRUITY CHOCOLATE FUDGE

[MAKES ABOUT FIFTY SQUARES]

1½ cups evaporated milk
2 cups sugar
2 6-ounce packages
semi-sweet chocolate
pieces

1 1-pound jar ready-
to-use mixed fruits
and peels

In a saucepan combine evaporated milk and sugar and bring to a full, rolling boil, stirring constantly. Cook for about 10 minutes. Remove from heat, add chocolate pieces, and stir until mixture is smooth. Fold in the fruits and peels. Line an 8-inch-square pan with waxed paper and pour the stuff into the pan. Let it cool, then refrigerate. Cut into 1½-inch squares.

CASTAGNE

[SERVES FOUR TO SIX]

1 pound raw chestnuts
1½ cups water
⅛ teaspoon salt
2 tablespoons butter
2 tablespoons cream
6 tablespoons confection-
ers' sugar

1 teaspoon vanilla
2 tablespoons brandy
4 egg whites
sweetened whipped cream

Slash and boil the chestnuts for 20 minutes and peel them. Throw this dirty water away. Put the chestnuts and 1½ cups water into blender container, cover it, and run at high speed for 15 seconds. Now add everything else except egg whites and cream, cover the container again, and run it at high speed for 10 seconds. Beat the egg whites stiff, and pour everything that's in the blender container over the stiff egg whites. Fold in egg whites. Now grease a casserole, put everything into it, and bake it for 35 minutes in an oven preheated to 350 degrees. Top with whipped cream and serve. This is a wonderful cold dessert, too. If you want it that way, let it cool after baking, refrigerate for hours and hours and then, just before serving, top with whipped cream.

SOUR-CREAM ICE CREAM

[SERVES TWO TO THREE]

1 10-ounce package
frozen, sliced
strawberries

1 pint sour cream
1 cup sugar

Ice cream made from sour cream? You know whose
idea that is? Somebody who gives his name as
Smith, from Landgrove, Vermont. And do you
know? It's just great, that's all, just great! What
you do is, thaw the strawberries and agitate them
all around with the sour cream and the sugar. Then
you pour it all into an ice-cube tray and freeze it
for 2 to 3 hours. We tried it just like this and once
we added some brandy to it—it was great both
ways. Thank you, Smith.

STRAWBERRY ICE-CREAM SAUCE

1 10-ounce package
frozen strawberries

1 tablespoon lemon juice

Partially defrost the strawberries and put into
your blender container with the lemon juice. Cover
the container and run it at high speed for 10 seconds. Get sauce well chilled and pour over ice
cream. We think it's best on vanilla. Maybe you
prefer another flavor?

If your husband persists in telling stories,
like the one about the woman who said to her husband when he came home at 5 A.M., "So, you
finally decided to come home?" and the husband
answers, "Well, dear, it was the only place that's
open," he'll quit if you beat him with a:

STRAWBERRY (or other fruit) WHIP

[SERVES THREE TO FOUR]

2 egg whites (my, you
sure got a lot of
yolks piled up if
you've been
listening to us)

½ cup powdered sugar
1 cup strawberries,
crushed (or other
fruit, as we said)
whipped cream

Beat up the egg whites until they are stiff and, while you are beating on them, add the sugar slowly. Now fold in the crushed berries or fruit, put all the stuff in sherbet glasses and refrigerate. Before serving, squirt some whipped cream on top. If this doesn't shut him up, nothing will, hey?

We like coconut on almost anything, don't you? In that case, try this:

COCONUTTY BANANAS

[SERVES SIX TO EIGHT]

4 bananas
2 tablespoons butter, melted
¼ teaspoon salt
1 cup coconut flakes

3 tablespoons orange juice
½ teaspoon orange rind, grated

Peel bananas and split them in half lengthwise. Put them cut-side down in a lightly buttered, shallow baking pan, brush with melted butter, and sprinkle with salt. Put the pan in broiler about 4 inches from heat for about 3 minutes.

Combine coconut, orange juice, and rind. Turn the bananas over gently, sprinkle them with the coconut mixture, and put it all back under the broiler until the coconut is browned. It's a good dish with meat, fish, or fowl.

CRANBERRY PARFAIT

[SERVES SIX TO EIGHT]

1 1-pound can jellied cranberry sauce
2 tablespoons powdered sugar
1 egg white, beaten stiff

½ pint heavy cream whipped
½ teaspoon almond extract

Beat the cranberry sauce and powdered sugar together with a fork. Add the beaten egg white, the whipped cream, and the almond extract. Pour it in a freezer tray and let it get firm. Real good with a shot of rum or brandy added before freezing.

GRAPE SHERBET

[ABOUT ONE AND ONE-HALF PINTS]

1 pint grape juice	½ cup sugar
2 tablespoons lemon juice	2 egg whites (save yolks
pinch of salt	in a jar, in the
¼ cup water	fridge, hear?)

Stir up the grape juice, lemon juice, and salt and freeze in an ice-cube tray—you know a better place? Boil the water and sugar, beat the egg whites, and add the sugared water slowly to the egg whites, beating mercilessly. Let it stand until it's lukewarm. Now take that tray with the fruit-juice mixture out (it's frozen, isn't it?) of the re-frigerator, fold the stuff into the egg mixture, and put everything back into the ice-cube tray again and back into the refrigerator to freeze once more. You can put whipped cream on it if you like, even maraschino cherries.

id you ever get a:
PEACH PICKLED?

4 quarts peaches	4 3-inch pieces cinnamon
3 pounds sugar	(or 3 4-inch
3 cups cider vinegar	pieces?)
	4 teaspoons whole cloves

You skin a peach by putting it in a strainer, dipping it in a kettle of boiling water for about 30 seconds, and then rinsing it with cold water. Skin then comes off easy. Do that to about 6 peaches at a time. Now boil everything else except the cloves for 20 minutes or until syrupy. (Hold on to the cloves, we'll tell you what to do with them.) Put 6 peaches at a time into the syrup and cook them until they're tender, about 5 minutes. Take them out and put them into jars with a teaspoon of cloves in each jar. Keep doing that until you've cooked all the peaches and jarred them. Then fill the jars with the syrup and seal them. The jars have to be HOT before you put the hot peaches in or they'll crack. We didn't tell you to sterilize the jars, but we didn't have to tell you to wash your hands either, did we?

HONEY FRITTERS

[SERVES SIX TO EIGHT]

1 cup milk
1¼ cups self-rising
    cake flour
oil

honey
unsalted nuts, chopped
cinnamon

Pour the milk into the flour gradually, beating it until it is thick and full of bubbles. Get 2 inches of oil good and hot and drop the batter into pan by the tablespoonful. Fry fritters on both sides until they are nice and brown. Drain them on a paper towel and spread them on a large platter. Pour on as much honey as you like, sprinkle with chopped nuts, and then cinnamon. The name the Greeks have for these fritters is *loukoumades*.

GLAZED APPLES

[SERVES FOUR]

½ teaspoon cinnamon
½ cup sugar

4 apples, cored
½ cup water

Toss the sugar and cinnamon into the water and cook the stuff over a low heat for 5 minutes, stirring all the while. Steam the apples in a pan with a tight cover until tender, for about 20 minutes. Put the apples in a shallow baking dish, pour the syrup you've made over them, and place about 4 inches from source of heat in moderately hot broiler. Keep basting the apples until they are glazed. If you'd like to get a little glazed yourself, pour a shot of brandy or rum into the apples just before serving.

BAKED PEARS

[SERVES FOUR TO EIGHT]

4 pears, cored
1 tablespoon butter
½ cup honey

¼ cup lemon juice
½ teaspoon cinnamon

Peel and halve the pears. Butter a casserole and put the pears in. Mix the honey and lemon juice, pour mixture over the pears, and cover with cinnamon. In 350-degree oven bake for ½ hour. Very good with ice cream under or over the pears.

When we visited our sister-in-law, Mrs. J. Grunwald, in Puerto Rico, where she has lived for years, she told us she had prepared a fine dinner. And, she added, she had a dessert that was "a fiasco."

Well, the dinner was fine, and when the dessert was served, she said, "Here's the fiasco." We remarked that we had never eaten a "fiasco," and she became hysterical. When she calmed down, she explained that the real name of the dessert is "flan," and that it is a custard, but that she had botched up the recipe and that's why it was a fiasco. But if you follow these directions, which we got from a Puerto Rican lady, you'll have no fiasco, but a real tasty, invigorating:

RUMMY FLAN

[SERVES EIGHT]

1¾ cups sugar
8 eggs
1 quart milk
1 teaspoon vanilla extract

½ cup coconut flakes
6 tablespoons white
    Puerto Rican rum

In a deep pan—make sure you have an even larger pan into which you can put this one for the baking of the custard—put 1 cup of the sugar and cook it over a medium flame, stirring constantly, until the sugar melts and becomes a nice golden color. Take it away from the heat, and tilt the pan so the sides become coated with the sugar. Beat up the eggs with the milk, the rest of the sugar, and vanilla. (Much easier if you toss everything except the coconut flakes into an electric blender.) Mix in the flaked coconut and pour it all into the pan with the caramelized sugar.

Get hold of a larger pan, put in some hot water and into this set the pan with the flan. Preheat your oven to 350 degrees and bake flan until a knife stuck into the middle comes out clean, which will take about 1 hour. Cool it, turn it out on a nice serving platter, and chill it for hours.

When you are ready to serve it, warm the rum, ignite it at the table, and pour it flaming over the flan. What a sight! What a treat! In Puerto Rico they say, *"Barriga llena, corazón contento,"* which means, roughly, "A full belly makes a heart happy."

TROPICAL CREAM

[SERVES FOUR]

1 banana
2 tablespoons brown
    sugar
1 cup sour cream

1 9-ounce can pineapple
4 tablespoons coconut
    flakes

Put everything but the coconut flakes into your blender container, cover, and run at high speed for 20 seconds. Top each serving with a tablespoon of the coconut.

MAPLE PARFAIT

[SERVES FOUR TO SIX]

6 egg yolks
¾ cup maple syrup
1 pint heavy cream

½ cup unsalted nut meats,
 chopped

In a double boiler, cook the egg yolks and maple syrup, stirring constantly until thick. Now pour the stuff into a bowl and beat it up until it gets cold and you get hot and arm-weary. Whip up the cream, fold it into the custard, stir in the nut meats, and put it all into the refrigerator, where it will get icy cold if you are not careful.

COCONUTTY ORANGES

[SERVES FOUR TO FIVE]

4 oranges (icy cold)
coconut flakes

1 quart ice cream

Peel and carefully remove all fibers from oranges. Now slice them as thin as you can (you got to use a sharp knife, see?) and arrange slices in bowls, saucers, parfait glasses, or whatever you like and pour some coconut over them. Now put in ice cream, some more orange slices in sides of bowls, saucers, or whatever, and finally some more coconut flakes over all.

!

We will bet you never imagined in your wildest dreams that at home you could make your own:

HALVAH!

2½ cups sugar
3 cups water
1 cup sweet butter
1 14-ounce box regular
 farina

½ cup unblanched
 almonds, split
 lengthwise
cinnamon

Stir up sugar and water in a saucepan and bring it to a boil, letting it boil for 10 minutes until it gets syrupy. Stir occasionally. Now take it off heat and set it aside. Melt the butter in another pan, but don't let it brown. Stir the farina into melted butter and cook it over very low heat for 45 minutes, being careful not to let farina turn brown. Add the almonds and stir the syrup in slowly. Keep stirring as it cooks, until it resists spoon. Now pour it all out into a mold and let it cool. Turn it out of mold when cool and sprinkle cinnamon lavishly on it. Cut it into squares.

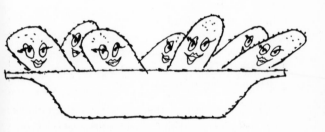

DRUNKEN LADYFINGERS

[SERVES SIX TO EIGHT]

2 cups milk, scalded	pinch of salt
4 egg yolks, beaten	1 tablespoon brandy
¼ cup sugar	25 ladyfingers

You scald milk by stirring it constantly in a saucepan over low heat. Don't let a coat form on top and remove it from heat as soon as it steams. In double boiler, stir the yolks gently, adding sugar and salt. Pour in the scalded milk slowly as you stir and cook until the mixture gets thick. *Don't let it boil.* Strain it, let it cool, then pour in brandy. (If you want to use more than 1 tablespoon brandy, go ahead.) Put the ladyfingers in a large serving dish, pour the custardy mixture all over them, put the whole business into a refrigerator and serve when it is all good and cold.

*A*ll Saints' Day is a Catholic Holy Day of Obligation. On this day, favors are not asked of the saints, but, instead, prayers are offered in behalf of all saints, canonized and uncanonized, known and unknown, as well as for holy men and martyrs whose records have not survived.

And the next day is All Souls' Day, when prayers are offered for the dead, especially for those who were members of the family. In some places, especially in Sicily, virtuous children who have heeded their religious duties all year are rewarded with gifts, presumably left by the dead, like:

FAVE DEI MORTI
("beans of the dead")

¼ pound almonds (unblanched)	1 teaspoon cinnamon
	2 tablespoons flour
¼ pound sugar	1 tablespoon butter
½ lemon peel, grated	1 egg

Crush the almonds without pity, mix the crumbs with the sugar, and put all through a sieve. Combine the resulting paste with all the remaining ingredients and mix and agitate it all until it is as smooth as a baby's hinterland. When it gets to this state, roll it up into several thin rolls, cut them up into small pieces, and shape them so they look like lima beans. Get hold of a baking pan, grease it well, put the beans on the pan, and in an oven preheated to 350 degrees bake them until they become a lovely light brown. When they cool they get hard, but they melt in the mouth. A *mechiah!* In Mexico they do:

PAN DE MUERTOS
("bread of the dead")

[TWO LOAVES]

1 yeast cake	3 cups sugar
¼ cup lukewarm water	6 eggs, separated
5 cups flour	⅓ cup orange juice
1 teaspoon salt	⅓ cup milk
1 cup butter	¼ cup anisette (or rum)

Dissolve yeast in water and sift flour with salt. Add yeast to half the flour, mix, and let it rise in greased bowl until its bulk doubles. Combine butter and sugar; add egg yolks and orange juice. Now add remaining flour, milk, and anisette (or rum) and knead it. Add egg whites gradually, kneading all the time. Now add the risen dough and beat and knead it all until you are pretty arm- and handweary. Put it all in the greased bowl and let it stand in a warm place until it is doubled in bulk. When that happens, knead it again, divide it into two hunks, and shape them into loaves. Moisten the tops slightly with water and sprinkle with sugar. In an oven preheated to 375 degrees, bake loaves for about 50 minutes, and they will be glazed, and so will you if you've nibbled on that anisette (or rum) while doing all this.

BUTTERSCOTS
(pretty funny joke, don't you think?)

[MAKES ABOUT TWENTY TO TWENTY-FIVE]

½ cup milk
¼ cup sugar
½ teaspoon salt
2 tablespoons corn-oil margarine
¼ cup water, warm
1 cake (or package) active dry yeast
1 egg
2¼ cups flour, unsifted

1 stick corn-oil margarine (Yes, we know we listed 2 tablespoons margarine before. Just shut up and pay attention.)
⅔ cup brown sugar
2 teaspoons corn syrup
½ cup pecans, chopped

Scald milk, stir in sugar, and add salt and 2 tablespoons margarine. Allow this to become lukewarm. Into large mixing bowl put warm water (about 110 degrees) and crumble in the yeast, stirring noisily until the yeast is dissolved. Stir into this the lukewarm milk mixture, the egg, and half the flour. If your husband is a prosperous man and you have an electric mixer, beat all this up in your mixer at medium speed. If you've got no electric mixer, you know what you've got to do? You've got to beat this stuff by hand 300—yes, we said 300—

angry, furious strokes with a spoon. Stop your whining, now stir in the rest of the flour, and you'll have a soft dough.

Scrape down dough from sides of bowl and cover it, letting it rise in a warm place until it is doubled in bulk (about 50 minutes). Keep the bowl out of drafts. While this dough is propagating madly, melt the stick of margarine, stir in sugar and corn syrup, and bring it all to a rolling boil. Spread it speedily in a pan 13 by 9 by 2 inches. Sprinkle chopped pecans over it. Now, back to the dough. Stir it down and turn it out on a well-floured board. Rub margarine on your hands so you can handle the dough easily. Shape dough into 2-inch balls, place in pan where you have put sugar, syrup and nuts, and put them away to double in bulk again. (This stuff sure does double up, don't it, sisters?) Bake in oven preheated to 400 degrees, for 20 to 25 minutes. Turn pan over on large platter and remove them, of course. You just made yourself some butterscots, you lucky, hot things, you.

CREAMY MACAROONS WITH SHERRY

[SERVES FOUR TO SIX]

⅓ cup drinking sherry
20 macaroons
2 cups heavy cream
½ teaspoon vanilla

Do all this hours before you're going to serve it, because the colder the better. Pour the sherry over all the macaroons and let them soak for 30 minutes or so. (We sometimes use rum or brandy instead of sherry.) Now whip the cream, adding the vanilla as you go. Get hold of a serving platter and arrange a layer of macaroons, cover them with the whipped cream, cover that with a layer of macaroons, then cream again, until you have used up everything.

BAVARIAN CREAM

[SERVES FOUR]

1 package flavored gelatin
    (any kind you like)
½ cup water, boiling
¾ cup ice, crushed
1 cup heavy cream

Put in your blender container the gelatin and the boiling water, cover and run the machine on high speed for 20 seconds. Now add the ice. (We crush cubes by putting them in an old towel and bludgeoning them with a blunt instrument until they are as crushed as a rejected suitor.) Now cover the container again and run it on high speed until the ice is blended—about 30 seconds. Let the motor run, take the cover off, and pour in the cream. When that's blended, put it into a mold, and refrigerate it until it becomes firm. It'll take about 30 minutes.

COCONUTTY CHOCOLATE COOKIES

[MAKES ABOUT TWENTY-FIVE TO THIRTY]

3 squares semi-sweet chocolate
¼ cup cream-style peanut butter
1 cup sweetened condensed milk
¼ teaspoon salt
1 teaspoon vanilla
1⅓ cups coconut flakes

Melt chocolate over hot water and then remove from heat. Add peanut butter and stir until smooth. Add milk, salt, vanilla, and coconut, stirring vigorously to mix all ingredients. Drop mixture from teaspoon onto a greased baking sheet. Bake in oven preheated to 350 degrees for 10 to 12 minutes and remove from baking sheet while still warm. Now store them in a tightly covered container. Put them where small boys won't think of looking for coconutty cookies.

CANDIED APPLES

[SERVES FOUR TO SIX]

½ cup butter   6 apples
1 cup brown sugar
½ cup nuts, chopped (any
      kind, but not salted
      ones)

Cream the butter and sugar and then stir in the nuts. Peel and slice the apples and put them in a buttered baking dish. Pour the mixture over them and bake for about 20 minutes in a 400-degree oven.

Here's a lovely dessert we got from a Puerto Rican lady named Carmen Aboy Valldejulli. It is candied milk, called:

LECHE COSTRADA

[SERVES SIX TO EIGHT]

⅓ cup sugar   4 egg yolks
½ teaspoon salt   3 egg whites
1 quart milk   1 teaspoon vanilla

Add the sugar and salt to the milk and bring it to boiling point. In another pan, stir, but do not beat the egg yolks and whites and then pour the hot milk mixture over the eggs, stirring wildly. Add the vanilla and stir again. Now strain it all into a baking dish and in oven preheated to 400 degrees bake it for 30 minutes. Cool and then refrigerate the *leche costrada* for hours and hours.

When the obnoxiously bright young man brought his boss home for dinner for the first time, his young wife baked a special treat, a pie. It was a terrible pie, for the crust was burned, and the filling was soggy and unappetizing. To her great surprise, the boss praised it fulsomely.

Months later, the pushy young fellow brought his boss home for dinner again, and the wife, seeking to make up for the last time's fiasco, baked the very same pie, but this time she had the sense and decency to follow directions, and the pie was perfect. But the boss said not a word about it. Finally, she asked why he had praised the pie so mightily the last time, when it was terrible, and didn't say a word this time, when it was perfect.

"Because," said the boss with a condescending leer, "that first pie was so bad, it needed an encouraging word." This is how to bake a perfect:

PINEAPPLE PIE

[SERVES SIX]

pastry for a 9-inch pie shell, plus some extra	½ cup sugar
	½ cup brown sugar
	2 teaspoons vanilla
1 13½-ounce can pineapple chunks	¼ teaspoon salt
	3 eggs, beaten
1 tablespoon flour	½ cup sour cream
½ cup butter	whipped cream

Line a 9-inch pan with the pastry—it will look pretty if you flute the edges. Roll out the extra pastry dough and cut out a number of small, roughly pineapple-shaped pieces. In an oven preheated to 425 degrees, bake the pastry shell for 5 minutes and the pineapple-shaped cut-outs until they are crisp and slightly browned. Drain the pineapple chunks well and sprinkle them with flour. Cream the butter with the 2 sugars, vanilla, and salt, add eggs, keep beating until the mixture is like velvet.

Now add to this the sour cream and the floured pineapple chunks. When everything is mixed, pour the whole thing into the pie shell and bake it for 50 minutes to 1 hour in a slow oven, 325 degrees. Let it cool and when you are ready to serve, garnish it with a rim of whipped cream and line the edge with the pineapple-shaped pastry cut-outs.

Here's a quick and easy way to bake:

MACAROONS

[MAKES ABOUT TWENTY]

5 egg whites	½ pound almond paste
1 cup sugar	¼ cup white cornmeal

Beat up the egg whites until they are stiff but not dry and then gradually add the sugar, beating like crazy all the time. Now get the almond paste and cornmeal all stirred up and fold in the egg whites-and-sugar mixture. Grease a cooky sheet lightly and drop the mixture on it with a teaspoon. With a wet knife, flatten the cookies a bit and bake in an oven preheated to 350 degrees, or until they are browned prettily.

Oh, the many terrible, unfunny so-called Valentine cards that pour into the U. S. mails on St. Valentine's Day! It used to be that this was a sweet, sentimental day, and boys and girls were made happy when we were younger by the thought that someone, even though anonymous, felt tender enough to send a hand-made message of love, or, at least, affection, on this day dedicated to the patron of lovers.

In the old days, it was believed that birds on this day chose their mates, and the poet John Gay wrote: ". . . the day when birds of kind/ Their paramours with mutual chirping find." Isn't that sweet? Also sweet are:

APPLE DUMPLINGS

[SERVES SIX]

2 cups flour
1 teaspoon baking
    powder
1 teaspoon salt
4 tablespoons shortening

1 cup milk
sugar
1 teaspoon cinnamon
6 apples, pared and cored

Sift together the flour, baking powder, and salt. Now cut in the shortening, add the milk slowly, and work into a smooth dough, using just enough milk to make the dough easy to handle. Roll the dough out about ¼-inch thick on a lightly floured board and cut the dough in sections big enough to enclose an apple. Put some sugar and a little cinnamon into the center of each apple, fold the dough all over the apple and press it together. Put the apples on a greased baking sheet or in a pan, and now make this:

SAUCE

⅔ cup granulated sugar
1 tablespoon cornstarch
1 cup water, boiling
2 tablespoons butter

1 teaspoon vanilla
dash of nutmeg
few grains of salt

Mix everything together and cook it over medium heat until it is thickened. Pour it over the apples and then bake the dumplings about 40 minutes in oven preheated to 350 degrees, when the pastry should be a light brown and the apples tender. Serve them in deep dishes and pass the cream.

you know what the Mexicans have that we haven't got? They have three national holidays that are just like our July 4th! Isn't that wild? November 20th is one of them, and it is known as Revolution Day, to celebrate the anniversary of the revolt in 1911 which freed them from a long, rough dictatorship by a general named Diaz.

In some parts of Old Mexico, there are hot springs and cold springs, sometimes right near each other. A silly tourist we heard about was watching some Mexican women wash their clothes in a hot spring and then rinse them in the cold spring.

"My, my," she my-myed, "I guess everybody here is very grateful to old Mother Nature for providing such natural laundry facilities!" An old Mexican regarded her quizzically. "No, señora," he said, "there is much grumbling because she does not also provide soap." Here's a wonderful dessert adored by rich Mexicans:

BLACK-BOTTOM PIE

[SERVES SIX]

1 envelope unflavored gelatin
1 cup sugar
1¼ tablespoons cornstarch
4 eggs, separated
2 cups milk, scalded
2 unsweetened chocolate squares, melted
1 teaspoon vanilla
1 9-inch pie shell, baked
⅓ cup coffee-flavored Jamaican liqueur
¼ teaspoon cream of tartar
2 semi-sweet chocolate squares, grated

Mix the gelatin with ½ cup of sugar and the corn starch in a double boiler. Beat the egg yolks up with the scalded milk, add to the gelatin mixture and keep stirring wildly until the spoon is coated with the mixture. Now pour off half the stuff into another saucepan. Add the melted chocolate and vanilla to this half, mix it all up well, and turn it into the pie shell. Add the coffee-flavored liqueur to the other half and put it in the refrigerator until it starts to get thick. When that happens, beat the egg whites up viciously with the cream of tartar until frothy. Add the remaining sugar gradually and keep agitating the egg whites until they hold their shape. (If you are worried about your shape, lay off things like black-bottom pie.) Fold this into the chilled custard, and pour it on top of the other layer. Now sprinkle it all with the grated chocolate and chill it, chill it.

One of our readers, a man who said he had "been baking cakes the last few years," wrote to ask how to make a pound cake. He said he tried, but had terrible disappointments in his efforts. Among the other ingredients he used, he said, was a pound of raisins. "What to do," he asks piteously, "to prevent raisins sinking to the bottom of the cake?"

What we would like to know is, what are you doing putting raisins in a pound cake? You want raisin cake, that's different. But you say you want a pound cake. Well, here's a recipe for pound cake. Forget the raisins, fellow.

POUND CAKE

[SERVES TEN]

1 pound butter (That's why we call it pound cake, see?)
1 pound sugar
10 eggs, separated

4 cups flour
1 teaspoon baking powder
½ teaspoon salt
1 teaspoon vanilla extract

Cream butter and add sugar slowly, creaming until you have a fluffy mixture. Beat yolks of eggs and pour them slowly into butter mixture, beating strenuously all the while. Sift flour, baking powder, and salt together thoroughly and add slowly to the butter-and-egg mixture, stirring like a mad one all the time. Now add the vanilla, and beat! beat! beat! If you think you are too beat to beat any more, you are a quitter, because you got some more beating to do. Courage! Victory is in sight! Whip the egg whites stiff BUT **NOT DRY** and fold them, with loving, tender care, into all that other stuff you beat up so bravely before. Now you butter two 12-inch loaf pans and then dust them with flour. Pour half the mixture into each pan (if you don't want 2 cakes, throw half the mixture away) and bake in oven preheated to 300 degrees until toothpick comes out clean (about 1 hour, maybe 10, 15 minutes more.) Where did the toothpick come from? Why, you got it from a toothpick box! You stuck it in the cake to test it, and then you took it out. Let's have no more talk about raisins in a pound cake, if you please.

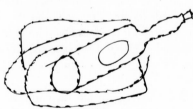

now here's a wonderful Italian dessert which can be made with brandy, rum or sherry. It's called:

ZABAGLIONE

[SERVES FOUR]

6 egg yolks
3 tablespoons sugar

5 tablespoons brandy, or
    rum, or sherry

Put the egg yolks in double boiler, getting the water in bottom part boiling. Beat them wildly with a rotary beater, gradually adding the sugar. Beat, beat, beat, without mercy, until the yolks are quite frothy, and then add the booze or wine, gradually, while you keep beating. Don't let it come to a boil, but cook, beating all the time, until the stuff gets thickened and bubbly. As soon as it starts bubbling, remove the top pan from the heat, let it cool and pour the stuff into sherbet glasses and refrigerate it.

Coffee is the traditional way of ending a meal, of course, whether it is breakfast, lunch, or dinner. And the best way to do it, at any of these meals, and especially for a late weekend breakfast, is with:

IRISH COFFEE

strong, very hot coffee   Irish whiskey
sugar   heavy cream

It doesn't really make any difference what you serve this delight in—a cup, mug, or anything handy. But a long-stemmed glass goblet is really best because it looks most attractive that way. Pour into each goblet enough coffee to reach about ½ inch from the top. Melt a teaspoon of sugar in each one, pour in a shot of Irish whiskey, and top it all with the heavy cream, pouring over back of spoon, so it floats. You had better have a spoon in the glass before you pour in the coffee, so the heat won't crack it. But you don't, of course, stir the coffee—you drink it through the cream.

Kosher Cookery for our Catholic Cousins on Fridays and Lenten Days

(Also for High Episcopalians, Lutherans, Methodists, Baptists, Unitarians, Moslems, Zen Buddhists, Sun-Worshippers and Hot-Rodders.)

Some of our best friends are Catholics—oh, we know a couple of Lutherans, one Unitarian, and a couple of Hot-Rodders—and for many years, every Friday and all through Lent, they were all very unhappy at the table because of the religious restrictions on meat at those times. Most of them got to hate fish and loathe eggs and cheese, because every Friday, and all through the Lenten season, they had to eat fish and eggs and cheese. Generally, they had their fish fried, their eggs fried, and their cheese uncooked, since most Catholic ladies are just as bored with cooking these dishes as are their families with eating them.

From time to time, we would persuade them to try a kosher dairy recipe that was utterly foreign to them, and they were delighted with the new food vistas that were opened to them. Here are some of those recipes. And, of course, many more so-called dairy dishes may be found in the index under EGGS, FISH and SOUPS. Happy Fridays and a less dreary Lenten season to you all!

You know the hollowed-out pumpkin with a candle in it that's always used on Halloween? Well, of course you do, but maybe you don't know the origin of that jack-o'-lantern. It seems that there is a folk tale in Ireland about a fellow named Jack, who was so rotten that when he died not only could he not get into Heaven, but he was so awfully nasty they didn't even want to accept him in Hell!

So he was doomed to wander around the earth until the end of time carrying a candle in a pumpkin, which is called "jack-o'-lantern" in his honor. His honor? Well, everyone will honor you if you sometimes give them:

KASHE VARNITCHKES

[SERVES SIX TO EIGHT]

⅓ cup butter
1 cup onions, minced
2 cups buckwheat groats (kashe), browned and cooked

3 cups bow ties or broad noodles (varnitchkes), cooked
1½ teaspoons salt
¼ teaspon pepper

Hot up the butter and brown the onion in it. One time, a lady wrote and asked, "How many onions make a cup of minced onions?" How can you answer a question like that? Maybe you got small onions, maybe you got medium or even large ones; how should we know? So what we told her was to mince onions, one at a time, until she had a cupful, no? Now, about those buckwheat groats. What you should do is brown them in a pan before you cook them, stirring all the time they are browning. This gives them a fine, nutty flavor. You cook them according to directions on the package, and you'll be fine. Now, about those noodles. If you do use noodles, cut them up into 2-inch pieces, after they are cooked. But you know what's best? The macaroni called "bow ties." Okay, you've got the onions browned, the *kashe* browned and cooked, and the *varnitchkes* (macaroni) all done? So put them all together with the seasoning, and what have you got? *Kashe varnitchkes*, that's what.

One of the parishioners of a small synagogue on the East Side of New York—not the fashionable uptown East Side, but the downtown, lower East Side—was asked how their rabbi could exist on the terribly small amount of money the congregation was able to give him. "Luckily," the man replied, "our rabbi is a very holy man. Not only does he fast on Yom Kippur, of course, but he also fasts every Wednesday and Saturday. Otherwise, he would starve to death." That unhappy fate will never come to anyone devoted to:

FRIED MATZOS

[SERVES FOUR TO SIX]

6 matzos	½ teaspoon salt
½ cup milk	¼ teaspoon pepper
4 eggs	½ stick of butter

Break up the *matzos*—unleavened bread used during Passover, but obtainable all year 'round—into pieces about 1-inch long. (It doesn't matter, really, what the size is.) Soak them in the milk, stirring them around so that each piece of *matzo* becomes softened. Now squeeze out the milk and save it. Beat the eggs with the milk, salt, and pepper and now put the *matzos* into the egg-milk mixture, turning steadily until all the egg-milk is absorbed by the *matzos*. Melt the butter in a large frying pan and pour the egg-coated *matzo* pieces into pan. Now there are two schools of thought on how a proper *matzo brie,* which is what fried *matzos* are called, should be made. One school believes that the *matzo* pieces should be pressed down in pan with a spatula and that when the bottom is browned, it should be turned, like a pancake, to brown on the other side. The other school believes that the *matzo* should be stir-fried. Well, we like it both ways. Try it once each way and see which you prefer.

*V*eteran's Day—remember when they called it Armistice Day?—reminds us of the story about the officer who became very angry because the brand-new soldier passed him right by without saluting.

The officer, a sharp young second lieutenant, raced after the soldier and stopped him. "What's the matter with you, soldier?" he barked. "Don't you know what this uniform is?"

The soldier reached out his hand, felt the lieutenant's uniform, and nodded. "Yes, sure I recognize it. It's all wool and it's a fine uniform. Just look at the terrible one they gave me." We think it's terrible the way some people always serve potatoes fried, boiled, or mashed, and no other way at all. So why not try a:

POTATO KUGEL?

[SERVES FOUR TO SIX]

3 eggs
3 cups potatoes, grated
⅓ cup potato flour
    (sometimes called
    potato starch)

½ teaspoon baking powder
1 teaspoon salt
dash of pepper
½ cup onion, chopped
4 tablespoons butter

Whip the eggs viciously and then stir in the grated, drained potatoes, the potato flour, and everything else listed up there. Put the mixture in a well-greased baking dish and bake it for one hour in your oven, which you have preheated to 350 degrees. It should be nice and brown all over the top. If you like, you can cover top with grated cheese—Parmesan, American, Swiss, whichever you prefer—before baking. And one other time, how about making:

POTATO LATKES (pancakes)?

[SERVES FOUR TO SIX]

3 cups potatoes, grated
3 tablespoons onion,
    grated
2 tablespoons cracker or
    matzo meal

2 eggs, beaten
1 teaspoon salt
¼ teaspoon pepper
½ cup butter

Mix up everything except the butter. Now get hold of a frying pan, melt some of the butter, and drop the potato mixture into the pan one tablespoon at a time. When bottom of *latkes* are browned, turn them and brown the other side. Add butter to the pan as required. A learned friend of ours says this is *"Ah meichel fah der beichel,"* which translates into, *"Quel joie!"*

A boy on our block just out of high school went to his school's guidance counselor and asked for advice on picking out his life's work. "Everything I've tried," he told the counselor, "I've failed at. When I became a newspaper deliverer, the newspapers were out on strike. When I bought an umbrella to walk people home from the subway, it stopped raining. What should I do?"

After much thought, the counselor advised him to become a baker. "People always have to eat bread," the wise man said. "Yes," said the boy, "but what will I do if I can't afford to buy flour to make bread with?" The counselor shrugged his shoulders. "So, you won't be a baker," he said philosophically. Have you ever baked an:

ONION KUGEL?

[SERVES THREE TO FOUR]

6 eggs, separated	⅓ cup cracker meal
3 cups onions, chopped	1½ teaspoons salt
4 tablespoons butter	¼ teaspoon pepper

Separate the yolks and the whites of the eggs and beat them—*separately,* you hear?—until the yolks are thick and the whites are stiff. Mix the onions, butter, cracker meal, salt, and pepper into the yolks and then fold in the whites. Grease a casserole, pour all that stuff into it, and bake in an oven, preheated to 350 degrees, until it is set—about 40 minutes.

Here is a recipe for *gefilte* fish, but first we want to tell you a *gelfite*-fish experience we once had. We looked over the menu in a restaurant, a long and fascinating menu, and for the first course chose *gefilte* fish. The waiter came back from the kitchen, treading gently and sadly on his flat feet. "The *gefilte* fish is all over," he said morosely. "All over what?" we asked. "With," he said funereally. So we chose, for our first course, stuffed derma instead of:

BAKED GEFILTE FISH

[MAKES ABOUT TEN FISH CAKES]

2½ pounds whitefish
2½ pounds pike
¼ cup oil
2 pounds onions, chopped
1 head of garlic (we'll talk about this later)
1 tablespoon salt
¾ teaspoon pepper

½ teaspoon paprika
3 eggs
¼ cup (maybe less) water
¼ cup matzo meal
2 carrots, 1 grated, 1 sliced
½ cup oil
4 bay leaves
8 cloves

This is a fairly unusual version of *gefilte* fish, because most of the time it is boiled; this is baked, and it is best eaten cold. You've got to start working on this the day before—two days before is even better—you want to eat it. You know, nobody can explain to us why this is called *gelfite,* which means "filled," doesn't it? Why isn't it called, instead, *gehakte,* which means "chopped," because goodness knows, there's an awful lot of chopping, chopping, chopping goes into this *gefilte* fish. If it was a fish that was stuffed, we could understand *gefilte.* But it isn't stuffed, it's chopped! Oh, well.

Anyway, the fish have to be filleted and skinned, then washed, ground fine, salted, and put into the refrigerator overnight. Also, the day before you bake the fish, fry the chopped onions in the ¼ cup of oil in an uncovered pan over low heat, stirring often. The onion has to get quite brown. Let it cool, then refrigerate the onion overnight.

Next day, put the garlic through a garlic press or mash it up fine with a blunt instrument. You think a whole head of garlic, which is about 15 or so cloves, is too much? Well, we are old-timey garlic lovers, and the *gefilte* fish tastes great with this much garlic, but if you are scared, why, use less if you want to. In your own kitchen, you are the boss and don't forget it.

Now get hold of a wooden bowl—a large one— and you got to have an old-fashioned metal chopper. Put into the bowl the chopped fish, the onion you fried the day before, the garlic, salt, pepper, and paprika. Now you chop, chop, chop. No fooling, if your arms don't get tired, believe us, you haven't chopped enough. The more you chop, the better. So chop. Add one egg. Chop. Chop. And keep mixing it around with the chopper, understand? Add some water. Chop. Add second egg. Need we tell you to keep chopping? Add a little more water. Chop. Add third egg. Chop, chop, chop. Add matzo meal. Chop. Add grated carrot. Chop, chop, chop.

Now put the ½ cup of oil into a large baking pan, which should be about 2 inches deep. Put the pan into oven and set heat for 350 degrees. Take out pan after 5 minutes. Form the fish mixture into flat cakes about 1-inch thick, wetting your hands before shaping each one, and put cakes into the pan. Put a slice of carrot on each fish cake. Put 1 bay leaf and 2 cloves in each corner of the pan. Bake the fish until it is browned all over—45 to 60 minutes. Baste it at least 3 times with oil in pan. And you know what you've got? Baked *gefilte* fish! Of course, if you want to, you can eat it hot, but we tell you, it's better cold! With strong horseradish. We'd tell you how to make your own strong horseradish, but we can't. Our arms are too tired. From all that chopping.

A college boy we heard about was summoned to the dean's office and confronted with the accusation that he had a barrel of beer in his room. "Yes," he said, "I do have a barrel of beer in my room. But my doctor ordered that I drink beer, sir."

The dean was shocked. "Your doctor ordered you to drink beer?" he asked incredulously. The boy nodded. "Yes, sir," he said. "My doctor said it would make me stronger." The dean asked sarcastically whether it had worked. "Oh yes, sir," replied the sturdy lad, smirking evilly, "when I first got the barrel I could hardly move it, and now I can lift it over my head, easy as anything." The reason he had a great thirst was because he was addicted to:

NORWEGIAN-BAKED HERRING

[SERVES EIGHT TO TEN]

2 salt herrings
½ cup milk or sour cream
⅓ cup flour
5 tablespoons sweet butter

3 medium onions, sliced
3 tablespoons bread crumbs
coarse black pepper

Cover the herrings with water and let them soak overnight. Next day, drain and rinse the herrings and then fillet them. (Of course, you can buy herrings that are already filleted.) Dip the fillets first in the milk or sour cream, then in the flour. Melt half the butter in a baking dish and put the herrings in the dish. Put onion slices on the herrings, pour over it all the milk or sour cream in which you dipped the herrings, sprinkle with the bread crumbs and coarse black pepper, and dot with the remaining butter. Preheat your oven to 375 degrees and bake for 30 minutes and will you be thirsty!

The nightclub audience was enthralled by the small performing dog which sang, danced, told jokes, played several musical instruments, with all of the verve and talent of a Sammy Davis or a Danny Kaye. All of a sudden, in the middle of his exciting performance, another dog, much larger, jumped up on the stage, seized the small dog by the neck with her mouth, and began carrying him off the stage.

The small dog shook himself loose and, turning to the startled and frightened audience, explained, "It's all right, folks, this is my mother. She wants me to be a doctor." This is how Swiss mothers make:

FRIED SALMON

[SERVES SIX]

6 salmon steaks	3 tablespoons stock
2 teaspoons salt	1 teaspoon paprika
1 teaspoon pepper	1 teaspoon parsley
3 tablespoons flour	6 slices lemon
¼ pound butter	
2 medium onions, chopped fine	

Wipe salmon with damp cloth. Mix salt, pepper, and flour and rub it into the fish. In a skillet (where else?) melt half the butter and fry the steaks until they are brown on both sides (about 5 minutes).

Take salmon steaks out of skillet and keep warm.
Melt the rest of the butter, sauté the onions until
soft, dump them over the salmon. Pour stock into
skillet in which salmon steaks were browned and
scrape up the particles in it. Then pour hot stock
over salmon steaks. Put steaks on serving platter.
Sprinkle with paprika and parsley. Serve with
lemon slices.

There's a judge in Brooklyn who hates lawyers even though, when he was practicing law himself, almost every judge he ever came before grew
to hate him. Anyway, that's neither here nor there.
Once, when an unfortunate barrister died broke not
long ago (he was a gambler, that's why he was
broke, because we all know, don't we, that there
are very few poor lawyers?), his fellow attorneys—
my, there are a lot of names for lawyers, aren't
there?—took up a collection. They asked the lawyer-
hating judge for a dollar to bury the poor slob.
"Only one dollar?" the judge cried out in astonishment. "Here's $21, go bury 20 more." You won't
have to bury your head in shame if you cook:

FISH CUTLETS

[SERVES THREE TO FOUR]

1 pound fish, boned
    (any white-meat
    kind)
2 slices bread
4 tablespoons cream
1 tablespoon dill,
    chopped

½ teaspoon salt
¼ teaspoon pepper
1 egg white
¼ pound butter
½ cup bread crumbs

Bone and skin the fish and then chop it fine. Cut
the crusts off the bread and soak it in the cream.
(You can eat the crusts or throw them away. Just
don't use them in the dish, see?) Smash the chopped
fish and the bread together, getting them thoroughly mixed up. Add the dill, salt, pepper, un-
beaten egg white, and one tablespoon of the butter,

melted. Mix it all up good and put it into the re-frigerator for three or four hours. Sift the bread crumbs onto a board or on waxed paper. Form the fish mixture into cakes or stick shapes, whichever you like, and roll them in the bread crumbs. Get them heavily coated. Now melt the rest of the butter in a pan and fry the fish cakes, sticks, or whatever, turning several times so they brown on all sides. Fine with lemon and tartar sauce. Sometimes try a mixture of horseradish and ketchup. This is great with fish.

*m*an we know went to a restaurant one Friday recently. "I'll have a broiled abalone steak," he told the waiter. "Sorry, sir," said the waiter, "we don't have abalone steak." Our friend said with a sly grin, "Then I'll have a whale steak." The waiter looked worried. "Whale steak?" he asked. "We don't have . . ." "All right," said the customer, "then I'll have shark fins on toast." When the waiter threw up his arms in desperation, our friend sighed. "Well, then," he said, "give me the roast beef. Heaven knows I've tried." The poor waiter might have had less trouble with our friend if he'd suggested:

BEER-SAUCED SALMON

[SERVES SIX]

6 salmon steaks	2 cups beer
2 teaspoons salt	1 tablespoon sugar
¼ teaspoon pepper	2 cloves
1 onion, chopped	1 tablespoon parsley,
4 tablespoons butter	chopped
2 tablespoons flour	lemon wedges

Wash and dry fish, rub in salt and pepper. Sauté onion 5 minutes in melted butter in deep frying pan, add flour, and stir until golden. Add beer slowly, stirring constantly, until mixture reaches boiling point. Put fish in pan, then add sugar and cloves. Cover and cook for 30 minutes over low heat. Put fish on serving platter, then taste sauce and add seasoning if necessary. Sprinkle with parsley and garnish with lemon. If the man in your family hates fish, make more beer sauce for him. Very tasty sopped up with garlic bread.

O ne Friday night recently, a well-to-do beneficent man told us, he invited a mutual acquaintance of ours, who is a prominent free-loader, to his home for dinner. "As a rule," he said, "I avoid this fellow assiduously, but this one time I couldn't help myself. I had to invite him home for a meal."

They met at the well-to-do man's office, and they were walking toward his home, when the w-t-d man suddenly stopped. "I think," he said to the free-loader, "that we are being followed." The free-loader looked back down the street. "Oh, him," he said. "That's all right. That's my son-in-law. He's following us to your house for dinner. I'm supporting him."

This is what they all had that Friday night, a fish dish so delicious that even the famous Jennie Grossinger serves it this way to her guests, a great many of whom are free-loaders:

LEMONY FISH

[SERVES SIX]

1 cup salad oil
2 cups onions, sliced
6 fish fillets (pike, whitefish, salmon, etc.)
2 teaspoons salt
½ teaspoon pepper
2 tomatoes, diced

2 lemons (slice thin but don't peel)
½ cup water
1 tablespoon cider vinegar
2 teaspoons sugar
1 bay leaf

Heat oil in deep skillet and brown onions. Arrange fish fillets over onions and sprinkle them with salt and pepper. Add tomatoes, lemon slices, water, vinegar, sugar, and bay leaf. Cover and cook over low heat for 35 minutes. Remove bay leaf before serving. Some like it hot, some like it better cold. But when we say cold, we mean cold, not not-hot, see? Either way it's terrific!

shlemiehl (dope) we know paid a visit to his rich uncle, who noticed that his nephew looked very unhappy. "Why are you so unhappy?" asked the uncle. "I'm in terrible trouble financially," the *shlemiehl* replied. "I have to pay for my son's college tuition; I have to buy him new clothes; my wife needs a new dress; I have to make a payment on my car; and I have to get some money to pay my income taxes."

"Don't worry," said the uncle, taking out a pen and a piece of paper. "For tuition, how much do you need?" "$1,500," said the *shlemiehl*, and the uncle wrote that down. "For your son's clothing and your wife's new dress?" The dope said, "$250," and the uncle wrote it down. "For your car?" And the man said he needed $75 for the car, so the uncle wrote that down. "For taxes, how much?" $350 was what he needed for taxes. The uncle rapidly added it all up.

"Okay," said the uncle, "now you don't have to worry about tuition, clothing, the car and taxes.

Now you have only one thing to worry about—where are you going to get $2,175?" You won't have anything to worry about with:

LOX SOUFFLÉ (smoked salmon)

[SERVES TWO TO THREE]

1 tablespoon butter	¼ cup butter
1 cup milk	3 eggs, separated
1 tablespoon flour	dash of pepper
¼ pound lox	

Melt the tablespoon of butter. Add the milk and then the flour, stirring until smooth, and simmer it all slowly until it is thickened. Chop the lox up fine, sauté it gently in the ¼ cup of butter in another pan, and pour into it the milk-flour-butter mixture. Then add the egg yolks and pepper and stir it all around to blend. Remove from heat. Beat the egg whites stiff and fold them in with everything else. Now butter a casserole and pour it all in and bake for 25 minutes in oven preheated to 375 degrees. We're sure you know that lox is smoked salmon, and that it's pretty salty; if you don't like it too salty, soak it for awhile in some milk, drain it, and throw the milk away. And if you don't like lox, you can try this soufflé with chopped ham. If you don't like lox OR ham, try it with some chopped clams or maybe chopped shrimp. And if you don't like lox, ham, clams, OR chopped shrimp, well, what can we say?

They used to tell a lot of wonderful stories about Supreme Court Justice Oliver Wendell Holmes—you know the one about how he and Justice Brandeis were out walking one day, when a pretty girl passed them, and Holmes said, sighing, "Oh, to be eighty once more!"—but you seldom hear any these days. One of the best concerns the lady who was seated next to the Chief Justice at dinner one evening. She was very excited. Seems that a burglar had been caught in her house the night before.

"I went down to the jailhouse," she told Holmes, "and I talked to that thief. I told him that he should mend his ways; I told him how sinful it was to steal; I told him that he should see the light! I talked to him for three whole hours!" Justice Holmes shook his head sorrowfully. "Poor man," he murmured, "oh, that poor, poor fellow." What Justice Holmes and that lady were eating was:

COLD BORSCHT

[MAKES ONE AND ONE-HALF QUARTS, ABOUT]

6 large beets	3 tablespoons sugar
2 quarts water, boiling	(brown, preferably)
1 onion, chopped	1 egg
1 tablespoon salt	1 cup sour cream
⅓ cup lemon juice	potatoes, hot, boiled,
	and peeled

Grate 4 of the beets; cut the others into 2-inch slices, after scraping them, of course. Boil the 2 quarts of water and put in the beets, onion, and salt. When it comes to a boil again, reduce the heat and simmer, covered, for 1 hour. Now add the lemon juice and sugar and simmer for 30 minutes. The soup at this point should be sweet-and-sour. Add sugar or lemon juice or both if necessary. Now beat the egg and add 2 cups of the soup to the egg slowly, beating all the time. Add this mixture to the pot slowly, beating all the while. When you've got this mixture in the pot, remove it from the heat, and let it cool. If you want a clear soup, strain it; we like the beets in the soup. Refrigerate the borscht—it should be real cold—and when you serve it, pop a generous dollop of cold sour cream into each portion, and put a hot potato in the middle of the cold sour cream.

We remember an old silent movie from the days when movie houses were in stores called nickelodeons, because it cost a nickel to get in, in which a poor but honest man came to the kitchen of a rich man's house to ask for a handout, and the master of the house told the butler, "Give him a cold potato and tell him to go." We cried. A cold potato is terrible. So serve this borscht with a hot potato.

We all know individuals who are so ill-natured or so benighted they can't, or won't, understand that good food and drink and good conversation are natural companions and that a wise mixture of these boons to the human race distinguishes us from the beasts. Such a one is a man we know whom we'll call Hamish, because that's not his name.

Hamish visited relatives in a distant town. They immediately plied him with food and drink and eager questions about the health and welfare of friends and relations.

"And how is William?" asked one. "William," said the traveler, grunting, "has gone to his reward." Loud lamentations!

"Margaret?" someone else asked anxiously. "What of her?" Hamish helped himself to more soup. "Margaret," he slurped, "is no more." Sadness! But then someone asked, "What has happened back there? A plague?"

Hamish put down his spoon. "Listen," he growled, "when I'm enjoying good food, far as I'm concerned, everyone can go to hell!" This is the soup that churlish Hamish was eating:

SORREL SOUP (Tschav)

[ABOUT ONE AND ONE-HALF QUARTS]

1½ bunches scallions	2 tablespoons salt
1½ quarts water, boiling	½ quart sour cream
	4 tablespoons sugar
1 pound sorrel (also called "sour grass")	juice of 4 lemons
	1 cucumber
3 eggs (1 hard boiled)	pepper

Chop scallions fine and put 1 bunch into the boiling water for 20 minutes. Wash sorrel very carefully, add to pot, and cook for 10 minutes more. Beat two eggs with 1 teaspoon salt, then slowly add sour cream, beating mixture steadily. Remove sorrel soup from heat, let it cool for 5 minutes, then slowly add half the contents of pot to egg mixture, beating steadily. Pour this back into pot slowly, stirring constantly. Add sugar and lemon juice. Put contents of pot through coarse sieve to remove sorrel stems. Cool and then chill in refrigerator for several hours. Before serving, garnish with chopped ½ bunch of scallions—use stems, too—slices of cucumber, and the 1 chopped, hard-boiled egg. Add salt and pepper to taste, serve icy cold.

A rich philanthropist friend in a state of shock told us about a frightening experience he'd had one day recently. Walking along Fifth Avenue, he was accosted by a panhandler. "Please, sir," the fellow said, "could you let me have just one cent?

I haven't eaten for a whole week." Our friend says he reeled in astonishment. "But what can you do with just one cent?" he says he asked. The panhandler smiled with pity. "I want," he said, "to weigh myself." If you serve your family this meal, it won't cost very much, and no dieters among them will have to jump on the scales:

FISH SOUP

[SERVES FOUR TO EIGHT]

6 perch	salt to taste
2 bay leaves	4 eggs, hard boiled and
5 peppercorns	chopped

Clean fish and place in pot with enough salted water to cover fish. Put bay leaves and peppercorns into a cheesecloth bag, put that into pot, and cook fish until they are tender. (Use salt sparingly, you can always add seasoning later.) When fish are tender, drain and save liquid. Skin fish, remove bones, and flake the fish meat. Put a layer of fish into soup bowls and then sprinkle with chopped egg. (This should feed four teenagers or eight adults.) Add layers of fish and then chopped eggs until you've used them all up. Did we tell you to throw away the cheesecloth with the bay leaves and peppercorns? Well, do it now. Reheat the liquid in which the fish have been cooked, pour it into the bowls, and serve.

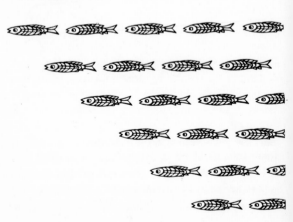

*B*efore we tell you this one, we have to explain that in Yiddish the affectionate diminutive is usually formed for a name, an object, anything at all, by adding the suffix *"eleh,"* as in Shloimeleh for Shloim, Beckeleh for Becky, etc. Okay? You got it? So there was this woman who reached into the pickle barrel and pulled out a big pickle, and asked the pickle-store man, "How much does this pickle cost?" That pickle, the pickle-store man said, costs a nickel. The woman put the pickle back into the pickle barrel and pulled out another one, which might have been a twin, for it was the same size as the first one. "And how much," she asked, "for this little pickeleh?" The pickle-store man grinned. "That pickeleh," he replied, "costs a nickeleh."

One of the recipes we are asked about most often is for kosher-style pickles. Well, this is a pretty tricky business, and you will probably have to experiment a couple of times to get the hang of it, because temperature has a great deal to do with the pickling process. Most recipes say, "Let them stand at room temperature for 1 week." Well, who knows what the temperature of your room is, hey? One book we have says, "Let it stand at 68 degrees F."

Well, how are you going to do that, hey? Anyway, here's how to make:

KOSHER-STYLE PICKLES

10 small, hard cucumbers	1 tablespoon salt
2 cloves garlic, sliced	¼ cup white vinegar
1 tablespoon mixed	dill
pickling spices	boiling water

These quantities are for a 1-quart jar of pickles, for experimental purposes. The cucumbers have to be scrubbed most carefully or they'll spoil. Sterilize a 1-quart jar and put the cucumbers into the hot jar. Now put in the garlic, pickling spices, salt, and vinegar. Add enough boiling water so that the cucumbers are completely covered. Now add enough dill to cover top of jar and seal it. If you have a place where the temperature is about 70 degrees most of the time, the cucumbers will be half-sour in 4 or 5 days, which is the way many people, including us, like them best; if you like them fully pickled, keep them sealed for about 10 days. *Remember:* the warmer the place, the faster the pickling. *Listen:* after 4 days, try one; if you like it the way it tastes after that length of pickling, put the jar in the refrigerator. The cold stops the pickling process. How did we ever get ourselves in such a pickle?

The city fellow bought a farm—it's a pretty good device, you know, for claiming a loss for income tax purposes—and on the farm he had two cows. The man who sold him the farm had taught him how to milk the cows, but he never thought of asking how long he should milk them. This troubled him for a long time, so finally he wrote to the U. S.

Department of Agriculture. "Will you please let me know right away," he wrote, "how long cows should be milked?" By return mail, he got this reply: "Long cows should be milked the same way as short ones."

When we were a boy living in the country at our father's hotel, one of the summer boarders—from New York—asked us to show him which cows gave the sour cream. You know, we have heard that in some parts of the country, it is not possible to buy sour cream? Imagine! How dreadful! How can one go through life without sour cream? Well, if you live in such an uncivilized place, here's how to make:

SOUR CREAM

½ cup milk
8 ounces (1 cup) cottage cheese (or, maybe, farmer's cheese)
1 tablespoon lemon juice

¼ teaspoon salt (maybe more, maybe less, according to your taste)

If you have an electric blender, this is a cinch. Just put the milk in the container, then the cheese—if you use farmer's cheese, you may need more milk, because it is pretty dry—the lemon juice, and the salt and run the motor on high until it is all well blended. If you don't have a blender, you'll have to cream everything together with a fork, until it is all quite smooth. If you want to fancy it up, you can add pimientos, green pimiento-stuffed olives, or pitted black olives. But remember that the olives are salty, so cut down on the salt if you use them. And if you like, you can use a combination of equal parts of cottage cheese and cream cheese. What do you do with sour cream? My goodness, there are a million things you can do with sour cream!

How about sour cream with vegetables, for a start? Cut up some cucumbers—yes, peel them, first, if you like, but we like them unpeeled, and we suggest you try it this way, one time—some scallions, green parts and all, and some radishes. Mix them all together, douse the vegetables lavishly with sour cream, give one or two turns with the pepper mill, and you have a delightful lunch dish, with pumpernickel or rye bread liberally buttered. Oh, yes, the sour cream and the vegetables should be icy cold.

And how about sour cream with strawberries? Maybe you like strawberries with sour cream better? Put some strawberries in a saucer, cover them heavily with sour cream, and eat. We know a clot from Devonshire who loves strawberries this way. You know who came from Devonshire? Sir Walter Raleigh came from Devonshire, where they have a famous clotted cream they eat with strawberries. We saw a play about him and Queen Elizabeth I on the telly one night, and Bette Davis, who was the queen, naturally, kept calling Sir Walter "Rally" all through it, just like someone from Boston saying "really." The way we learned it in school, it was pronounced "raw-lee." But you never know, do you?

In our city there are two brothers who are vastly different, not only in temperament, but also in occupations. One of them is a social-climbing chiropodist, and the other brother, sad to relate, is a panhandler. One day the two brothers were walking toward each other on Park Avenue. The chiropodist turned around hurriedly and tried to escape, but the panhandler caught up with him and angrily stopped him.

"Why are you so stuck-up?" he shouted, as a curious crowd gathered. "What have you got to be stuck-up about, anyhow? I got a right to be stuck-up, because I got a brother who is a social-climbing chiropodist. But all you have is a brother who is a panhandler." You'll have a right to be stuck-up if you make:

TAIGLACH

2½ cups flour	¾ cup brown sugar
⅛ teaspoon salt	1 teaspoon powdered
1 teaspoon baking powder	ginger
4 eggs	½ teaspoon nutmeg
4 tablespoons salad oil	2 cups nuts, chopped
1 pound dark honey	

Sift flour, salt, and baking powder into a bowl. Make a well in the center and drop in eggs and oil. Mix it all together—with your hands, how else? Mix until you have dough. Break off pieces as thick as a thick pencil, cut them into ½-inch pieces and on a greased cooky sheet bake them for 20 minutes until browned in an oven preheated to 350 degrees. While they are cooling, cook the honey, sugar, ginger, and nutmeg, stirring for 15 minutes. Drop the baked dough pieces into this pot with the honey and let it cook for another 5 minutes. Now drop in the chopped nuts and keep cooking, stirring constantly, for another 10 minutes. Now turn it all out on a wet board and let it cool. When you can handle it, wet your hands and form the stuff into 3-inch balls, and refrigerate. Jewish people make and eat this delicious, sticky confection to symbolize their hope for a sweet New Year.

The bashful bride told her new husband that she would die of embarrassment if everyone at the resort hotel knew that they were honeymooners, so he tipped the bellboy magnificently, as well as the desk clerk, to keep their big mouths shut about the old shoes tied to their car, the rice in their hair, and all the other giveaway signs of a newly married couple. But every time the two showed themselves, in the dining room or anywhere else about the place, they noticed that everyone stared and giggled at them.

So the bridegroom asked the desk clerk and the bellboy if their secret had been given away. "Oh no, sir," said the bellhop, "I kept your secret. I told everybody you weren't married at all, that you were just very good friends." Everybody will be your friends if you give them:

HONEY CHREMSELS (CHREMSLACH?)

[MAKES ABOUT FIFTEEN]

½ cup water, hot	3 eggs, separated
2 tablespoons butter	1 teaspoon sugar
1 lemon (juice and grated rind)	⅛ teaspoon salt
3 cups matzo meal	1 cup shortening

First make the dough by stirring together the hot water, butter, lemon juice, and rind and then adding *matzo* meal slowly, stirring strenuously all the time. The dough should be fairly stiff and smooth, and you may not need all of the cups 3 of *matzo* meal. Beat the egg yolks with sugar and stir into the dough. Beat the egg whites with the salt until stiff and fold into the dough. Let dough stand while you make the:

CHREMSEL FILLING

1 cup prunes cooked, pitted, and chopped	honey (lots of honey)
½ cup almonds, blanched and chopped	

You know what we do with prunes? We don't cook them at all, really. Instead of cooking them the usual way (which is OK, too), you can make a gash on one side of each prune and put them in a crock with orange juice to cover. Let them stand and soak for a couple of days at room temperature, then refrigerate, and are they ever good that way. They surely are.

Well, what you do about the *chremsel* mixture is mix together the chopped, cooked (or soaked) prunes, and the almonds, with a couple of tablespoons of honey. Remember that dough? Sure you do. Tear off pieces and press them flat into ½-inch-thick ovals, put a tablespoon of filling in center of each piece, fold them over and press the edges together. In the hot shortening, fry them until they are well and truly browned all over, take them out and drain on paper towels, put them on a large platter and drench them with honey. These *chremsels (chremslach?)* are lovely hot, but we like them better cold. We loved them so much as a boy that we used to pester our mother into baking them for weeks after Passover was over.

The guide was conducting a group through the botanical garden, and everyone oohed and aahed at the sight of the first banana tree; everyone adored the real, live, growing orchids and all the other flora on display in the wonderful place. "And this," said the guide, pointing, "is a fig tree."

Everyone in the crowd regarded the tree with great interest, but the tree brought only one audible response. "This is a fig tree?" one of the ladies asked with a strong note of doubt in her voice. "My goodness, I thought the leaves would be much bigger!" Here's a dish that will go over real big:

BAKED FIG PUDDING

[SERVES FOUR TO SIX]

¼ cup butter
1 egg, beaten
½ cup molasses
1 cup figs, chopped fine
¼ cup nut meats
    (unsalted)
¼ teaspoon lemon rind,
    grated

¼ teaspoon soda
½ cup milk
1½ cups flour, sifted
1 teaspoon baking powder
½ teaspoon salt
½ teaspoon cinnamon

My, that's a long list, isn't it? But don't let it scare you; nobody expects you to do more than one thing at a time, so just take it easy and take one step at a time and suddenly you'll find you've accomplished a fig pudding that's great. Mash the butter and beat it soft, slowly add the egg, beating all the while, and then very slowly, like molasses, add the molasses, beating, beating, beating. When it's nice and fluffy, add the chopped figs, the nuts and grated lemon rind. Now mix the soda into the milk and add this to the mixture. Sift the sifted flour together with the baking powder, salt, and cinnamon and stir this into the pudding. Grease a pan and bake it for an hour in oven preheated to 325 degrees. What's good with this is a:

HOT BRANDY SAUCE

½ cup butter
1 cup sugar

¼ cup brandy
nutmeg

You like rum better than brandy? So use rum. Combine the butter and sugar in a saucepan over low heat, then bring to a boil. Soon as it boils, remove it from heat, stir in the brandy or rum, pour in some nutmeg—just a little bit—and pour it all over the fig pudding. You don't want the kiddies to have brandy or rum? Okay. So top the pudding with whipped cream. And if your taste runs that way, top it all with a maraschino cherry. Who's going to stop you?

A small boy was staying at a summer hotel with his family, and one afternoon he walked over to an old lady who was dozing in a chair after lunch and stood before her until she opened her eyes. "Hello, dear," she said.

"Listen, lady," he said, "can you crack nuts with your teeth?" The old lady smiled sweetly. "No, my dear," she said, "I am sorry to say that I lost all my teeth years ago." Now it was the boy's turn to smile sweetly.

"Okay," he said, "will you hold these nuts for me, while I go get some more?" Even with store-bought teeth, you can enjoy:

NUTTY-PRUNE KNAIDLACH

[MAKES ABOUT TWENTY]

1 pound prunes
orange juice
juice of 1 lemon
3 eggs, separated
⅛ teaspoon salt
3 tablespoons butter,
    melted

¾ cup matzo meal
raisins
chopped nuts (almonds,
    walnuts, any kind, as
    long as they're
    unsalted)

Wash the prunes thoroughly, slash them, and let them stand for at least 2 days in the refrigerator, in orange juice and the juice of one lemon to cover. (If you do this it isn't necessary to cook them; they're much tastier like this.) Now you make the *knaidlach*. (This is the plural of *knaidle*.) Beat the whites and yolks of the eggs separately, then fold one into the other. Into the eggs, put the salt and melted butter, then add the *matzo* meal gradually, mixing all the while, until you have a nice batter. Form it into balls. Into each ball, press a raisin and some chopped nuts and close opening. Put the *knaidlach* into a pan, casserole, or heat-proof dish, toss in the prunes, along with the juice, and bake for about 30 minutes in oven preheated to 350 degrees. No one will think you are nutty if you make:

NUTTY DRUNKEN FISH

fish fillets (any kind of firm-meat fish, fresh or frozen)
lemon or lime juice
dry white wine
almonds, toasted and slivered

If the fish are frozen, thaw them. Cut them into bite-size pieces and put them into a crock. Cover the cut-up fish with a mixture of equal parts of lemon or lime juice and wine. Put the crock of fish into the refrigerator and let it stand at least overnight, maybe for two nights. When you are ready to serve it, drain the fish pieces, arrange them on a large platter, sprinkle the fish pieces with slivered, toasted almonds. Nobody will suspect, unless they've had it before or you tell them, that this delicious fish dish isn't cooked!

*P*urim is a joyous holiday which celebrates the deliverance of the Hebrews in ancient Persia from the wicked prime minister Haman, through the intercession of Queen Esther. It was proved that Esther's uncle, Mordecai, had once saved the life of her husband, King Ahasuerus, so Haman was hanged from the very scaffold he had ordered erected to hang Mordecai and to this day that happy circumstance is celebrated with feasting, giving of gifts, and general merriment.

A bitter story used to be told about Hitler asking an astrologer to tell him when he was going to die. "You will die," said the astrologer, "on a Jewish holiday, *mein Führer*." But which Jewish holiday, Hitler wanted to know. "Any day that you die," the man said, "will be a Jewish holiday."

On this holiday the children—and the adults, too —eat:

HAMANTASCHEN

[ABOUT TWENTY]

1 cup milk, scalded
1 cake or package yeast
½ cup sugar
2 eggs, beaten

½ teaspoon salt
½ cup butter, melted
3½ cups sifted flour

First scald the milk (hot it up until steam rises, but don't let it boil). Let it cool until it is lukewarm. In ¼ cup of the milk put the yeast and 3 tablespoons of the sugar, and when the yeast and sugar are softened, mix it with the eggs, salt, butter, and the rest of the milk and sugar. Add the flour slowly, stirring until dough is formed. Flour your hands and knead dough until it is nice and smooth. Now grease a bowl, put the dough in, cover it with a towel, and set it aside in a warm place for a couple of hours until it is doubled in bulk. While this dough is propagating is a good time to make the:

HAMANTASCH FILLING

¾ cup milk
¾ cup honey
pinch of salt

2 cups ground poppy seeds
1 egg, beaten
1 egg yolk

Put the milk, honey, salt, and ground poppy seeds into a saucepan and cook over low heat, stirring steadily, until it is pretty thick. Add the beaten egg, stir, and let it all cool. Now let's get back to the dough. When it has risen, punch it down, knead it for a couple of minutes, and roll it out until it is less than ¼-inch thick. Cut it into 4-inch squares. Put some of the filling into each square, fold over into a triangle and press the edges together. Preheat your oven to 350 degrees, brush each *hamantasch* with the egg yolk, and bake on a greased baking sheet until the tops are browned and glazed —about 20-25 minutes. If you want to get a little glazed yourself, add some brandy or rum or slivovitz or sherry to the filling mixture when you remove it from heat. Just 3 or 4 ounces of the booze will do nicely.

On Feasting

he Bible says that Ahasuerus, the king of the Medes and the Persians, once gave a feast that lasted for 180 days. These days such carryings-on would seem a little ostentatious, don't you think? So let us just talk about ten different dinners that you can serve at ten different parties during the year, which is more than enough parties to give in one year, for goodness' sake, don't you think? After all, who has all that time for parties? And who, for goodness' sake, wants to *know* so many people that he'd have to give more than ten parties?

We know a fellow who all the time keeps talking about "dinner parties" that he goes to, which conjures up, of course, visions of formal dress, butlers, four kinds of wine, oh, you know, the kind of thing you see in the movies? Well, we realized after awhile that any time he didn't get his wife's dreadful cooking, that to him was a party. What we mean—we're trying to avoid the use of the phrase "dinner party," which we think is a dreadful phrase —is a party where you will serve booze and food to more than five or six people, and still spend all or most of your time with your guests, having as good a time —if not better— as your guests.

In the index, under "Appetizers," you'll find an assortment of *hors d'oeuvres,* any one of which, or a combination of two or three, makes a marvelous thirst-and-hunger provoker, which, after all, is the primary function of the stuff that's served before the regular meal, with or without drinks. And under the "Meats," "Fowl," "Fish," and "Eggs," you'll find many main courses which are splendid for party fare, especially those dishes whose making can be finished, or mostly finished, before your company comes, so that all you have to do when your guests are ready to eat is to serve the food.

Just to start you off, however, here are suggestions for those ten parties we were talking about, all of them to be found in this cook book, with full instructions on the preparation and cooking.

DINNER #1

APPETIZER—*Guacamole* (page 14), a spread or dip that can be as hot to the taste as you like, depending on the amount of seasoning you use.

ENTRÉE—*Yankee pot roast* (page 118), a dish which not only needs no messing around with after you start cooking, but which requires very little time and effort to prepare.

DESSERT—*Pineapple pie* (page 311), a simple but elegant and delicious ending for a meal, which doesn't require much effort, for the principal ingredients are a can of pineapple chunks and pastry, which can be made from any of the commercial mixes, which are just fine.

The beauty of a meal like this for company is that it can be a sit-down affair or a buffet. Of course, you may choose to be lavish at a sit-down dinner and serve soup and then a fish course before the entrée. In that case, the soup should always be a light one, an unadorned consommé, because anything heavier would ruin the appetite for the main course. There are many fish dishes in the index.

DINNER #2

APPETIZER—*Knishes* (page 15), a delicious *hors d'oeuvre,* composed of mashed potatoes, onion, eggs, and seasoning, which serve to encase any kind of filling you choose—chopped meat, fish, chicken, shrimp, lobster, clams, or oysters. They can be prepared early and then just hotted up when company arrives.

ENTRÉE—*Chicken cacciatore* (page 181), an Italian classic—*cacciatore* means "hunter's style"—which also is suitable for both sit-down and buffet dinners and takes very little time to prepare and no time at all to supervise, once the cooking starts.

DESSERT—*Biscuit tortoni* (page 292), an Italian delicacy which naturally follows such a dish as *chicken cacciatore,* and one which, though easily made at home with an electric blender and a refrigerator, will startle and delight your friends, who may never have dreamt that it could be made at home.

DINNER #3

APPETIZER—*Pizza* (page 280). Every city and almost every town, village, hamlet or cross-road in America probably has a *pizzeria* which is more or less authentic, and, of course, frozen pizzas are to be found in the supermarket, as are pizza mixes complete with toppings. But we offer you the opportunity to do a genuine hand-made, home-made pizza.

ENTRÉE—*Shrimp-stuffed red snapper* (page 75), which presents a pretty picture and a surprise, too, when the shrimp come tumbling out. We say red snapper, but any whole fish may be used—striped bass, sea bass, small salmon, any fish big enough to take a stuffing.

DESSERT—*Cool rum pie* (page 291), about which we could rhapsodize, but we will restrain ourselves.

DINNER #4

APPETIZER—*Chicken-liver balls* (page 269), and we caution you to make a lot of them, and the dinner, consequently, will be much *lighter*, for these are *rich* and vastly tempting, and no one will want much more food.

ENTRÉE—*Turkey and ham* (page 207), a great combination with a great sauce.

DESSERT—*Coconutty oranges* (page 304), a simple, refreshing, final touch. (This dinner is just right for a buffet, but it will also do for a sit-down that's quite informal.)

DINNER #5

APPETIZER—*Kishke* (page 168), a quite simple dish to prepare, which will be exotic to you if you don't know Jewish *haute cuisine*.

ENTRÉE—*Veal paprika* (page 136), a Hungarian delight which runs a close second to Hungarian goulash, which you'll also find in the index.

DESSERT—*Halvah* (page 305), a Turkish delight which is, indeed, known as "Turkish Delight."

DINNER #6

APPETIZER—*Maryland crab cakes* (page 91), which would make the state it honors lovable, if there were nothing else—which there is, of course—in its history.

ENTRÉE—*Baked stuffed lamb chops* (page 140), which will be a surprise offering, for lamb chops are rarely considered party fare. But this has a rich stuffing which will please enormously, for few people have ever considered stuffing a lamb chop.

DESSERT—*Drunken ladyfingers* (page 305). Ladyfingers, of course, are for kids, but drunken ladyfingers? Ah!

DINNER #7

APPETIZER—*Baked smoked whitefish* (page 74), a Scandinavian invention which is found only on the gaudiest smorgasbords. And we all know, don't we, that when it comes to appetizers, the Scandinavians are the champs?

ENTRÉE—*Flaming ham steak* (page 148), not our kind of dish because not only does it call for marshmallows, for goodness' sake(!), but it also has maraschino cherries, may heaven help us all! But we won't deny that it is colorful to look at, and when it is flamed with Scotch liqueur, it is more than a little sensational. And it seems as though a great many people like meat with not only marshmallows, but also maraschino cherries. But we promise you, this is the only such dish in this collection.

DESSERT—*Black-bottom pie* (page 314), a beauty which has as one of its ingredients a coffee liqueur that is splendid.

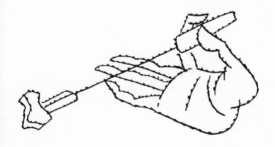

DINNER #8

APPETIZER—*Chicken sausage* (page 20), a Caribbean invention that is impressive, rare, but not difficult to make. It's done in advance.

ENTRÉE—*Hung shao* (page 59), a beautifully garnished steamed fish that is served only in a few Chinese restaurants in this or any other country, and then only on special order given in advance. Gin—yes, gin—is one of the ingredients. It takes care to cook, but it really isn't difficult.

DESSERT—*Zabaglione* (page 316), a rich Italian dessert that is simple to make and pretty to serve in parfait glasses.

DINNER #9

APPETIZER—*Caviar blinis* (page 9), delicate pancakes with either red salmon caviar, if you are just plain folks, or authentic sturgeon caviar, if you are rich—a Russian classic which is served with sour cream.

ENTRÉE—*Roast goose* (page 208) is our favorite fowl, but we have to caution you that it is a great deal of work. We think it is worth all that work and we have it several times each winter. It is a wonderful bird—much tastier than turkey, which we think is highly overrated—and its by-products, the wonderful goose fat, which is better than butter for frying, and the *gansene griebernüsse* which is the skin, fried crisp, are added boons. We have a splendid stuffing for this bird made with chicken livers and all manner of other goodies. Most, if not all, of the work on the roast goose can be done before your company arrives, and you know, don't you, that most people really are impressed with the meal you give them if they know that you've gone to a great deal of work in their behalf? And the beauty part is that all of the work is done before they arrive.

DESSERT—*Grape sherbet* (page 300) or something as simple, maybe just fresh fruit, is the thing after a great dinner of roast goose.

APPETIZER—*Cold baked marinated fish* .(page 11), a spicy, thirst-and-appetite provoker which should be made a day or two before your party. It is as delicious as it is unusual.

ENTRÉE—*Rack of lamb* (page 137), a truly festive dish to put before your guests.

DESSERT—*Leche costrada* (page 310), a cold, wonderful, candied milk dessert which comes from the Caribbean, and it is easily made hours before your guests arrive.

In this section we haven't mentioned any steak dishes because we figured you already know about steaks. But even in the steak department, we think, you will find exotic party recipes in our index, like: *Wino-coffee steak, Steak with blue cheese, Winey filet mignon,* and a couple of others.

We haven't mentioned vegetables at all here; we think you can find all you'll want in the index. And we trust you'll find some new ideas and that they will please you. As we said, these ten dinner suggestions are only suggestions; you'll probably be happier picking out your own combinations of foods for your parties, which is the way it should be done and which we want to encourage. Be daring! Have fun!

Spiritual Cookery,
or
The Gentle Art
of Cooking
with Spirits

Sam Spelunker, who lived in a cave 1,000,-000 years ago, give or take a month or two, was huddled over the fire in the fastness of his squalid dugout one squally evening, gnawing on a slab of brontosaurus steak, when suddenly the meat slipped out of his greasy little hands and fell into the flames. Old Sam screamed with rage and cursed fervently but inarticulately and then snatched the meat out of the fire. Sam was singed and the meat was quite charred, but when it cooled sufficiently to enable him to hold it in his paws, Sam bit into it, tore off a hunk, chewed, and then swallowed. His squinty little eyes opened wide in astonishment, and a look of intense pleasure came over his wonderfully revolting face. It was good! It was delicious! Primitive man had had his first lesson in cooking food!

If you doubt this theory of how cookery began you are not alone; many anthropologists think that some primitive slob discovered the joy of cooking when he came across a beast that had been roasted in a forest fire. (If you don't like *either* of these theories, you are entitled to make up one of your own.)

We like to believe that boozy cookery was invented by accident in some such similar manner. Sam Spelunker—a great-great-great-grandson of the first Sam—was huddled over *his* fire, stirring his dinosaur stew (in the same cave where his great-great-great-grandfather had discovered cookery), getting noisily stewed on an alcoholic beverage, whose ingredients it would be best not to speculate upon, and which also had been discovered accidentally. It would be most unkind, reader dear, if you were to doubt us when we say that Sam Spelunker staggered and spilled a pint or so of his home brew into the stew. And that when young Sam tasted his stew he found that the brew had vastly improved the dull old dinosaur mishmash to such an extent that the Spelunker cave became famous all over the land for its exotic and unique cuisine. (You got a better theory? So propound it.)

Wine cookery was known to the ancient Greeks and Romans, and it is recorded that in the third century B. C., when the Great Wall was being built around China, one of the Emperor's chefs accidentally invented rice wine by forgetting about some rice which he had left soaking. This forgetful but daring Oriental gentleman took a cautious and then a longer sip of the ferment, found it to be tasty, and then, to his unbounded joy, most refreshing and exhilarating. (The art of whisky manufacture, it is believed, was not invented until the fifteenth century.)

Most people know about cooking with wine, but we keep running across men and women who express amazement when they hear for the first time about beer and booze cookery. Even the cookers with wine often are unaware of the effect of alcoholic beverages on food—that the beer, wine, or booze has a catalytic effect on the other ingredients, heightening whatever flavors are in them in somewhat the same way as does monosodium glutamate, the compound known to every housewife as M. S. G. or by one of the well-advertised brand names. This stuff, of course, doesn't have the exhilarating effect of boozy cookery.

The exhilaration is, however, all in the mind of the person who cooks with booze, for, sad to say, alcohol is evaporated instantly when it is heated. It is difficult to convince people of this fact, especially when they are told that it is quite all right to give kiddies food cooked with booze, because after cooking there is no alcohol in it. (People who are themselves devoted boozers are apt to be most horrified by the idea of feeding children on dishes concocted with something spirituous.)

Aside from the subtle flavor changes wrought in food by alcohol, there is, then, the added aesthetic pleasure—to a drinking man or woman—of slopping at least a modicum (a modicum in our set is about one-half a pint) of booze into a stew, a soup, or whatever.

Many women have told us—with great pride, generally, of their daring—that they often, or habitually, cook with wine. All too often, however, we find that what they have been using is an obscenity called "cooking sherry." This is a so-called sherry-type wine which can be found in delicatessens and supermarkets. It has salt added to it, and only a devout Sterno guzzler would drink it straight or even diluted. Few people would disagree with the dictum that inferior or poor products should never be used in cookery; why not, then, follow the same rule when it comes to wine or booze? If this "cooking sherry" is not fit to be drunk, why use it in cooking?

It saddens us when a woman—or a man—says that cooking is sheer drudgery. We know, of course, that it can become exceedingly irksome when one must cook two, three, or more meals each day.

However, it is difficult to convince the unfortunates who have that problem that there is great joy to be found in cooking, and that when the task is undertaken with imagination and an inquisitive, daring approach, the feeling of gratification is akin to that achieved by any worker in the creative arts.

Let us, then, all be daring! Next time you make a stew or a casserole, slop into it half a cup of rye, or bourbon, or brandy, or wine, or beer; flavor the fruit salad with a little kirsch; enhance your apple pie with some rum or applejack; follow an old Scottish custom: pour a small beaker of Scotch into the hot morning cereal! Make a batch of beery biscuits, using beer instead of any other liquid to make the batter. Try some such *bizarrerie* as schlivovitz— a plum brandy to which Eastern Europeans are addicted—in an omelet.

Here now are some dishes we have worked up and served to our friends and family, all with some sort of booze—you'll find many such dishes, indeed, all through the book—and we wish you and yours every happiness.

RUMMY LIVERWURST BALLS

[MAKES ABOUT FIFTY]

4 to 5 slices bacon
1 pound liverwurst
2 eggs, separated
1½ cups soft bread crumbs
½ cup green pepper, minced fine
1 tablespoon Worcestershire sauce
salt and pepper to taste (careful, because liverwurst is pretty salty)
3 tablespoons light rum

Fry the bacon crisp, dry it on paper towel, and crumble it. With a fork, mash up the liverwurst and get it quite soft. Beat the yolks of the eggs and mix them into the liverwurst and add the bacon and all the other ingredients—except the egg whites and the rum. When all these ingredients are thoroughly combined beat the egg whites stiff and fold it into the mixture, along with the rum. Drop it by the spoonful into hot, deep fat and fry the balls until they are nicely browned. Drain them on paper towel. These rummy liverwurst balls are good hot or cold, and you should have about 50 of them. You can vary this by using chopped, cooked calf's liver or chicken livers instead of liverwurst.

t was a class in American history and the teacher, who had just told the children that it was Eli Whitney who had invented the cotton gin, was shocked when a small boy in the back of the room suddenly burst into loud, hysterical weeping. The teacher took the lad to the office of the school nurse, and after awhile his tears abated and his convulsive sobs ceased. "What's wrong, Johnny?" asked the teacher solicitously. "Oh please, teacher," the boy gasped out, bursting into tears once more, "please don't let my father find out that you can now make gin from cotton!" Here's how to make a:

GINNY FISH

[SERVES THREE TO FOUR]

¼ pound butter
1 3- to 4-pound fish (a whole bass or any kind you fancy)
2 tablespoons flour
1 large onion, sliced
2 tomatoes, sliced

3 tablespoons green pepper, chopped
6 green pimiento-stuffed olives
1 bay leaf
4 peppercorns
1 teaspoon salt
3 tablespoons gin

Melt the butter in a baking dish large enough to hold the fish, which should, of course, be cleaned. A fish looks pretty when served with its head and tail, but if you don't think so, why, go right ahead and behead it and de-tail it and you won't hurt our feelings. Now put the fish into the butter and turn it from side to side so it is thoroughly coated with the melted butter. Sprinkle the flour all over the fish, put onion slices on the fish, then tomato slices. Toss the chopped green pepper over the tomatoes, arrange the olives on top of that, and drop the bay leaf, peppercorns and salt into the baking dish. Preheat your oven to 350 degrees and bake the fish, covered, until the fish will flake easily when tested with a fork. Baste it at least 3 times and add the gin, sprinkling the fish with it, in the last 15 minutes of cooking. Lift fish out carefully—two spatulas are the best tools for this job—so that the delicate creature doesn't break, and put it on serving platter, surrounded by the vegetables. Remove the bay leaf and pour the sauce from dish over fish.

Scotch for breakfast? Well, my old man fed me bourbon for breakfast, so I don't see why not Scotch for breakfast, especially when it's used in this delicious:

SCOTCHY CHICKEN-LIVER OMELET

[SERVES TWO]

4 tablespoons butter	1 tablespoon parsley
3 chicken livers	flakes
1 small onion, minced	1 tablespoon flour
¼ cup consommé	salt and pepper to taste
3 tablespoons Scotch	4 eggs

Get the butter hot in a frying pan, separate the chicken livers, wash them under cold running water, removing the fat and membranes, and then dry the livers and fry them gently on both sides. Remove the livers from the pan, keep them on a warm platter. Now pour the minced onion, consommé, Scotch, parsley flakes, flour, and seasoning into pan and simmer, uncovered, until reduced to half of original quantity.

In a separate pan, meanwhile, make your omelet. Put chicken livers on half of omelet, fold it over, pour the sauce all over it, serve it and enjoy Scotch for breakfast.

For all we know, the temperance people (oh yes, they are still with us) are still using a story —attributed, for some peculiar reason best known to them, to Arabic folklore—about the fellow who got into some kind of trouble with the devil. "The only way you can prevent me from striking you dead and taking your soul to hell," the devil was supposed to have said to this poor devil of an Arab, "is to choose one of three alternatives. You can beat your wife with a stick, you can kill your servant or drink this bottle of brandy."

The Arab asked for time to think for a few minutes. "It would be very naughty to beat my wife with a stick, for I love her," he thought out loud, "and it would be shameful to slay my good and faithful servant, so I guess I'll just have to drink that bottle of brandy, won't I?" The devil said it was up to him, entirely, so the Arab drank the whole bottle of brandy, and, of course, he got himself very drunk. And being drunk, he got into an argument with his wife, grabbed a stick, and began beating her.

Well, sir, the fellow's servant rushed into the room and tried to save the Arab's wife from the beating, and this infuriated the drunken Arab, so he killed his good and faithful servant. If there is a moral to this charming little nursery tale, we don't think it is to make:

COLD BRANDIED APPLE SOUP

[SERVES THREE TO FOUR]

6 large apples, peeled and cored (tart ones are best)	1 cup sugar
	3 cloves
	½ cup brandy
4 cups water	

Dice the apples and bring the water to a boil. Put the diced apples, sugar, and cloves into the boiling water and when it comes to a boil again, reduce the heat and let it simmer slowly, covered, until the diced apples are mushy. That should take about 15 to 20 minutes. Remove the pot from heat, add the brandy, stir it all around, let it cool and then refrigerate this for hours and hours until it is icy cold.

you have probably suspected, at one time or another, that someone was giving you the cold shoulder. And you know, of course, that the phrase "giving the cold shoulder" means a snub. Well, you know how that silly phrase originated? In medieval days, when the master of a great house wanted everyone in his set to know that he had taken a dislike to someone, there could be no misinterpretation of his feelings because the way he administered the snub was clear not only to the snubbee, but to everyone else present. While all the company ate hot roast meats, the person who was in disfavor was given some cold shoulder of beef or mutton. Shoulder of beef, or chuck, as it is often called, is one of the more inexpensive cuts. But despite what those medieval snobs thought, shoulder of beef, when it is properly prepared with thought and some imagination, is delicious cold as well as hot. Here's how to make:

BEERY POT ROAST

6 pounds chuck, rump, or round	½ teaspoon thyme
3 cloves garlic, sliced	1 bay leaf
4 tablespoons butter or oil	3-4 peppercorns
2 onions, sliced	1 teaspoon salt
1 teaspoon parsley	½ cup water, boiling
	1 bouillon cube
	1 can beer (or more)

This will serve 6 pretty good eaters or 8 fair eaters; when you pot roast meat, you know, the long cooking period causes some shrinkage. You should allow ½ to ¾ of a pound for each adult, and, really, you should have some extra, because this beef is so very good cold in sandwiches.

Make tiny slits all over the meat and stick slivers of the garlic into them, a little piece here, another one there. Now, in a large pot that has a tight-fitting cover, hot up the butter or oil and brown the meat all over. Now toss into the pot all the other ingredients except the boiling water, the bouillon cube, and the beer. Dissolve the bouillon cube in the boiling water and add that to the pot. Add the beer, bring it to a boil, reduce the heat, cover the pot, and let it simmer. Figure on 20 to 25 minutes for each pound of meat. After an hour of slow simmering, uncover the pot and look into it. If it needs more liquid, add some more beer, and turn the meat. When you serve it, put it on a hot platter and remove the peppercorns and bay leaf. Slice enough of the meat to allow for one generous piece for each serving, pour the gravy over the meat, and bring it to the table on a platter surrounded by mashed potatoes, noodles liberally buttered, or whatever you fancy. But you should have some nice rye, corn, or pumpernickel bread to sop up that nice gravy, don't you think? We like this with horseradish; not horseradish sauce—we mean horseradish, see? The hotter the better. Some commercial varieties are pretty good.

T

℞

he Scottish gentleman didn't feel very well —why does it have to be a Scottish gentleman and not some other nationality? Well, this is leading up to a Scotch recipe, that's the only reason why—so he went to the doctor. The doctor gave him a prescription for some pills to tone up his appetite and told him to take one pill and one small glass of whisky before each meal and to come back in a week for a check-up. Which he did.

"Are you doing what I told you?" the doctor asked. "I'm a wee bit behind wi' the pills," said the patient, "but I'm six weeks ahead wi' the whisky, Doctor." Here's a prescription for:

SCOTCH-LIQUEURED DUCKLING

[SERVES FOUR TO FIVE]

1 5- to 6-pound duckling	2 medium onions, minced
giblets	1 clove garlic, minced
liver	2 cups red wine, dry
1 teaspoon salt	4 to 5 ounces Scotch
⅛ teaspoon pepper	liqueur
	¼ pound mushrooms

Cut the duckling into serving pieces, removing visible pieces of fat under the skin, but save the fat for later use. Wash the parts in cold water and dry them thoroughly. Wash and dry the giblets, removing and throwing away any fat or membranes. Put the liver into the refrigerator, to be used later. Rub the duckling parts with salt and pepper and put them into a Dutch oven or a large casserole. Chop the giblets, removing any gristle, and add them and all the other ingredients, except the mushrooms, to the casserole. We'll tell you when to use the mushrooms.

Let the Dutch oven or casserole stand at room temperature for several hours, turning the duckling pieces from time to time, so that everything is properly soaked in the marinade. (Lay off the wine and Scotch liqueur, will you, because we don't want to get soaked ourselves before we finish cooking this dish, do we?) Now drain the duck, holding on to the marinade for use later. Melt some of the duck fat you've been saving over medium heat and brown all the duck and giblet pieces thoroughly. Reduce the heat to low and cook, uncovered, for 20 minutes or so, turning the parts occasionally and pouring off excess fat. After 20 minutes, pour off all fat and add the marinade you've been saving.

Cover the Dutch oven or casserole and cook over medium heat for another 35 to 40 minutes, when the duck should be nice and tender. In the last 15 minutes of cooking add the sliced mushrooms. Remember that duck liver we told you to put into the refrigerator and save until later? Well, you want to know what we do with it? What we do with 1 duck liver is to fry it over low heat for 2 to 3 minutes in a little duck fat. Then we put it on a piece of rye, pumpernickel, or corn bread, salt it lightly, put on a pinch of pepper, and sprinkle it with a little bit of chopped onion. And then we eat it, all by ourselves! Look, there's only enough for one person in one measly little duck liver, so why don't you keep quiet, the way we do, and eat it all by yourself? You've earned a little treat.

Well, when the duck is finished cooking, arrange the duck parts on a hot serving platter, and pour over it the marinade in which it soaked and cooked, along with the giblets. If you want to add a spectacular touch, heat some Scotch liqueur in a ladle, put a match to it, and pour it, flaming, over the dish at the table. (When we were a kid, we pronounced "ladle" as though it were spelled "laddle," and we thought it meant a small lad. Wasn't that stupid? Well, we also pronounced "needless" as though it were spelled "needles," and we couldn't imagine what writers meant when they wrote, "needless to say . . ." because we thought they were writing, "needles to say . . ." which, when you come right down to it, is not much sillier than "needless to say . . ." because, after all, if something is needless to say, why the hell say it? Hey?)

man in the hash house ordered hash. "One," shouted the counterman to the short-order cook, "for a gambler." Another man came in just then and he, too, ordered hash. "Another sport," yelled the waiter, "wants to take a chance!" You won't be chancing a thing if you make:

BOOZY HASH

[SERVES FOUR]

1 tablespoon fat, butter, or oil
1 large onion, chopped
2 cloves garlic, chopped
3 cups roast or corned beef, cooked and diced

1 cup potatoes, boiled and diced
½ cup brown sauce (canned, or look below)
½ cup bourbon
salt and pepper
4 eggs, poached

Hot up your fat, butter, or oil and fry the chopped onion and chopped garlic until they are well browned. Add the meat and then the potatoes, stir-frying until the potatoes are slightly browned. Now grease a baking dish and pour in the meat and potatoes, add the other ingredients—except the poached eggs, for goodness' sake—and stir it all around. Pack it all down tight in the baking dish and in your oven, preheated to 350 degrees, bake it uncovered until the top is well browned.

Leftover meats are fine for this dish, of course. If you are making corned beef hash, use salt sparingly, because corned beef, of course, is already salted. If you have an egg poacher—hardware stores sell them, and they're handy little things because they make egg-poaching so simple—here's something real sporty you can do with poached eggs. Grease the egg cups, break an egg into each one. Put into the egg a pinch of minced onion, a small cherry tomato or a couple of small pieces of chopped tomato, and sprinkle it all with a pinch of chopped parsley. Steam the eggs until the whites are set and a film forms over the yolks. And won't they look pretty, all white and yellow and red and green sitting on top of each portion of hash! Remember the brown sauce that goes into the hash? Well, here's how to make a:

WINEY BROWN SAUCE

1 tablespoon butter
1 tablespoon flour
1 bouillon cube
1 cup water, boiling

1 bay leaf
¼ cup sherry
dash of commercial
    caramel coloring

Hot up the butter, blend in the flour, and let it brown. Dissolve the bouillon cube in the boiling water and slowly add it to the pan, stirring all the time. Let it cook for 1 to 2 minutes, stirring it steadily. Add the bay leaf and the sherry. Let it simmer for 10 minutes, add the caramel coloring, and bring it to a boil. Remove from the heat and strain the sauce. You'll have a little more than the ½ cup you need for the hash, but you can keep what's left over in your refrigerator for several days and you can use it for gravy another day. (Of course, you can buy canned brown sauce.)

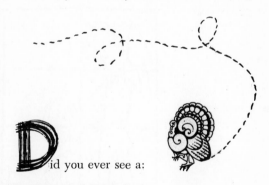

Did you ever see a:

DRUNKEN TURKEY?

[SERVES THREE TO FOUR]

1 4-pound turkey,
    cleaned and dressed
3 cups dark Puerto
    Rican rum
½ cup butter
1 pound small white
    onions

1 can (1¼ pounds)
    whole tomatoes
1 bay leaf
2 teaspoons salt
1 3-ounce jar pimiento-
    stuffed green
    olives

Dissect turkey into serving pieces, rinse them all in cold water and dry with paper towels. Put the turkey pieces in a large, long dish or pan for which you have a cover and pour the rum over them. Cover the thing and let the turkey marinate overnight in the refrigerator. From time to time, turn the turkey pieces so they'll all get loaded on the rum. When you are ready to start cooking next day, drain off the rum and hold on to it.

Now melt ¼ cup of the butter, hot it up in a frying pan, and brown the turkey pieces on each side. Turn the heat down low and add the rest of the butter, the onions, tomatoes and their juice, the bay leaf, the salt, and the rum you used as a marinade. Cover the pan and cook over low heat for 30 minutes. Then take the cover off and cook for another 30 minutes. After that, add the olives and cook the drunken turkey for another hour, stirring everything around with crazy abandon from time to time. When you serve the turkey, remove bay leaf and pour the sauce all over it.

The teacher had a problem in mathematics for the class which went like this: "If it takes your father two hours to wash the windows in your house, and it takes your mother two hours to wash them, also, how long would it take them if they worked on the task together?" A little boy in the back row raised his hand and he stood up and said, "It would take them four hours." The teacher looked disappointed, and asked sarcastically how he had arrived at that figure. "That's counting the time," the little boy said, smirking evilly, "that they'd be fighting about it." It won't take you much time to make:

STEAK IN RYE SAUCE

[SERVES THREE TO FOUR]

½ teaspoon salt	3 tablespoons butter
1 teaspoon coarse black pepper	1 tablespoon olive oil
	¼ cup bouillon
2 pounds boneless sirloin, 1½ inches thick	2 tablespoons heavy cream
	¼ cup dry white wine
	¼ cup rye whisky

This will serve 3 or 4 people. Rub the salt and pepper into the steak. You can buy coarsely ground black pepper or you can crush peppercorns yourself. Put the butter in a pan large enough to hold the steak comfortably, add the oil and hot it all up. (The combination of butter and oil adds a certain something to the flavor.) Quickly brown the steak on both sides over high heat, but don't let the butter-oil mixture smoke. The steak should be 1½ inches thick, so cook it over medium heat for 3 to 4 minutes on each side for rare or 7 to 8 minutes or longer, depending on how well done you want it. When you have the steak done the way you want it (cut into it to be certain), remove it from pan to a hot platter. Hot up some water in a large pot, turn off heat, and put the platter on top of pot. Cover the platter with another plate.

Now add the bouillon—you can make this by dissolving a bouillon cube in hot water or you can buy it canned—the cream, the white wine, and the rye whiskey to the pan, and let it all simmer for 4 to 5 minutes, stirring all the time. Pour sauce over the steak and serve.

Now, a nice way to finish up a boozy meal, we suggest, is a nice piece of cake like *Biscochos Borrachos,* which is what the Spaniards call:

DRUNKEN CAKES

[MAKES THREE SMALL CAKES]

6 tablespoons sugar
12 eggs, separated
1 pound flour

½ cup (1 stick) butter, softened

Beat the sugar with the egg yolks, mix in the flour a little at a time, and cut in the butter. Beat the egg whites and fold into the mixture. You'll need 3 small cake tins. Grease them and then fill them half-way with the batter. Preheat your oven to 400 degrees and bake the cakes until they are lightly browned, which will take maybe 10 to 12 minutes, and make the:

DRUNKEN TOPPING

1 pound sugar
½ pint Malaga, port,
    or dark rum

powdered cinnamon
maybe some nuts
    chopped and
    unsalted

In a pan, heat the sugar until it becomes caramelized. Add the wine or rum. Take the cakes out of the tins, let them cool, and pour the topping over them. Sprinkle with cinnamon and the chopped nuts, if you are using them.

If you want to wind it all up with IRISH COFFEE (which is a recent invention of the distillers of Irish whiskey or their agents, and which is largely unknown in Ireland), you'll find it in the index, and: ENJOY! ENJOY!

How NOT to Brew Coffee

It was the best restaurant in Sydney, we had been told, and therefore undoubtedly the best eating-place in all of the vast Australian continent. And it lived up to its reputation until, alas, the very end. The coffee was abominable. It was so inconceivably bad, indeed, that we asked the manager of the place how they managed to achieve such a fantastic brew. As we meant him to, the fellow beamingly accepted our statement as a compliment. "Thank you, sir," he said modestly, "but there's really no trick to it at all; we just make it in the ordinary way." But what, we pressed on, was the ordinary way in Australia?

"Why," he said, looking puzzled at our great interest, "we just put the ground-up coffee in the pot, add sugar, then the milk, and we boil it."

What we said was, "Oh," and from then on in Australia we always ordered tea, which is a good rule to follow in England, also.

According to Betty Wason, whose wonderful book, "Cooks, Gluttons and Gourmets," is a treasure trove of weird and wonderful facts about the history of food, coffee was supposed to have been discovered in Arabia sometime in the 9th or 10th century by a shepherd who saw his sheep gambol wildly after eating a certain plant. So the shepherd munched some of the beans and found that it kept him awake. What this silly fellow had to stay awake for, Miss Wason does not say. It is not surprising to learn that coffee became known very early in its history as "the black enemy of sleep"; but why did it also become known as "the enemy of copulation"?

We should think otherwise, and our belief was up-
held by a spokesman for the Coffee Brewing Institute, who said that the Institute's lengthy and intensive research would lead them to say, "*Au con-
traire.*"

When coffee was brought to Europe in the 16th
century, certain churchmen denounced it as an
instrument of Satan and forbade its use. But wise
Pope Clement tasted it. "This Satan's drink," he
said, "is so delicious it would be a pity to let infi-
dels have exclusive use of it—we shall baptize it and
make it a Christian beverage."

The Coffee Brewing Institute, which doesn't care
what brand of coffee you buy as long as you prepare it properly, has conferred its Golden Cup
Award to about 3,000 restaurants and hotel dining
rooms in the United States. They don't make these
awards to individuals, but you can become pretty
famous in your set if you'll just follow their rules
for proper coffee brewing.

As we've said, it doesn't make any difference
what brand you buy; each is a blend, and you have
to experiment to find the one you like best. First,
you have to use the grind that is right for your
coffee-maker. For a percolator, use regular grind;
for a drip pot, use drip grind; for a vacuum-style
coffee-maker, use drip or fine grind.

Your coffee-maker must be absolutely clean.
After each use, all parts must be washed in hot
water with a light-duty detergent and thoroughly
rinsed with cold water. And before it is used again,
it should be scalded.

Whatever method you use, there should be two level tablespoons of coffee for each serving and three-quarters of a measuring cup—six ounces—of water. (Most people get a watery brew because they use a full measuring cup of water and then add one spoon of coffee "for the pot.") The water should be freshly drawn cold water; hot-water pipes may have mineral deposits, which spoil the taste.

NEVER brew less than three-quarters of your coffee-maker's capacity; NEVER let coffee boil after it has been brewed, for this will ruin the flavor.

A percolator should perk for six to eight minutes (the Institute says "gentle minutes"). Drip pots should drip not less than four minutes or more than six. In a vacuum coffee-maker, the brew should return to the lower bowl in three minutes.

The recipe for the best iced coffee we ever tasted came not from the Coffee Brewing Institute, but from our wife. She says: "Put 2 level teaspoons of instant coffee into a glass—put a spoon in the glass—add 2 tablespoons boiling water, and dissolve the coffee. Half-fill the glass with milk, add ice cubes, fill glass with milk. And if you don't want the coffee at all diluted by melting ice, make enough coffee to fill a refrigerator ice-tray, freeze it, and use the frozen coffee instead of plain ice cubes."

The doctor was talking to his patient's wife. "Your husband must not drink strong coffee," said the doctor, "because it might make him too excited." The wife disagreed. "Listen, doctor," she said, "you should see how excited he gets when I give him weak coffee."

Index